LEARNING TO USE THE INTERNET AND WORLD WIDE WEB

ERNEST ACKERMANN

Mary Washington College

KAREN HARTMAN

Mary Washington College

FRANKLIN, BEEDLE & ASSOCIATES, INCORPORATED
8536 SW ST. HELENS DRIVE, STE. D
WILSONVILLE, OREGON 97070
503/682-7668
WWW.FBEEDLE.COM

President and Publisher	Jim Leisy (jimleisy@fbeedle.com)
Manuscript Editor	Michelle Williams
Production	Tom Sumner
	Jeni Lee
	Stephanie Welch
Cover	Ian Shadburne
Illustrations	Oliver Ackermann
Developmental Editor	Sue Page
Marketing	Chris Collier
Order Processing	Krista Brown

Printed in the U.S.A.

Library of Congress Cataloging-in-Publication data is available from the publisher.

Dedication

To Lynn, Karl, and Oliver
                                                      —E.A

_____

To Jack
                                                      — K.H.

CONTENTS

chapter 5 ▶COMMUNICATION ON THE INTERNET   99

chapter 6 ▶ELECTRONIC MAIL   123

chapter 7 ▶DISCUSSION GROUPS AND USENET NEWSGROUPS   141

PREFACE

Learning to Use the Internet and World Wide Web is designed primarily as a text for students in a college-level introductory Internet course. It gives the reader the skills necessary to use the Internet for communication; to search for, access, and evaluate resources; and to design, author, and publish Web pages.

This book is based on the best elements of our successful textbook *Internet and Web Essentials: What You Need to Know*. Each chapter includes a statement of objectives for the learner, an activity that shows step-by-step instructions for using necessary software, a list of important terms introduced in the chapters that are then defined in an extensive glossary, several chapter review questions, and exercises that give the student practice using the concepts and tools covered. We also include information about supplemental material that is on the CD that accompanies the text. Previous experience with the Internet and the Web isn't necessary to successfully use and learn from the text. Students in any discipline will find the book useful. The text is interesting, informative, and accessible.

We've been teaching and writing about the Internet and the Web for several years. That work and our personal involvement in using and providing Internet services brings us to the belief that an informed and discriminating user of the Internet needs to know:

- ☑ The basic technology that supports the Internet
- ☑ Effective means of using the Internet for communication
- ☑ How to search for and access, evaluate, and use information from the Internet
- ☑ How to produce and publish information so it can be effectively shared with others on the Internet
- ☑ The social, ethical, and legal issues surrounding the use of the Internet and the World Wide Web

The book contains ample material for an eight or ten-week introductory course about the Internet. It also makes a good choice as a supplement to a course that uses the Internet. If you incorporate the supplemental material on the CD, the text is suitable for a one-semester, three-credit course. Consider using our book *Internet and Web Essentials*, ISBN 1-887902-46-0, for a course that would benefit from a more complete discussion of communication, searching, and publishing on the Internet.

Important Features of the Book

Each chapter begins with an introduction to its topic. This is followed by a list of goals and objectives for the reader and a list of the major topics in the chapter. The text of each chapter includes one guided activity that includes step-by-step instructions learners can follow to enforce and enhance their understanding of the skills and concepts introduced in the chapter. In most cases the activities access sites on the Internet; in some cases we've provided the files needed for the activities on the CD included with the book. Each chapter also contains several short lists of Web resources titled "FYI." A reader can use these as a means to further explore some of the topics introduced. A summary, a list of important terms, and exercises conclude each chapter.

The book includes a glossary of the important terms listed in the chapters and four appendices. The first appendix is an extensive section on how to manage and use information found on the Internet. The second is an informative essay on how to evaluate and cite information from the Internet and the Web. The third appendix is an overview of Internet privacy and security issues.

Both Netscape Navigator and Internet Explorer are used for activities and examples. The browsers are similar enough so that using one or the other makes very little difference in most cases. We do point out the differences and give specific and separate instructions for using the features of each when it is important to do so.

Organization of the Book

Learning to Use the Internet and World Wide Web introduces students to the important aspects of using the Internet and the World Wide Web. The book is organized as follows:

Chapter 1 **Quick Start — Getting Connected and Using the Internet**
Basic terminology and technology associated with the Internet and the Web; connecting to the Internet

Chapter 2 **Internet and Browser Basics**
Browser details, concepts, and techniques covered; discussion of the differences between Netscape and Internet Explorer

Chapter 3 **Searching for Information**
Features of search engines, constructing search strategies, brief introduction to copyright, and social and ethical issues surrounding content on the Internet

Chapter 4 **Beyond Search Engines**
Overview of other types of information resources, such as directories, virtual libraries, and specialized databases.

Chapter 5 **Communication on the Internet**
Covers the types of communication technologies available, behavior and etiquette guidelines, legal and ethical issues

Chapter 6 **Electronic Mail**
How email works, common email features, email in text and non-text formats

Chapter 7 **Discussion Groups and Usenet Newsgroups**
Essential information about discussion groups, how to find them, proper etiquette and behavior in a group, details of working with Usenet News

Chapter 8 **FTP and Downloading Web Resources**
Downloading files using anonymous FTP, locating FTP archives, downloading software files from archives, using an FTP client program

Chapter 9 **Writing Web Pages**
The details of using HTML for basic Web pages; using images, colors, and tables; contains an activity that goes through all the steps to create and link Web pages

---

Chapter 10 **Web Publishing: Putting Information on the Web**
Considers the issues related to Web publishing or putting information on the Web, including Web page and Web site design, technologies used to produce Web pages, and putting Web page sources on a Web server; evaluating Web page design, and publicizing Web information

---

Appendix A **Managing and Using Information from the Internet and the World Wide Web**
Common file types; copyright guidelines; methods for capturing text, images, and data from Web pages; and using that information in other applications.

Appendix B **Evaluating and Citing Information from the Internet and the World Wide Web**
Important information for people interested in using the Internet and the Web for research; deals with issues related to critically evaluating content; and guidelines for citing information.

Appendix C **Privacy and Security on the Internet and the World Wide Web**
Several topics that deal with the issues of privacy and security. These include the basics of computer and network security, the trail you leave behind as you browse the Web, viruses, cookies, and things to consider before giving out personal information.

Chapter Selection

Chapters 1 and 2 are fundamental to the rest of the material in the text. After you've read them, you can go through the rest of the material in the order it's presented in the text, or you can proceed to later chapters if that is preferred. Essential for a short course are chapters 1 through 6, and 9; while a basic introductory course would cover the first nine chapters.

If the primary focus of the course is on producing information for the Web, it would be advantageous to concentrate on the following chapters:

Chapter 1	**Quick Start — Getting Connected and Using the Internet**
Chapter 2	**Internet and Browser Basics**
Chapter 3	**Searching for Information**
Chapter 4	**Beyond Search Engines**
Chapter 7	**Discussion Groups and Usenet Newsgroups**
Chapter 8	**FTP and Downloading Web Resources**
Chapter 9	**Writing Web Pages**
Chapter 10	**Web Publishing: Putting Information on the Web**
Appendix A	**Managing and Using Information from the Internet and the World Wide Web**
Appendix B	**Evaluating and Citing Information from the Internet and the World Wide Web**

If the primary focus is using the Internet for research, emphasize the following:

Chapter 1	**Quick Start—Getting Connected and Using the Internet**
Chapter 2	**Internet and Browser Basics**

If the primary focus is on communication, then the following chapters should be emphasized:

Supplemental Materials

The CD that accompanies this text contains supplemental material for each of the chapters. For each chapter we include material that enhances both learning and teaching what is in the text:

- ☑ all URLs mentioned in this chapter in hypertext format
- ☑ selected terms discussed in this chapter with hyperlinks to the glossary
- ☑ copies of the review questions in quiz format

We also include supplemental material that expands on or gives more detail about topics covered in the text. We've designed the material on the CD so that it may become an integral part of a course that uses this book.

We maintain a Web site with the URL **http://webliminal.com/LTU** to accompany this book. The Web pages that make up the site contain up-to-date links to all the resources mentioned in the book. We'll be updating the Web pages regularly, so please check the Web site to see what has changed since the book was printed. It's likely that some of the URLs will change because that's the nature of the Web, but the concepts we discuss in the book stay the same.

For teachers using this book, an instructor's guide is available from the publisher, Franklin, Beedle & Associates. The publisher can be contacted through its Web site, **http://www.fbeedle.com**, or by phone, 1-800-FBA-BOOK.

About the Authors

As a professor of computer science and a reference and instruction librarian, we've been using the Internet and the World Wide Web for over a decade in our professional work. We have also had the chance for the last several years to teach others about using the Web and the Internet for communication, research, and Web publishing. On top of this good fortune we've also had the chance to write several textbooks that deal in one way or another with those same topics.

Acknowledgments

There are many people to thank for helping us with this project. First, what must be inadequate thanks goes to our families. They, more than anyone, have made it possible for us to complete this work. It's more than their helping with specific tasks, such as proofreading, fielding ideas, checking URLs, and doing our share of chores. What is so special is that they allow us the selfish pleasure of writing. Ernie wants to thank his wife Lynn for her help and love. His sons Karl and Oliver have been a constant source of encouragement. Oliver is responsible for the excellent illustrations in the book. Karen wants to especially thank her husband Jack for his ideas, which have prompted creative solutions in many aspects of her work; his unwavering support of all her pursuits; and his enduring faith in her abilities as an educator, writer, and mother. She also wants to thank her daughters, Tracy and Hilary, for keeping her up to date with new trends, especially MP3.

Our friends, colleagues, and students in Fredericksburg and at Mary Washington College deserve a great deal of thanks. We get a much better view of what's important about using the Internet because of working with them. We would also like to thank Jack Bales for allowing us to use a piece of his writing in an example of citing Web pages in Appendix B.

Franklin, Beedle & Associates has been a very supportive and cooperative publisher and has helped us greatly throughout this project. We'd like to especially thank Sue Page, developmental editor; Stephanie Welch, Ian Shadburne, and Tom Sumner, production; Jim Leisy; Chris Collier, and Krista Hall.

The reviewers listed below critiqued portions of prior manuscripts or the complete manuscript for this book. Their input has been invaluable and has greatly improved the quality of our effort.

> Steve St. John, Tulsa Community College—Northeast
> Debbie Crowley, Santa Ana College

We hope you enjoy this book and find it useful. Please send us email to let us know your opinions and suggestions. When you have the time, add something to our guestbooks that are accessible from our home pages on the Web.

Peace.

Ernest Ackermann
Department of Computer Science
Mary Washington College
ernie@mwc.edu
http://webliminal.com/ernie

Karen Hartman
James Monroe Center Library
Mary Washington College
khartman@mwc.edu
http://users.mwc.edu/~khartman

Quick Start—
Getting Connected
and Using the Internet

▶ a quick start is what we're after. You've no doubt heard a lot about the Internet and the World Wide Web, and you are interested in learning how they work and how to use them effectively. You probably have some experience using email, the Internet, or a Web browser.

We'll start here with some introductory material about the Internet, how it can be used, and how to get connected. We're not going to go into much technical detail here or later in this book. We're interested in dealing with the basic and essential material to get you started using the Internet and the Web.

You'll see that this chapter, and each chapter in this book, begins with a list of goals and objectives. We listed these from the point of view of someone reading the book. These goals and objectives tell you what you can expect to learn or understand and what skills you will gain by reading the text and working through the activities and exercises.

Let's get started!

Goals/Objectives:

☑ Know the basic concepts of the World Wide Web (WWW) and the Internet
☑ Become familiar with some of the basic issues related to getting access to the Internet

Topics:

☑ Introduction to the Internet and the World Wide Web
☑ Connecting to the Internet; Selecting an ISP
☑ Using a Web Browser

Introduction to the Internet and the World Wide Web

The reports are appearing everywhere: in the newspaper, on the radio, and on the television news. Go to any magazine display, and you'll see the words *World Wide Web* and *Internet* on several of the covers. Your friends and family are telling you about the Web and asking you for your email address. The Internet has caused a momentous change in society, the reports say. The Internet is transforming the way people communicate with each other. It has revolution-ized the way people do research and conduct business. It has changed the way research is published and distributed and the way products are marketed and sold.

You keep hearing and reading about all of this, but you want to know what isn't talked about much. You want to know what exactly is the Internet? How does it work? Where does the World Wide Web fit in? How do you get connected? How can the Internet make your life fuller, richer, more productive, and more fun? The aim of this book is to answer all these questions and more. But for now, let's begin at the beginning and talk about what the Internet actually is.

The **Internet** is an international collection of computer networks that exchange informa-tion according to a fixed set of rules. A network is a group of computers that are linked together so that they can exchange information. The computers and networks on the Internet communicate with each other by exchanging data according to the same rules, even though the individual networks and computer systems may use different technologies. The rules for exchanging information are called **protocols**. Since the Internet is a collection of computer networks on a worldwide scale, your computer can retrieve information from networks throughout the world.

The **World Wide Web** is the collection of infor-mation accessible through the Internet. The informa-tion is linked together like a web through **hyperlinks**. This information may be any type of content, including text, video, audio, or graphical images. We can refer to these types of content on the Web as **hypermedia**. Each link is specified or written using a **Uniform Resource Locator**, or **URL**, which acts as an address for the information. The protocol that's used to exchange information through hyperlinks is called **hypertext transfer protocol**, or **HTTP**. There's no definite starting point on the Web, and the path you take is your choice. You can move around in many ways: by going backward, forward, up, down, right, or left.

☑ F Y I **History of the Internet and the World Wide Web**

The Internet has been around since 1968, and the Web got its start in 1991. To learn more about their histories, take a look at some of the items listed at this resource:

☑ "Internet Histories,"
http://www.isoc.org
/internet/history/
index.shtml

Many people who use the Internet use it for communicating with others through *electronic mail* or *email*. Others use the Internet primarily for research, employing the vast resources found on the World Wide Web. The World Wide Web has popularized the Internet for millions of people throughout the world. The Web has revolutionized learning, communication, and commerce by allowing people to simply click on an image or a block of text and be taken to documents that enrich and expand on the text with graphics, sounds, and video.

☑ F Y I   **Guides to Netiquette**

"Netiquette" is the term used to describe rules for proper behavior on the Internet. Take a look at these sites to see what's expected of you and how to behave on the Internet.

☑ "The Net: User Guidelines and Netiquette,"
http://ns1.fau.edu
/netiquette/net

☑ "Netiquette Home Page,"
http://albion.com
/netiquette/index.html

☑ "RFC 1855: Netiquette Guidelines," http:/ /
marketing.tenagra
.com/rfc1855.html

The beauty of the Internet is that it is interactive. People are encouraged to contribute to its development. It doesn't matter who you are, where you live, or what work you do, it's the quality of the communication and interaction that's important. You can send an email message to someone who lives in a different country as easily as to a friend who lives across the street. You can search for and read documents that have been placed on the Internet from all over the world. It's a decentralized entity; there is no one company, organization, or government running it, nor is there any control over what information is accessed through it. The Internet, by its very nature, is an evolving and expanding creation.

When you are connected to the Internet, you're able to communicate with others and access Web sites using your browser to browse or search for information. Having the ability to do these things means there's a lot of technology supporting you, including hardware—networks, computers, modems, and other devices that make the connection possible.

Before explaining how to get connected to the Internet, we want to briefly mention some terms and concepts that will make it easier for us to give you the straight story. We'll go over this and other information in more detail in Chapter 2.

☑ Two basic protocols used for exchanging information on the Internet are *Internet Protocol (IP)* and *Transmission Control Protocol (TCP)*.

☑ Each network on the Internet has a unique address, called an *IP address*, and each of the computer systems making up a network has an IP address, which is sometimes based on the network's IP address. At a basic level, the addresses are numeric—209.196.179.233, for example. Often, a descriptive name, called an *Internet domain name*, is used instead of an address: **www.webliminal.com**.

☑ The translation of domain names to IP addresses is handled automatically by the *domain name system*.

☑ Packets of characters, similar to envelopes holding messages, are used to carry information on the Internet.

With these details as background about how the Internet works, we'll next explain how to get connected to the Internet.

Connecting to the Internet; Selecting an ISP

If you already have Internet access, congratulations! It is still worth your while to read this section to get an understanding of some of the issues involved and some of the alternatives available. If you're reading this because you'll be getting an Internet connection, congratulations! There are lots of good things in store for you.

Here are the major topics we'll cover:

☑ What You Need to Connect to the Internet
☑ Selecting an Internet Service Provider
☑ Getting Connected: Two Scenarios

What You Need to Connect to the Internet

We will go over the concepts and terms you need to know when you're thinking about getting connected to the Internet. There is more than one way to establish a connection to the Internet, so you'll want to be knowledgeable enough to find an affordable connection that meets your needs.

You need a computer or some other digital device that has the software and hardware necessary to implement TCP/IP and other protocols.

Personal computers are the most common devices used to access the Internet, but you also can use hand-held digital communication devices, game machines, WebTV, and specially outfitted telephones. There are some differences in the technology used to access the Internet, but the essential concepts are the same. To simplify the discussion, we'll focus on the details of connecting to the Internet using a personal computer. The necessary software is included on most modern computers or is readily available from the company or organization that provides your network and your access to the Internet.

Your computer must include a device—a network card or a modem—that permits a connection to a network that will be providing the Internet services.

The device must either come as part of your computer, or you will need to obtain a network card or modem to connect to a network. If your school, organization, or company has its own network, then you'll probably use a network card. You'll also use a network card if you connect to the Internet through what's called a cable modem or other high-speed service to the home. The card, a collection of integrated circuits and chips on plastic, sits inside your computer. It has a cable attached to it that plugs into a wall jack (or similar receptacle) to connect to the network. In this case, you're likely to have relatively high-speed access to the Internet.

If you don't have such immediate access to a network—for example, if you want to connect to the Internet from your home in a relatively inexpensive manner—you'll use a modem to connect to a network. (The term "modem" comes from a combination of **mod**ulate and **dem**odulate.) A modem is necessary because the computers on the network only deal with information in digital format, and this information needs to be transmitted through an analog—not digital—medium, such as an ordinary phone line. In a typical setup, the modem, with dial-up networking software, dials a phone number, and then the call is answered by another modem, which also is connected to a computer.

Variations on this setup include using a high-speed connection on your existing phone line called a digital subscriber line (DSL)—a digital communications line that can be shared

☑ T I P ! **When You're Ready
to Get Connected**

☑ Obtain as much informa-
tion as possible concerning
what type of hardware and
software you'll need.

☑ Read over the Help
information available on
your computer. Click on
Help in the Start menu;
select the topic or type in
the keyword "Internet."

☑ Be sure to know whom to
call for assistance.

☑ Invite a friend over who has
gone through this before.

by voice telephones, computers, and fax machines—
or using a cable modem that connects to the Internet
using cable TV lines.

**The speed at which information is exchanged with
the Internet depends on the type of connection you
have to the Internet and on other factors such as the
total amount of information being transmitted over a
local network or the Internet backbone.**

The speed at which information is transmitted across
the Internet is measured in bits per second (bps).
Bits symbolize the fundamental 1s and 0s that all
computers use to represent information. If you have
a network card in your computer, then you likely have
a fast connection to the Internet, possibly in the
range of 1.5 to 44 Mbps (M represents million or
mega). Modems used with ordinary telephone lines
are rated at 56 Kbps, 33.4 Kbps, or 28.8 Kbps (K rep-
resents thousand.) Higher speed access usually costs more. The typical cost (when this book
was written) for Internet access is several hundred dollars per month for the fastest connection speeds, about $50 to $80 per month for DSL or cable access, and about $20 per month for
access with a modem at 56 Kbps or slower.

**You have to connect to a network that has a connection to the Internet. That network assigns
an IP address or domain name to your computer. You may have to select an Internet service
provider (ISP).**

It seems that the Internet is ubiquitous. It is everywhere, but you still need to become part of a
network that has established access to the Internet. Each computer on the network has to have
an IP address in order to send and receive packets of information. In most networks, the IP
address is assigned whenever you log on
to or connect to the network. In others,
your computer is assigned a permanent
IP address.

The organization that provides the
network that you'll connect to for
Internet access is called an *Internet
service provider (ISP)*. Sometimes it's up
to you to choose an ISP, but not always.
The authors of this book are provided
with an ISP through their employer for
work-related Internet usage, but each
has a different ISP for various off-
campus activities (such as writing this
book!). A number of considerations go
into selecting an ISP, such as the cost of
access and the speed of access.

☑ F Y I **Selecting an ISP
and Getting Connected**

☑ "ISP Finder," http://
ispfinder.com

☑ "Learn the Net:
Getting Connected,"
http://learnthenet.com
/english/html
/04connec.htm

☑ "Webmonkey Guide
to Finding an ISP,"
http://otwired.lycos.com
/webmonkey/guides
/web/isp.html

Selecting an Internet Service Provider

If you're setting up Internet access in your home for work or personal use, you'll have to select an ISP. The ISP is your link to the Internet, so it is an important choice. You'll want to choose one that provides reliable, convenient, and affordable service.

Here are some points to consider:

Access

The ISP is your link to the Internet. Be sure you can connect to the Internet without long delays or busy signals. Ask questions about local access. Dial the local number to be sure it's local. Call at different times of the day to see if you get busy signals. If you're planning on using the Internet when you travel, then you'll want an ISP with local access available nationwide or worldwide.

Reliability

Do a little checking into the reliability of services provided by the ISP and the satisfaction of current customers.

Service

Somewhere along the line, you'll need some assistance from the ISP or you'll need to report a problem. You'll want to know how to get help by phone and through email, as well as a place on the Internet where you can check to see if others are experiencing problems.

Speed

A faster connection is usually better, provided the cost doesn't become prohibitive. You'll want to know about the options you have for connecting to the ISP's network and its connection to the Internet.

Fees

Some services offer a discount if fees are paid yearly instead of monthly. Some ISPs offer different pricing depending on the amount of time connected. Be sure you understand the fee structure and don't underestimate how much you'll use the service. Charges for extra time are often at a rate of $1.50 to $2.00 per hour.

Features

Some ISPs offer only basic service—a reliable connection to the Internet. Others also offer Web page space and other services. Explore the features available from several ISPs and decide which features are important to you.

As you can see, there are a number of factors to consider when selecting an ISP. Take the time to consider the alternatives and get some recommendations before you decide which to use. Now that we've discussed selecting an ISP, it's time to move on to getting connected to the Internet.

> ☑ T I P ! Pay attention to and save any information you get from your ISP or network support group.

Getting Connected: Two Scenarios

Here, we'll cover two scenarios for getting connected to the Internet: one using a network card and the other using a modem. These match the two types of Internet connections previously mentioned. In both of the scenarios, we assume you have a computer that uses Microsoft Windows as the operating system.

Scenario I

You are connecting to a network through a network card in your computer. For example, your company or school provides access to its network or you are using a cable modem at home. Find out as much as possible beforehand about the type of network card you need and the software settings for a proper network connection. If possible, arrange to have a technician on hand or on call for the installation.

☑ Obtain a network card that meets the specifications provided by the people who provide network support.

☑ Install the network card and the network software. You may have to do this yourself. The computer will have to be opened to install a network card. Once the card is installed, determine if the connection to the local network is working properly. Try to send email to someone on the local network or print a file on a network printer. The exact steps you'll follow will depend on the type of network card you have installed, the network software, and the local procedures for connecting to and using your network.

At this point, your computer is directly connected to the network.

You may find that the software you've installed handles the proper configuration of your Internet connection. If it does, then that's all there is to it! If you're not in that happy situation, you'll have to deal with the settings yourself. It's not hard; you just have to go through it step by step.

> ☑ **T I P !** You may have to fill in some key addresses. You'll get the numeric IP addresses and domain names you'll need from your network support center or ISP. Be sure to have those numbers and addresses on hand before you start.

With your computer started, click on the **Start** button, select **Settings**, select **Control Panel**, and then select **Network**. Click on **TCP/IP** and then click on **Properties**.

We'll go through the properties you're likely to have to set.

☑ **DNS Configuration.** Find out whether the domain name system (DNS) will be disabled or enabled. If DNS is enabled, select that option. Put in the proper host and domain names and carefully enter the numeric IP addresses for the DNS. These are the addresses of the computers on your network that take care of the translations. If these aren't set correctly, you won't be able to retrieve anything from the Internet or view any Web pages.

☑ **IP Address.** In this panel, you assign, if necessary, the IP address for the computer. In many cases, the IP address is assigned dynamically each time the computer is started or a user logs on to the network. If your computer has a permanent IP address, you'll have to fill in the IP addresses assigned to the computer and a subnet mask. In many cases, the subnet mask 255.555.255.0 is used. The subnet mask may be used in conjunction with a technique to give one IP address to each subnetwork of a larger network. You don't need to worry about these details, but you do need to know what the mask should be.

☑ **Gateway.** If your network uses a gateway to connect to the Internet, you'll have to carefully enter the proper IP address of the system that acts as the gateway. You'll need this to be correct to connect to sites on the Internet through your network.

Scenario II

You've decided to establish dial-up access to the Internet from the computer in your home office or from the family computer at home.

You've selected an ISP and have obtained a login name and password from the ISP.

You'll use a modem to call and connect to a network. Your computer and the network you reach through the phone lines communicate with each other by using software called ***point-to-point protocol (PPP).***

Get a modem that meets the specifications provided by the folks who support the network.

☑ You'll want the fastest modem you can afford and one that's supported by your ISP. If a modem isn't already installed in your computer, get an external modem. It's easier to install and troubleshoot, but it costs a little more. An external modem is connected to your computer by a serial cable that's plugged into a serial port, usually labeled COM 1 or COM 2, on your computer. The modem connects to your phone line through a phone wire to a telephone jack. Most modems come with the necessary cables.

Follow the installation instructions that come with the modem.

☑ Turn off the power on your computer. If the modem is internal, you'll have to take the cover off the computer and plug the modem into a slot in the computer. If the modem is external, then connect it to a serial port; plug in the cable to the phone jack and the power cord. Boot the computer. Click on **Start**, **Settings**, **Control Panel**, and then **Add New Hardware**. Follow the instructions; Windows should detect the hardware and take you step by step through the installation.

Many ISPs supply the software to configure your computer so that it has the proper settings for TCP/IP. If you have that software, install it and then test your connection. If you don't have the software, here are instructions for configuring dial-up networking:

☑ Double-click on the icon **Dial-Up Networking**. Find the dial-up icon on the desktop or click on **My Computer** and select **Dial-Up Networking**. A folder with one or more entries will open. Each entry in this folder represents a dial-up connection to the Internet.

☑ Double-click on the icon labeled **Make New Connection**. If that icon isn't present, then click on **Connections** in the menu bar and select **Make a New Connection**. This takes you through a step-by-step process where you enter a name for the connection (give any name you'd like) and have the option of selecting a modem from the ones installed or connected to your computer. Clicking on **Next** takes you to a page where you enter the phone number for the modem to dial. Use the number provided by your ISP. Then click on **Finish.**

☑ Set the properties for the new connection. Move the mouse pointer to the icon for the new connection, click once with the right mouse button, and select **Properties**. A set of panels will appear. The one labeled **General** should have the information you just entered. Click on the tab labeled **Server Types**. For Type of Dial-Up Server, **select PPP: Internet, NT, Windows 98**. Don't change the Advanced options. Click on **TCP/IP Settings**. Check the instructions from your ISP to see if you have to set the IP address or DNS address. Check the instructions again to see if values have to be entered and make sure that the values you entered are correct. If these aren't right, you won't be able to make a connection to the Internet. Click on **OK.**

Test your connection. Click on the icon in the Dial-Up Networking folder and then select **Connect** to make the connection. Give the password you need to connect to your ISP. You'll probably hear a dial tone and then the phone number being dialed. In a minute or so, the modems will connect and begin to communicate. If you have problems, call the ISP or a knowledgeable friend for help.

Once you're connected, look for a Netscape or Internet Explorer icon on your desktop. Click on it. A browser will start, and a home page will be displayed. Bon voyage!

Using a Web Browser

The concept behind the World Wide Web was to develop a hypertext networked information system. One of the goals was to create a uniform means of accessing all the different types of information on the Internet. Since you only need to know one way to get information, you can concentrate on what you want, not how to get it. These concepts were first developed by Tim Berners-Lee at CERN, the European Organization for Nuclear Research, in Geneva, Switzerland.

You access the WWW by using a program on your computer called a **Web browser**. Several browsers are available. The first popular browser was Mosaic, and currently the most popular ones are Netscape Navigator and Microsoft Internet Explorer. Each has its special features and advantages, but they also have a lot in common. We'll use both browsers—Netscape's Navigator and Microsoft's Internet Explorer—in this book. In most cases, we'll be able to use one in the same way we use the other. When it's necessary, we'll specifically mention the way to use Netscape and the corresponding way to use Internet Explorer.

You move from place to place and item to item on the Web by using a mouse to select and click on a portion of text, an icon, or a region of a map or image. These hyperlinks, or *links* for short, represent information somewhere on the Internet. The browser also includes features that let you save files and print documents you've found on the Web. You also can use the browser to keep lists of sites and resources you'd like to visit again.

We'll go into the details of a Web browser in the next chapter. Now let's try a hands-on activity that will demonstrate some of the concepts of navigating the World Wide Web and using a browser.

In this activity, we'll explore the United States Census Bureau's Web site. The Census Bureau has made much of the 2000 census, as well as historical United States population information, available online for the public. Some people are interested in the data to determine demographic information. Business people and economists often need to find

About Activities

On the following page is the first of many activities in this book. Each activity is divided into two parts: "Overview" and "Details." In the "Overview" section, we discuss what we'll be covering in the activity and enumerate the steps we'll follow. "Details" takes you through the steps, shows you the results we got when we tried the activity, and discusses certain aspects of the particular skill being shown.

Follow the steps, use what's here as a guide, and pay attention to what you see. As you work through this and other activities in the book, **Do It!** will appear next to the action that you need to perform to move through the steps.

Remember that the Web is always changing, and the results you get may differ from those shown in this book. Don't let this confuse you. These activities demonstrate fundamental skills that don't change, even though what you see when you follow the steps may look different each time.

out population characteristics to further their understanding of business trends and make intelligent hypotheses regarding projected economic changes. Perhaps you're taking a job or moving to another part of the country and want to know something about the population in that area.

The United States Census Bureau is the most reliable source for this type of information, and its Web site is well-designed and filled with useful information. The following activity will give you practice browsing a Web site and will show you how easy it is to use the World Wide Web to find the information you need.

BROWSING THE U.S. CENSUS BUREAU'S WEB SITE

Overview

We're assuming that you have a browser program set up on your computer and that you have a way of connecting to the Internet.

In going through the steps of this activity, we'll start the browser, explain some of the items you'll see on your screen, and then type in a URL that will take us to the United States Census Bureau's home page. We'll locate a population clock for the United States and browse for census information for a county in Michigan. These are the steps we'll follow:

1. Start the Web browser.
2. Go to the United States Census Bureau's home page.
3. Explore the United States Census Bureau's Web site.
4. Exit the Web browser.

Details

1. Start the Web browser.

You start the Web browser by clicking on an icon or choosing the browser from a menu. You'll need to find the icon on the desktop or select the program from a list of programs you can run from your computer.

If you're using Internet Explorer, look for an icon that looks like this:

Internet
Explorer

If you're using Netscape, locate an icon that looks like one of the following:

Netscape
Communicator

Netscape
Communicator

Netscape

Double-clicking one of these icons starts the Web browser.

From here on, we'll give the steps for the activity assuming that Internet Explorer is being used as the Web browser.

A window similar to the one in Figure 1.1 will appear on your screen, although the contents will be different. In this case, the browser brought to the screen the home page for the computer that we are using for this activity. We will use this page as a starting point for this Web exploration exercise.

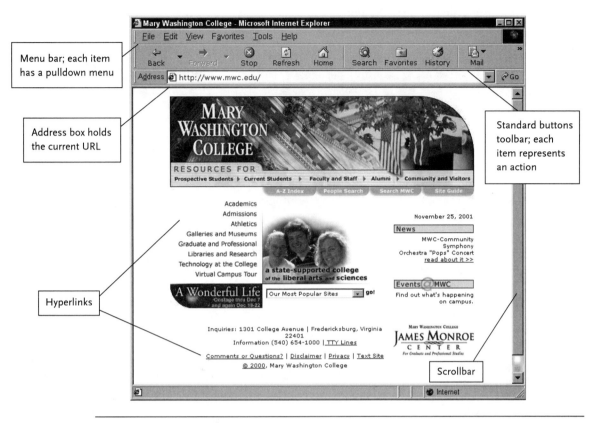

Menu bar; each item has a pulldown menu

Address box holds the current URL

Standard buttons toolbar; each item represents an action

Hyperlinks

Scrollbar

Figure 1.1   A Home Page

If you're familiar with a windowed environment, you should feel very comfortable using a Web browser. You can work with many of the items in this window in the same way as with any other window. The menu commands are listed across the top row. They include the following:

File   Edit   View   Favorites   Tools   Help

The menu bar contains items (such as File, Edit, and Help) that are common to several windowed applications. Each command has a pull-down menu; click on the command and a menu will appear.

The browser's window also has several items in the standard buttons toolbar, as shown in Figure 1.1. You can use them to go from one Web page to another, to print a Web page, stop the current page that is loading, and so forth. For example, you click on **Back** to go to the previous Web page.

2. Go to the United States Census Bureau's home page.

To go to the United States Census Bureau's home page, you need to know what its Uniform Resource Locator, or URL, is. We can assume that you have found the URL in a book or a newspaper article or a friend has given it to you. The URL, **http://www.census.gov**, will be typed in the address box of the browser window.

When you click on the Address box, it changes color. You can type a new URL to replace the current one.

☑ Do It! Type **http://www.census.gov** in the location field and press Enter.

After you type the URL in the Address box and press Enter, the Explorer icon will appear in front of it, as shown in Figure 1.2.

Figure 1.2—A URL Typed in the Address Box

☑ T I P ! **Typing Only Part of a URL**

You don't need to type the complete URL. You can always omit the leading **http://** and simply type the domain name (**www.census.gov**) in the location field. The browser may put **http://www.** in front of any partial URL you type in the location field.

If the URL doesn't start with http://www, then you'll have to type in the complete URL. We use the full form in this book so the URLs are complete and will work with any browser. Complete URLs **must** be used when you're creating a Web page using HTML.

When you press Enter, your Web browser sends a request to the Census Bureau's Web server, the computer that makes the U.S. census material available. The server then sends the Web page with the URL **http://www.census.gov** across the Internet to your computer. The United States Census Bureau's home page appears in Figure 1.3.

It's worth noting here that a URL gives us some information about a Web site. The first part of any URL after **http://** is the Internet domain name of the computer that hosts the Web site. In this case the domain name is **www.census.gov**. Only U.S. government sites can have a domain name that ends with **gov**, so the URL here indicates that this is a Web site associated with an agency of the U.S. government.

3. **Explore the United States Census Bureau's Web site.**

There are many ways to explore the U.S. Census Bureau. Let's start out by simply clicking on a hyperlink that looks interesting. In Figure 1.3, you'll notice the hyperlink **Population Clocks**. By clicking on this hyperlink, we can find out current population statistics for the United States and the world. Let's see what we can find out.

☑ Do It! Click on the hyperlink **Population Clocks**, as shown in Figure 1.3.

We can find out population statistics for the United States or for the world. Let's try clicking on the link for the United States.

☑ Do It! Click on **U.S. Population Estimate**, as shown in Figure 1.4.

Note the information retrieved in Figure 1.5. This population clock is a projection, which means that the numbers aren't exact—they are estimates. The Census Bureau uses the numbers it has in its databases from the last national census and adds numbers gathered from state and local governments to project a current population. The page shows the time intervals between births and deaths and other related information. One advantage of using a government site like this one for population data is that it provides reliable information. The U.S. Census Bureau stands behind its projections, using scientific data to formulate its predictions and other statistics.

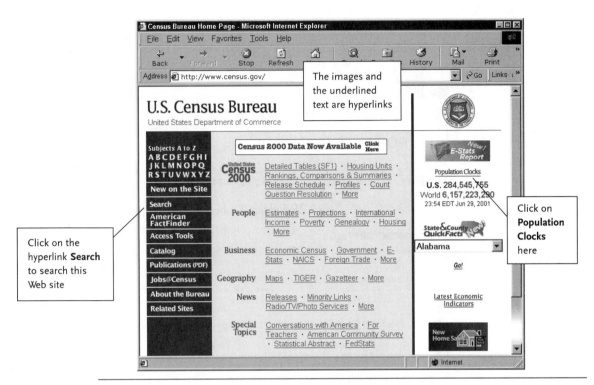

Figure 1.3   The U.S. Census Bureau's Home Page

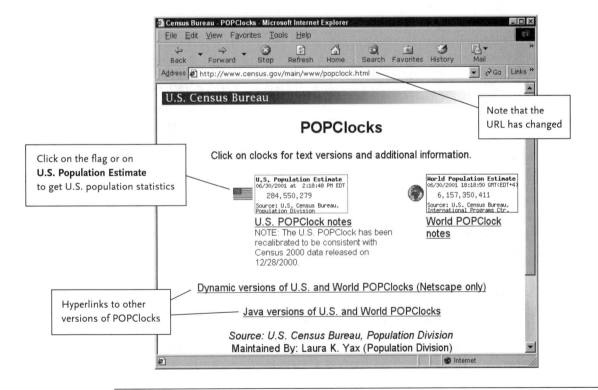

Figure 1.4   Population Clock Hyperlinks

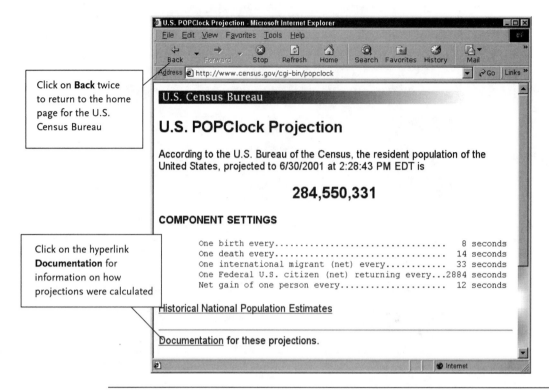

Click on **Back** twice to return to the home page for the U.S. Census Bureau

Click on the hyperlink **Documentation** for information on how projections were calculated

Figure 1.5   The Current Projected Population of the United States

Now let's explore some other areas of the Census Bureau. We want to return to the Census Bureau's home page, pictured in Figure 1.3. You'll need to go back two Web pages. You can do that by clicking on **Back**, in the navigation toolbar, twice.

☑ T I P !   **Using Back and Forward for Navigation**

Clicking once on **Back** or **Forward** in the standard buttons toolbar takes you to a Web page you previously visited. If you clicked a hyperlink on a Web page or typed in a URL to get to the present page, then clicking on **Back** will return you to the page where you were most recently. You can retrace your steps by continuing to click on **Back**. Once you've gone back, you can move in the opposite direction by clicking on **Forward**.

☑ Do It!   Click on **Back** twice, until you're at the U.S. Census Bureau's home page, as pictured in Figure 1.3.

Notice that in Figure 1.3 there is a hyperlink called **Search**. Let's look at the options for searching the Census Bureau's site.

☑ Do It!   Click on **Search**.

The browser retrieves the Web page called "Census Bureau Search." The form and hyperlinks on this page let you search by word, place, map, and staff. We're going to try a search by map, so use the vertical scroll bar to get the hyperlink **Map Search** in the browser's window, as shown in Figure 1.6.

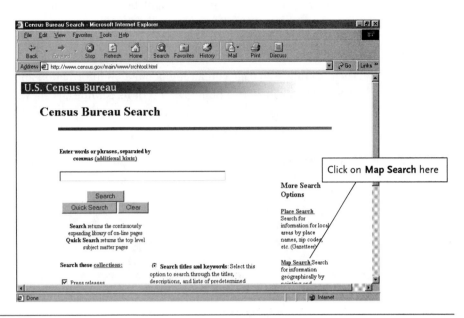

Figure 1.6   Ways to Search the Census Bureau's Site

The hyperlinks we've clicked so far in this activity have been either text links or, in the case of the population clock, icons. Now we'll demonstrate how a hyperlink can be part of a map.

☑ Do It!   Click on **Map Search**, as shown in Figure 1.6.

A map of the United States will appear, as shown in Figure 1.7.

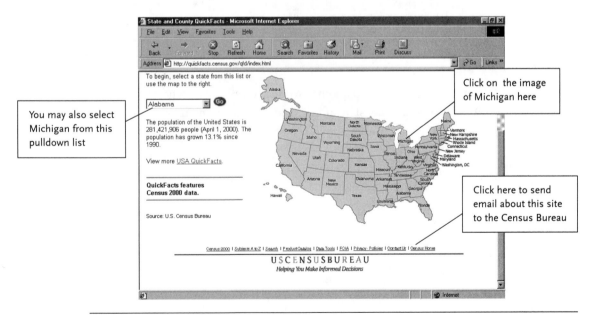

Figure 1.7   An Image Map of the United States

You can click on any state for population information. If you want, you can click on your own state. We'll click on the state of Michigan.

☑ Do It! Click on **Michigan**, as shown in Figure 1.7.

The resulting Web page containing population information and other statistics about the state of Michigan, with a pull-down list of its counties, is shown in Figure 1.8. Select the name of a county from the list, then click on **Go** to get information about that county. Let's try Washtenaw County.

☑ Do It! Select **Washtenaw** from the list of counties and click on **Go**, as shown in Figure 1.8.

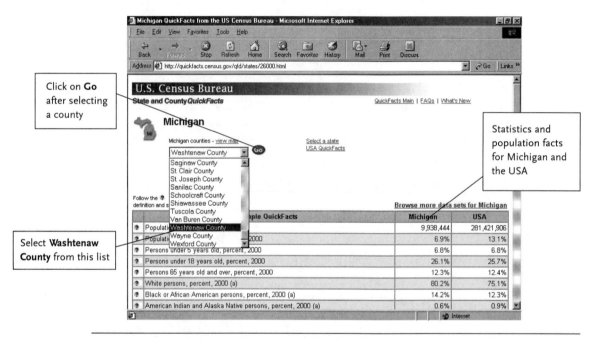

Figure 1.8   Michigan with Its Counties Outlined

This selection brings up another Web page with information about the selected county—Washtenaw—and the state of Michigan, as shown in Figure 1.9.

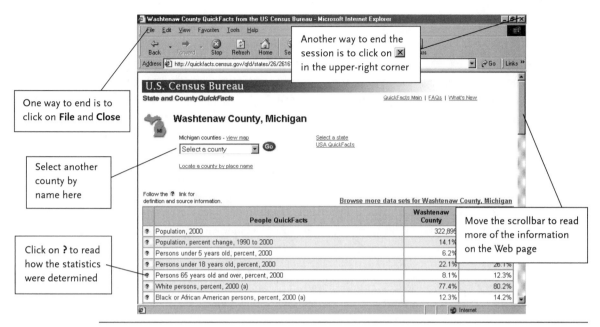

Figure 1.9   Washtenaw County Census Information Hyperlinks

We could spend hours exploring the U.S. Census Bureau's site, but let's stop now so we can talk about other things.

4. Exit the Web browser.

You can exit the browser in the same way you exit most other windowed applications. Here are two ways that work:

☑ Do It!   Click on **File** in the menu bar and select **Exit**.

☑ Do It!   Click on ⊠ in the upper-right corner of the window.

The window will close, and you will have ended this session with the browser. Make sure your connection is terminated if you are paying by the minute or the hour.

END OF ACTIVITY 1 ◀

In Activity 1, we introduced you to the Web browser and how to get started retrieving information from the World Wide Web by looking at a United States government Web site, the site of the Census Bureau. We'll be covering many more details of using a Web browser later on in the textbook. You may have noticed that some of the Web pages had a hyperlink called **text only**; you can use that link to bypass the graphic images. When the Internet is busy, you can save time by getting a text-only view.

Summary

The Internet is, by definition, a collection of networks throughout the world that agree to communicate using specific telecommunications protocols. However, this definition doesn't describe what makes the Internet so exciting. The Internet also can be viewed in terms of the people who use it and the ways they communicate with each other to share information and ideas. It also is a place for people to do research, conduct business, and find information that might enrich their daily lives. The major difference between the Internet and other media, such as television, is that it is interactive and provides immediate feedback. The World Wide Web is the collection of information that is available through the Internet.

Since the advent of graphical browsers like Netscape Navigator and Microsoft Internet Explorer, the hypertext environment on the Web has made it easy for people to access information by simply clicking on a hyperlink. These hyperlinks can connect the user to text files, programs, charts, graphical images, and digitized video and audio files. The possibilities seem endless, and the path you take is your own choice. A Uniform Resource Locator, or URL, represents each hyperlink. Web browsers use these URLs to specify the type of Internet service or protocol needed and the location of the item. For example, the URL for the Web page "POPClocks" (at the U.S. Census Bureau's Web site) is **http://www.census.gov/main/www/popclock.html**.

You can access the Internet by having a direct connection from your computer to a network. This is often the setup when your company or campus has a network installed in its offices, classrooms, labs, or residence hall rooms. To get connected to the Internet, you need the proper device to connect to your organization's network and (possibly) the IP address for your computer and for a domain name system. Another way to connect to the Internet is to use a modem to call an Internet service provider (ISP) and gain access through a point-to-point protocol, or PPP, connection.

Selected Terms Discussed in This Chapter

domain name system	Internet service provider (ISP)
electronic mail (email)	IP address
hyperlinks	point-to-point protocol (PPP)
hypermedia	protocol
hypertext transfer protocol (HTTP)	Transmission Control Protocol (TCP)
Internet	Uniform Resource Locator (URL)
Internet domain name	Web browser
Internet Protocol (IP)	World Wide Web (WWW)

Materials on CD for This Chapter

Here is a list of items for this chapter on the CD that accompanies the text:

- ☑ "Review of Fredericksburg.com," a review of the Web site Fredericksburg.com according to the directions in Exercise 5 below
- ☑ All URLs mentioned in this chapter in hypertext format
- ☑ Selected terms discussed in this chapter with hyperlinks to the glossary
- ☑ Copies of the review questions in quiz format

Review Questions

True or False?

1. Information is transmitted in packets on the Internet.
2. The concept of the World Wide Web is credited to the work of Tim Berners-Lee.
3. "World Wide Web" and "Internet" are terms that mean exactly the same thing.
4. A browser also can be referred to as an ISP.
5. You must always type the leading **http://** portion of a URL when trying to access a Web page.

Short Answer—Completion

1. The _____ is an international collection of computer networks that exchange information according to a fixed set of rules.
2. The _____ is the collection of information accessible through the Internet.
3. Many people who use the Internet use it for communicating with others through _____ .
4. Information on the Web may be text, video, audio, or graphical images. We refer to these types of information as _____ .
5. You access the World Wide Web by using a program called a _____ .

Exercises and Projects

1. Is there a person, office, or agency you can contact when you have problems or questions about using your computer or the Internet when you're at school or at work? If so, give the name, email address, URL of the Web page, or phone number of the place you can contact when you have a problem or a question. If there is no help desk or contact group for your organization, assume you're a student at Mary Washington College and start looking for this information at the Web page with the URL **http://inte.mwc.edu**.
2. Most organizations and Internet service providers (ISPs) have a set of policies about proper use and behavior on the Internet and the network used to access the Internet. Get a copy of these policies for your organization or school; many times it's available as a hyperlink from your organization's or school's Web site.
   a. What is the URL of the policy? If it's not available on the Web, then give the steps necessary to obtain a copy of the policy.
   b. Most policies give a list of acceptable uses or user responsibilities. List the three that are, in your opinion, most important.
   c. What activities are prohibited?
   d. How does the policy address the issue of protecting your privacy and keeping private information about you?
3. Use the same techniques as in this chapter's activity to find the following:
   a. The current U.S. and world populations.
   b. The percentage of the general population that are high school graduates and the percentage that are college graduates for the county where you currently live or where you call home.

4. Visit the Web site with the URL **http://nsrc.org/codes/country-codes.html**.
   a. Describe what you find at the Web site.
   b. What is the Internet domain name for the Web server that hosts this site?
   c. Using the domain name as a guide, state the type of network that hosts this server.
   d. Suppose you were to retrieve the Web page with the URL **http://hotline.pvtnet.cz/utility/nslookup.htm**. In what country is the network registered that hosts this Web site?

5. Take a look at some of the reviews or descriptions of Web sites at "Librarians' Index to the Internet," located at **http://lii.org,** or "The Scout Report" at **http://scout.cs.wisc.edu/index.html**.

   Write a review of a Web site for a local company or organization. On separate lines, give the title of the Web site and its URL. Follow this by the name of the author or hosting organization. Then include a few sentences (between 75 and 150 words) that state the purpose of the Web site and describe its content, usefulness, and design. On separate lines, write the date you viewed the Web site and the date it was last modified, if that can be determined. We've included a sample review on the CD that accompanies this book in the materials for Chapter 1.

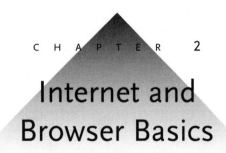

Internet and Browser Basics

▶ how does the Internet work? What are the basic terms and technical concepts? What happens when an email message, a file, a Web page, or any information is transported from one computer to another on the Internet? What does it mean to be connected to the Internet? We will give answers to these and related questions in this chapter.

The World Wide Web is a vast collection of information that is connected or linked together. You can access all this information through one program or tool, the Web browser. This is significant because it gives you essentially one way of doing things, one interface to many different types of information in a variety of media formats. Here we'll go over some of the details, concepts, and techniques that will help you become proficient in the ways you use your browser to explore the World Wide Web. This also helps you understand new concepts and terms that will surely come up as the nature of the Web and the browsers themselves change. The browser is what you use to access the Web, and you'll have a better time doing it when you're comfortable with the browser's features and capabilities.

Goals/Objectives:

- ☑ Gain a general understanding of the technical aspects of the Internet
- ☑ Learn the primary terms and concepts associated with using the Internet and the Web
- ☑ Learn some of the functions and capabilities of a Web browser
- ☑ Learn ways to navigate around the Web

Topics:

- ☑ An Overview of How the Internet Works
- ☑ Basic Terms and Concepts
- ☑ Using the Browser's Window
- ☑ Working with Netscape and Internet Explorer
- ☑ Navigating the Web

An Overview of How the Internet Works

When you are connected to the Internet, you're able to communicate with others on the Internet through email, Usenet news, and chat. You also can access Web sites using your browser to browse or search for information. The ability to do these things takes a lot of technical support. This includes hardware such as networks, computers, modems, and other devices to make the connection possible. It also includes software such as communication, client, server, and other programs.

Protocols

The Internet is designed so that computer systems within one network can exchange information with computers on other networks. The rules that govern this form of communication are called *protocols*. By using the same protocols, different types of networks and computer systems can communicate with one another. Each network and computer needs to have the software and hardware in place to deal with information in the form specified by the protocols.

Two basic protocols used are *Internet Protocol (IP)* and *Transmission Control Protocol (TCP)*. You often see them referred to together as TCP/IP.

☑ F Y I **Getting More Information About How the Internet Works**

- ☑ "Connected: An Internet Encyclopedia," http://www.FreeSoft.org/CIE/index.htm
- ☑ "How the Internet Works," http://www.sonic.net/~garyh/fstudy/section1_2.html#works
- ☑ "How Web Servers and the Internet Works," http://www.howstuffworks.com/web-server.htm

---

IP Addresses and Domain Names

The Internet is a collection of thousands of computer networks, each with its own address. Each network must have its own address so that information can be reliably routed from one network to another.

Each network on the Internet has a unique address, called an *IP address*, and each of the computer systems making up a network has an IP address, which is sometimes based on the network's IP address.

At a basic level, the addresses are numeric—209.196.179.233, for example. You don't need to memorize the numbers, however. The addresses also can be specified as names, such as **www.webliminal.com**. This is called an ***Internet domain name***. Domain names are included in URLs and email addresses. In the URL **http://www.webliminal.com/internet-today/it-gloss.html**, the domain name is **www.webliminal.com**. In the email address **jimleisy@fbeedle.com**, the domain name is **fbeedle.com**.

The translation of domain names to IP addresses is handled automatically by the ***domain name system***.

A domain name can tell you something about the site you're contacting. Some domain names are geographical, and the last two letters are an abbreviation for the country where the network is located. For example, the domain name **www.ee.ic.ac.uk** refers to a network in the United Kingdom. Some domain names registered in the United States end in three letters that indicate the type of network. Table 2.1 lists the major types of networks and their corresponding domain-name endings in the United States.

Domain Name Ending	Type of Network	Example
edu	Educational—usually a school, college, or university	**www.mwc.edu**
gov	U.S. government agency	**www.census.gov**
com	Commercial	**www.microsoft.com**
net	Network	**www.earthlink.net**
org	Organization— a nonprofit institution	**www.sierraclub.org**

Table 2.1   Domain Name Clues

Packets

Using Internet Protocol, a message consisting of at most 1,500 bytes or characters is put into a packet. Each packet has the address of the sender and the address of the destination. You can think of a packet in the same way you think of a letter that is sent by the postal service.

Packets of characters, similar to envelopes holding messages, are used to carry information on the Internet.

Using TCP, a single message is divided into a sequence of IP packets. The packets are passed from one network to another until they reach their destination. At the destination, the TCP software reassembles the packets into a complete message. If packets are lost or damaged, a request is transmitted to resend them. It isn't necessary for all of the packets in a single message to take the same route through the Internet or for the same message to take the same route each time it's sent. This concept of sending messages naturally applies to email, but it also applies to many of the other services on the Internet.

The Internet is a *packet-switched network.*

Emphasis is on transmitting and receiving packets, rather than on connecting computer systems to each other. Passing information and implementing the Internet services with packets keeps one system from tying up the networks with a connection dedicated to a single program.

Each computer system with a direct connection to the Internet has to have the hardware and/or software to allow it to work with packets. It's up to the individual computer systems to take care of sending and receiving packets.

The bulk of Internet traffic is carried on high-capacity communication lines that link communication centers throughout the world. These lines are sometimes called the Internet backbone. The lines are leased from major communication companies. Information on the Internet travels from individual users to a local network and from there (if necessary) to a larger network that provides a connection to another network until the information makes it to the backbone. Then it's carried on these high-capacity lines until it is passed off to a network that passes it to a smaller network, and so on, until it gets to its destination.

Basic Terms and Concepts

In this section, we'll discuss some of the terms and concepts that are important to know about when you're working with the Internet and the Web.

Digital Format

All the information on the Internet is sent, transmitted across networks, and received in a digital format. This has some significant consequences:

- ☑ Information is transmitted as electrons and then converted to other forms, such as Web pages or printed pages, at its destination. The person receiving the information has a choice of how to view, save, or manipulate it.
- ☑ Questions of distance virtually disappear because electrons travel at rates approaching the speed of light. A more relevant issue is the amount of information, measured in bytes, that can be transported through a network in a given period of time.

Client/Server

When you start a Web browser or follow a hyperlink, the browser sends a request to a computer on the Internet. That computer returns a file that the browser then displays. This sort of interaction, in which one system requests information and another provides it, is called a *client/server* relationship. The browser is the client, and it communicates with another program called a server, which provides the information. This relationship is illustrated in Figure 2.1. It's also common to use the term *client* to refer to the computer that's running the browser and to call the computer that is supplying the information the *server.*

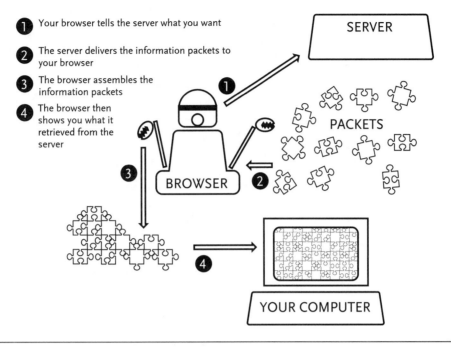

Figure 2.1   Client/Server: The Browser Is the Client and Receives Packets from the Server

Hypertext Transfer Protocol (HTTP)

Documents or pages are passed from a server to a client according to specific rules for exchanging information. These rules are called protocols. The protocol used on the WWW is called **HTTP**, which stands for **hypertext transfer protocol**, because the documents, pages, or other items passed from one computer to another are in hypertext or hypermedia form.

Hypertext Markup Language (HTML)

The rules for creating or writing a Web page are all specified as **hypertext markup language (HTML)**. This language provides the formal rules for marking text. The rules govern how text is displayed as part of a Web page. HTML is used, for example, to mark text so that it appears in boldface or italics. For text, an image, or an icon to represent a hyperlink, it has to be marked as a link in HTML and the URL has to be included. Web pages are usually stored in files with names that end with **.html** or **.htm**.

If the file is written using HTML, the browser interprets the file so that graphics and images are displayed along with the text. Figure 2.2 illustrates this.

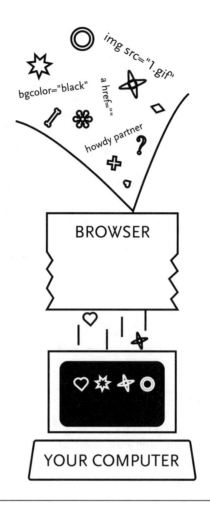

Figure 2.2   The Browser Interprets HTML to Display a Web Page

Here are a few lines to demonstrate what HTML looks like in a Web document:

```
This is a <b>very short</b> example of HTML.
For more examples, take a look at the Web page
<a href="http://www1.mwc.edu/~ernie/writeweb/writeweb.html">
Writing Your Own Web Pages.</a>
```

A Web browser would display the HTML above as:

```
This is a very short example of HTML. For more examples, take a
look at the Web page Writing Your Own Web Pages.
```

The tags used here are

- ☑ <b> and </b>: The text between them is displayed as bold.
- ☑ <a href="http://www1.mwc.edu/~ernie/writeweb/writeweb.html"> and </a>: The text between them is a hyperlink.

Uniform Resource Locator (URL)

A *hyperlink* is represented in a specific format called a ***URL,*** or ***Uniform Resource Locator.*** The URL is displayed just above the content area in a Web browser's window. Each Web page has a URL as its address. For example, the URL for the Library of Congress's Web page *Mr. Lincoln's Virtual Library* is **http://memory.loc.gov/ammem/alhtml/alhome.html.**

URLs that point to Web pages all start with **http://** because they are all transmitted according to HTTP. You'll see something different for URLs that access information through other Internet protocols. For example, information available by FTP, File Transfer Protocol, uses **ftp://** in its URL. The URL for the NASA collection of space images is **ftp://ftp.jpl.nasa.gov/pub/images.**

It's helpful to think of a URL as having the following form:

```
how-to-get-there://where-to-go/what-to-get
```

We will now show you the different parts of a URL so that you have a better idea of what information a URL conveys:

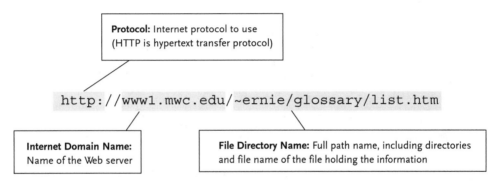

Most URLs have this format. By indicating which Internet protocol to use, they tell you how to retrieve the information. By naming the Web server and the file or directory holding the information, they tell you where the page is located. If only a server name is included in the URL, as in **http://www.loc.gov,** you will still retrieve a file; by default, the server will pass along a common default file, usually named **index.html** or **index.htm.**

Sometimes you'll see URLs written without **http://** in front. Generally, you can safely omit **http://** when you open a Web page or location by typing the remainder of the URL into the browser's location field. Most browsers assume HTTP is the protocol being used.

Error Messages

As amazing as some computer systems are, they generally need very precise instructions. You have to be careful about spacing (generally there aren't blank spaces in a URL), the symbols used (a slash and a period are not interchangeable), and the case of the letters.

For example, the URL for the frequently asked questions (FAQ) for finding email addresses is **http://www.qucis.queensu.ca/FAQs/email/finding.html.** Replacing "email" with "EMAIL," as in **http://www.qucis.queensu.ca/FAQs/EMAIL/finding.html,** would cause the server to report a message back to the browser, such as:

```
404
The requested URL was not found on this server.
```

☑ T I P ! **Dealing with 404 Messages**

1. Check the spelling, punctuation, and capitalization of the URL.

2. If the URL ends with **html** try **htm** instead.

3. Back up over the URL by highlighting everything past the last slash (/) and deleting it. It may be helpful to see a page or directory listing.

For more tips take a look at "Yikes! 404!," **http://plinko.net /404/yikes.asp**

This message tells us that there is a Web server with the domain name **www.qucis.queensu.ca** but that the file could not be found on the Web server.

A message such as this is called a ***404 error.*** You may see this error message if the URL is incorrect. Sometimes you'll also get this error message if a Web page has been removed from a Web server or is no longer available.

There are several other types of error codes you may see as you use the Web. Take a look at "Learn the Net: Decoding Error Messages," **http://learnthenet .com/english/html/96error.htm**, for a list of error messages and helpful advice for dealing with them.

With this information as background for working with the Internet, let's now take a look at how to use a browser.

Using the Browser's Window

When you start a Web browser, the browser's window appears on the screen. It's the Web browser's job to retrieve and display information inside the window.

Whenever you access a hyperlink, the browser, which is a computer program, sends a request to have a file transferred to it. The browser then interprets the information in the file so that it can be viewed in the browser's window or, in some cases, viewed through another program. For example, if a hyperlink points to a text file, then the file is displayed in the window as ordinary text. If the hyperlink points to a document written in HTML, then the browser displays it as a Web page. If the file is a sound file or an animation, then a different program is launched for hearing or viewing the file. Most of these facilities and capabilities are built into the browser, but in some cases, your computer must be equipped with special equipment or programs. For example, if you click on a hyperlink that points to a sound file, your computer must have a sound card, speakers, and the software to play back the sounds.

What is in the window will change as you go from site to site, but each window has the same format. The items that help you work with the Web document in the window include the scroll bar, the menu bar, and the toolbar, which are the same every time you use the browser. The major components of a Web page displayed by Netscape and Internet Explorer are labeled in Figure 2.3.

The browser lets you access, retrieve, work with, and enjoy the information and resources that make up the World Wide Web. To coin a phrase, the browser is your window to the Web.

In this section, we'll look at some of the functions available in a browser and techniques for working with them.

Ways of Working with Netscape and Internet Explorer

The windows for Netscape Navigator and Microsoft Internet Explorer are by and large the same. Here, we'll list and discuss the elements common to both.

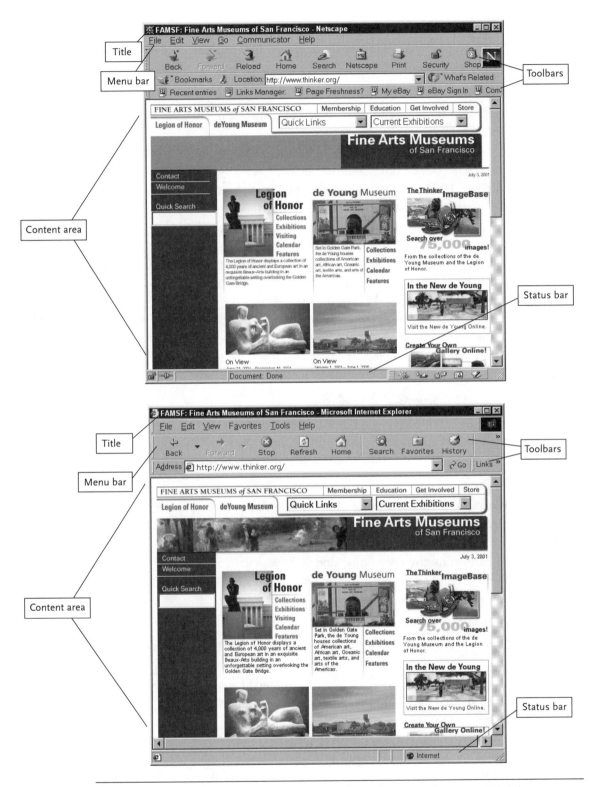

Figure 2.3   Netscape and Internet Explorer Windows with Common Components Labeled

Title

The title of a Web page is created when the page is written. A page's title is not the same as its URL, just as a book's title is different from its library call number.

Menu Bar

The *menu bar* is a list of items, each representing a menu from which you can choose an action.

To make a choice, simply move the mouse pointer to the item you want to choose and click on it. You also can activate one of these items by using the **Alt** key along with the underlined letter. For example, to display the menu associated with File, use **Alt**+**F**.

Selecting an item from the menu bar brings up a pull-down menu with several options. For example, if you click on **File** (or use **Alt**+**F**), you see the menu shown to the right.

Select any highlighted item in that menu either by clicking on it with the mouse or by pressing the underlined character in its name. To print the current Web page, you can click on **Print** in this menu or you can press **P** (upper- or lowercase). Some items on the menu are followed by **Ctrl**+ letter, such as the following:

Save As...   **Ctrl**+**S**

To select the command from the menu, you can either click on **Save As** using the mouse or use the keyboard shortcut given in the menu: **Ctrl**+**S**. This particular command allows you to save a copy of the Web page in a file on your computer.

Toolbars

Like other Windows software, Web browsers have one or more rows of icons or items called *toolbars* just below the menu bar. Each item works like a button. When you press it using the mouse, an operation or action will take place.

The icons give you a visual clue to the operation or action they represent. The commands they represent are all available through the items on the menu bar as well, but the icons give you a direct path—another shortcut—to the commands.

Content Area or Document View

The *content area* is the portion of the window that holds the document, page, or other resource as your browser presents it. It can contain text or images.

Sometimes the content area is divided into or consists of several independent portions called *frames*. Each frame has its own scroll bar, and you can move through one frame while staying in the same place in others.

The content area holds the Web page you're viewing, which likely contains hyperlinks in text or graphic format. Clicking on a hyperlink with the *left* mouse button allows you to follow the link. Clicking with the *right* mouse button (or holding down the mouse button without clicking if your mouse has only one button) brings up a menu that gives you options for working with a hyperlink.

Scroll Bar

If the document doesn't fit into the window, it will be displayed with vertical and/or horizontal *scroll bars*.

Status Bar

When you are retrieving a document, opening a location, or following a hyperlink, the bar along the bottom of the window (the *status bar*) displays the URL that's being used. It also lets you know whether a site is being contacted, if it's responding, and how the transmission is progressing.

Working with Netscape and Internet Explorer

Netscape Navigator and Microsoft Internet Explorer employ many of the same techniques for working with the browser. We'll discuss them here, noting where the two programs differ.

Starting the Browser

The Web browser is a program that runs or executes on your computer. You start it the same way that you start other programs. To start a Web browser session, double-click on the icon for the browser. Look for an icon that looks like one of the following:

To start Netscape: **To start Internet Explorer:**

Netscape   Netscape   Netscape   Internet
Communicator   Communicator   Explorer

Ending a Browser Session

You can stop a Web browser program in the same way that you end almost any other Windows-based program or application. Here are some ways to do that:

☑ Press **Alt**+**F4**.
☑ Click on ⊠ in the upper-right corner.
☑ Click on **File** in the menu bar, then click on **Close**, **Exit**, or **Quit**.

Getting Help

When you have a question about using the browser, check the online help by pressing **F1** or clicking on **Help** in the menu bar.

Changing the Size of the Text

Does it seem that the text on a Web page is too small or too large for your liking? Do you need to make the text larger so that your Web project shows up better when it's projected on a screen to a room full of interested people? It can be done! You can change the size of the text that's displayed by clicking on **View** in the menu bar, then selecting **Text Size**.

ON CD

The CD that accompanies this book includes a table that shows the keyboard shortcuts common to Internet Explorer and Netscape.

To view the table, click on the hyperlink "Keyboard Shortcuts" in the collection of items for Chapter 2.

Keyboard Shortcuts

You can access all the commands in a Web browser by pointing and clicking on a word, icon, or portion of the window, but sometimes you may want to give a command using the keyboard. To do this, use the key labeled **Ctrl** or **Alt**, along with another key. For example, to print the current Web page, you can select **Print** from a menu or use **Ctrl**+P. Using **Ctrl**+P means holding down the key labeled **Ctrl**, pressing the key labeled **P**, and then releasing them both. Pressing **Alt**+H will display a menu of online help information. To access the help menu, simply hold down the key labeled **Alt**, press the **H** key, and then release them both.

To see a complete list of keyboard shortcuts take a look at "Using Keyboard Shortcuts," **http://home.netscape.com/browsers/using/ieusers/browsing/shortcuts.html**.

Using the Right Mouse Button

Both Netscape and Internet Explorer take advantage of the *right* or *secondary* mouse button. If your mouse has only one button, then holding it down, rather than quickly clicking it, is usually equivalent to pressing the right button on a mouse with two or more buttons. While reading this chapter, try using the right mouse button as you work with the browser.

Here are some of the ways to use the right mouse button:

- ☑ **Back or Forward.** Clicking the right mouse button on either the **Back** or **Forward** icon brings up a list of sites that you have recently visited. You can move backward or forward to these sites by selecting one from the list and clicking on it.

- ☑ **Copy and Paste.** You can use the right mouse button to copy and paste information from a Web page, email, or other windowed source. Say that you're working with email or are in the content area of a Web page and are not on a hyperlink. Using the mouse, move the cursor or pointer to the beginning of a portion of text that you want to copy. Hold down the left mouse button and use the mouse to highlight the text, then click the right mouse button and select **Copy**. Now move the mouse pointer to where you want to paste the text—maybe you've copied a URL and want to put it in the location field. Press the right mouse button and select **Paste**. If you are pasting a URL into the location field or some other field in a form, be sure to click on the location field with the left mouse button first to highlight the text you want to replace.

- ☑ **Content area.** If the mouse pointer is in the content area but not on a hyperlink, clicking the right mouse button will bring up a menu with several useful items, many of which are part of other menus or toolbars. These include options to go **Back** or **Forward** to a Web page and to **Reload**, **Refresh**, or **Stop** loading the current Web page. Also, you can set the background image on a Web site as wallpaper for your desktop, save the image in a file on your hard drive, add the current page to your bookmark or favorites list, create a desktop shortcut to the page, or send the Web page via email.

- ☑ **Images.** When you place the mouse pointer on an image, you have the same choices as when it's in the content area and not on a hyperlink. In addition, you can view the image in a separate window, save the image in a file, or copy the URL for the image (in case you want to include it in a Web page that you're constructing).

☑ **Hyperlinks.** When you place the mouse pointer on a hyperlink, it will change into a hand. When you click the right mouse button, a menu will appear with all the same items as when the pointer isn't on a hyperlink. In addition, the menu includes items to open the link in a new, separate window. You also can save the Web page represented by the link to a file; you can copy the link, which means copying the URL for later use with the paste operation; or you can copy the link to your list of bookmarks (if you're using Netscape) or favorites (if you're using Internet Explorer).

◢ F Y I   **More About Browsers**

☑ "Browser News," http://upsdell.com/BrowserNews

☑ "Browsers," http://home.cnet.com/category/0-3773.html

☑ "Open Directory—Computers: Software: Internet: Clients: WWW: Browsers," http://dmoz.org/Computers/Software/Internet/Clients/WWW/Browsers

☑ "Web Browsers," http://webteacher.org/winnet/browser/browser.html

---

Copying and Pasting

You can copy the text on a Web page into another Windows-based application, such as a word-processing or spreadsheet program, or into a form or the location field in the browser's window. Highlight the text by pressing the left mouse button and dragging it over the text. Click the right mouse button and select **Copy**. Put the mouse pointer into another Windows application, click the right mouse button, and select **Paste**.

You can copy a hyperlink by moving the mouse pointer over the hyperlink, pressing the right mouse button, and selecting **Copy Link Location**.

Setting Preferences or Internet Options

Both Netscape and Internet Explorer let you set several preferences or options to customize your browsing experience. You can set a variety of preferences, including the location of your browser's home page, the default font and character set, and the information necessary for using the email program that comes with your browser. We won't go into the details here.

To set preferences in Netscape, click on **Edit** in the menu bar and then select **Preferences**. Another window with built-in online help will open.

To set Internet preferences in Internet Explorer, click on **Tools** in the menu bar and then select **Internet Options**. Press **F1** any time you need help.

Navigating the Web

Navigation and travel are two ways that people describe accessing and using the Internet. The Internet also has been called the "Information Superhighway." Netscape calls its browser Navigator and uses nautical imagery, such as a pilot's wheel and a lighthouse, as icons.

ON CD

The CD that accompanies this book includes more details about using Internet Explorer and Netscape.

To read them, click on either of these hyperlinks in the collection of items for Chapter 2.

☑ "Details About the Internet Explorer Window"

☑ "Details About the Netscape Navigator Window"

Microsoft has named its browser Internet Explorer. While the navigational theme is just a metaphor (the truth is you don't travel anywhere when you access the Internet), it is commonly accepted and useful for describing one primary function of a Web browser.

Starting at Home

When you start a Web browser, the first page or document that appears in the window is called the *home page* for the browser. It's where you start on the WWW. You can set this up to be any Web site that you choose. The term also is used in another way. Individuals, corporations, institutions, and organizations often have a page or document on the WWW that gives information about them. For example, the URL for the home page of the Smithsonian Institution is **http://www.si.edu**; the URL for the home page of MTV is **http://www.mtv.com**; and one of this book's authors has a home page located at **http://users.mwc.edu/~khartman**.

Moving Through a Page

Since most Web pages contain more information than can be displayed in one window, you need to know how to move through a page to view all the information. Here are some ways to do that:

- ☑ **Using the scroll bars.** You can move around or through a document by using the vertical and horizontal scroll bars on the right and bottom of the window.
- ☑ **Using the keyboard.** Pressing the up or down arrow will move you up or down one line. Pressing the **PgUp** key moves up one window length, and pressing **PgDn** moves down one window length. Pressing **Ctrl**+**Home** takes you to the beginning of the document, and pressing **Ctrl**+**End** takes you to its end.
- ☑ **Finding text or searching a page.** You can search a Web page for a word, a portion of a word, a phrase, or, more generally, any string of characters. To find a string, you first have to bring up the dialog box labeled "Find." Type **Ctrl**+**F** on the keyboard.

Moving from Page to Page: Hyperlinks

You can always tell when the pointer is over a hyperlink because it will change to an image of a hand with a pointing index finger. When this happens, you can click on the hyperlink and retrieve the item that the hyperlink represents. Also, the browser usually displays the URL of the target document in the status bar. Hyperlinks are often underlined or displayed in a distinctive color.

In some cases, a small pop-up text box will appear next to the pointer when it's moved over an image. This is called *alternate text*, and it's a description of the hyperlink put in by the author or designer of the Web page.

Following links from one document to another in a freewheeling way is what is meant by the phase "surfing the Web." When you surf the Web, you go with the flow by surrendering to the serendipity of unstructured exploration and discovery.

Moving Back and Forward

You'll be able to move backwards and forward through the documents that you have viewed during a session. The easiest way is to click on the items **Back** or **Forward** in the toolbar just below the menu bar.

Back and **Forward** always take you through all the Web pages that you have viewed in the same order or in the reverse order that you have viewed them.

You can go back or forward one site at a time or you can select from a list of sites. To go back one site at a time, repeatedly click on **Back**. To go forward one at a time, press **Forward**. To skip to a desired site, do the following:

☑ Place the mouse pointer over **Back** on the toolbar.

☑ Click the right mouse button.

☑ Click on any site from the list of previously visited sites that appears.

Returning to Visited Sites and the History List

The Web browser keeps a record of the path you've taken to get to the current location. To see the path and select a site from it, do the following:

Netscape

Click on Go in the menu bar.

Internet
Explorer

Click on View in the menu bar and select Go To.

The browser also keeps track of all the Web pages visited recently in the *history list*. You can use this list to go directly to a Web page without having to go through all the pages in between.

Netscape   Internet
Explorer

Press Ctrl+H on the keyboard.

If you're using Internet Explorer, the history list is displayed as a list of folders in a frame to the left of the content area. Netscape shows the history list as a list of titles and URLs. You can select and highlight any item by using the up or down arrow on the keyboard or by using the mouse. Once you've highlighted the location you want, double-clicking will take you to the selected page. Click with the right mouse button to copy or delete entries or to add an entry to the bookmark list.

The number of days an item may be kept on the history list is set as follows:

Netscape

Click on Edit in the menu bar, select Preferences, then select the panel titled Navigator.

Internet
Explorer

Click on Tools in the menu bar, select Internet Options, then select the panel titled General.

Keeping Track—The Bookmark List (Netscape) and the Favorites List (Internet Explorer)

The *bookmark* or *favorites list* is a collection of hyperlinks to Web pages that you want to save from session to session. They could be Web pages or sites you especially like, ones you find useful, or ones you've looked at briefly but want to return to in the future. This is particularly good when you're starting to research a topic.

Each item on the bookmark or favorites list is fundamentally a hyperlink. The browser includes software to manage and arrange the list. You can add items, delete items, arrange them into folders, and so on.

To display the list, do the following:

Use the keyboard shortcut Ctrl**+B. The bookmark list is displayed in a separate window.**

Netscape

Click on Favorites **in the toolbar. The favorites list is displayed as a list of folders and hyperlinks in a frame to the left of the content area.**

Internet
Explorer

Figure 2.4 shows a sample Internet Explorer favorites list. The Netscape bookmark list is similar. Click on a folder to display its contents, and double-click on an entry to follow the hyperlink.

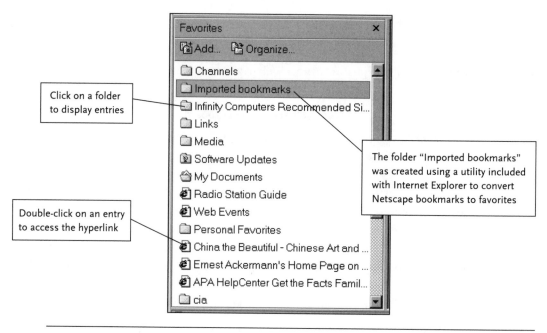

Figure 2.4   The Internet Explorer Favorites List

Press Ctrl**+D to add the Web page hyperlink you're currently viewing to either the bookmark or favorites list.**

Now that we've covered the navigational basics of using a browser, let's have some fun and practice. We're going to start at the World Wide Web Virtual Library, then take a look at some sites that deal with surfing and Hawaii, and then check out a few Web resources related to golf.

BROWSING THE WWW VIRTUAL LIBRARY—SPORT

Overview

This activity takes us to the WWW Virtual Library. It's a good site to keep in your bookmark or favorites list because it contains hyperlinks to information on all kinds of subjects ranging from Aboriginal Studies to Zoos. Going from site to site is sometimes called "browsing" or "surfing" the Internet. To show how easy it is to visit a number of sites, regardless of where they are located, we will look in the subject area Sport. We'll find information about surfing (on water), take a look at some sites in Hawaii, and then take a look at some information about golf—check out the links (oops, a pun!).

Although this example focuses on sports, you also will see hyperlinks along the way that could easily take you to different topics if or when you choose to follow them. It's this interconnection of sites and topics that makes the term "World Wide Web" really appropriate. We'll be using Netscape Navigator for this activity. If you use Internet Explorer, you'll see that the concepts and most of the details are the same.

> Remember that the Web is always changing and your results may differ from those shown here. Don't let this confuse you. The activities demonstrate fundamental skills. These skills don't change, even though what you see when you do this activity may look different every time.

We'll assume that the computer has established a connection to the Internet and that the browser is already started. Here are the steps we'll follow:

1. Display the home page for the World Wide Web Virtual Library (WWW Virtual Library).
2. Select the hyperlink to the Sport home page.
3. Find hyperlinks dealing with surfing in the Sport section.
4. Select the hyperlink for La Jolla Surfing.
5. Browse the La Jolla Surfing site for pictures about surfing and weather information.
6. Visit a site with information about Hawaii.
7. Use the history list to go back to the Sport home page.
8. Get information about golf (explore the links!).

While you're going through the steps in this example, practice using **Back** and **Forward** in the toolbar. As long as you click on **Forward** the same number of times as you click on **Back**, you won't lose your place.

Details

1. Display the home page for the World Wide Web Virtual Library (WWW Virtual Library).

When you start your Web browser, your home page will appear on the screen. There just might be a hyperlink to the WWW Virtual Library on that page. Browse through your home page to look for it. If you don't find a hyperlink to the Virtual Library, click on the location field, type **http://vlib.org**, and then press **Enter**. The home page for the WWW Virtual Library is shown in Figure 2.5.

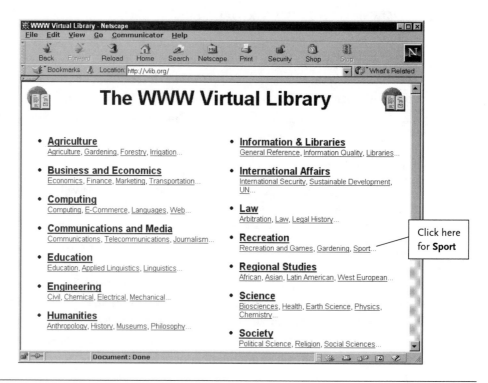

Figure 2.5   The Home Page for the WWW Virtual Library

2. **Select the hyperlink to the Sport home page.**

The home page for the WWW Virtual Library lists top-level categories and subcategories. There is one subcategory labeled Sport, as shown in Figure 2.5.

☑ Do It!   Click on the hyperlink **Sport** on the home page for WWW Virtual Library.

In a few seconds, you should see the Web page for the Sport section in the WWW Virtual Library, as shown in Figure 2.6.

We'll follow a couple of hyperlinks to get to the water surfing section.

☑ Do It!   Click on the hyperlink **Contents** on the home page for the Virtual Library of Sport (VLS).

Clicking on **Directory** brings us the Web page shown in Figure 2.7.

☑ Do It!   Look for the heading **Water Sports**—use the scroll bar, page down key, or down-arrow keys if necessary.

☑ Do It!   Click on the hyperlink **surfing** as shown in Figure 2.7.

The VLS section for surfing, as shown in Figure 2.8, will appear in a few seconds. Using the scroll bar, you can see that this collection has many links to information about surfing. You may want to explore some on your own. We're going to follow the hyperlink "La Jolla surfing." La Jolla is in California, near San Diego. It's the home of the Scripps Research Oceanographic Institute and a great place for surfing. The La Jolla Web site is also a great place for information about surfing.

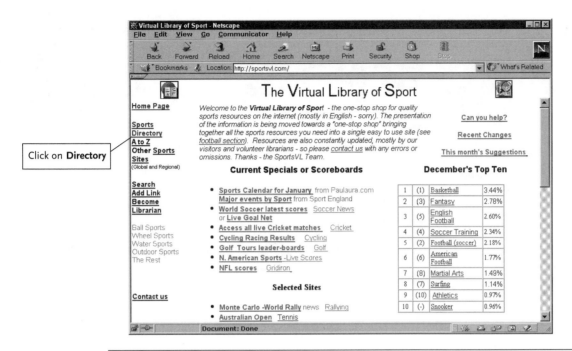

Figure 2.6   The Home Page for the Sport Section of the WWW Virtual Library

3. Find hyperlinks dealing with surfing in the Sport section.

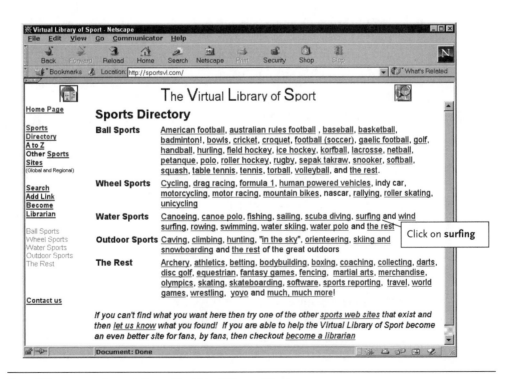

Figure 2.7   Contents Page of the Virtual Library of Sport

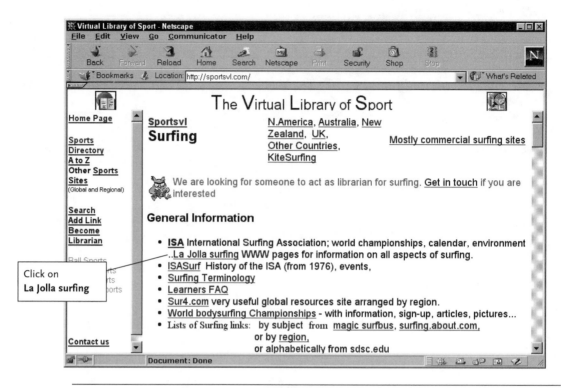

Figure 2.8   The Virtual Library of Sport—Surfing

4. Select the hyperlink for La Jolla surfing.

◪ Do It!   Click on the hyperlink **La Jolla surfing**.

The Web page titled "La Jolla Surfing" appears. It's shown in Figure 2.9. When we visited the VLS recently and clicked on **La Jolla surfing**, the Web page appeared in a frame of the Web page for the VLS. To make things more clear here, we're showing the La Jolla Web page in its own window. You also can get that effect. Instead of just clicking on the hyperlink, as shown in Figure 2.8, *right-click* on the link and select **Open in New Window**. In other words, put the mouse pointer over the hyperlink **La Jolla surfing**, press the right mouse button, and select **Open New Window** from the menu that pops up.

Viewing a Frame in a New Window

You can open a frame in a new window. That way, the contents of the frame can use all of the browser's content area. Move the mouse pointer to the frame and click the right mouse button. A menu pops up. Select **Open Frame in New Window**. This is available to you if you're using Netscape Navigator version 4 or greater.

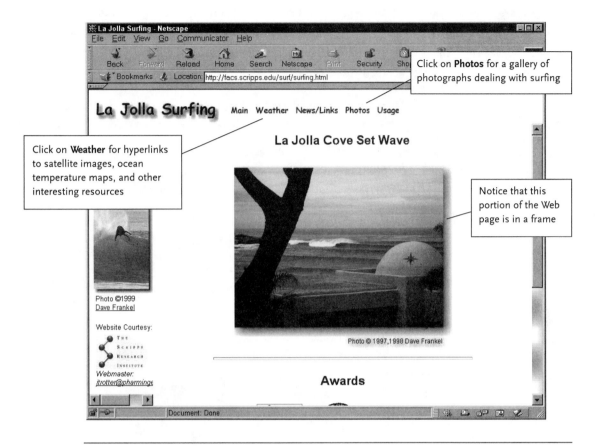

Figure 2.9   The Web Page "La Jolla Surfing"

5. Browse the La Jolla Surfing site for pictures about surfing and weather information.

This is a very nice Web site and has won several awards. The links across the top go to other sections of the site. The large picture and the information below it on the home page is inside its own frame. You'll see when you follow hyperlinks from this Web site that the resulting information is displayed inside that frame. This keeps the main menus in the window, but it also cuts down on the amount of available space for the information that's in a frame. The frame has its own scroll bar for viewing information that is in the frame but not present on the screen.

Take a look at the surfing photographs available through this Web site.

☑ Do It!   Click on the hyperlink **Photos**.

This brings up a collection of hyperlinks. Each link leads to a group of small images. (Just so you know, small images like these are sometimes called *thumbnails*.) Click on any of the small images and a larger one will appear in the frame. This presents a virtual photographic gallery—real surfing "eye candy." As you move through the collection, you may want to return to a previous frame or window. Use **Back** and **Forward** in the toolbar to navigate through frames or windows you've visited.

We could spend hours here! Take a look around, and then check out the weather. Since frames are used in this Web site, a link to weather resources is still on the screen.

☑ Do It!   Click on the hyperlink **Weather** on the La Jolla Surfing home page as shown in Figure 2.9.

Clicking on **Weather** brings up a new image in the frame and also changes the menu on the left. Figure 2.10 shows what we see after clicking on **Weather**.

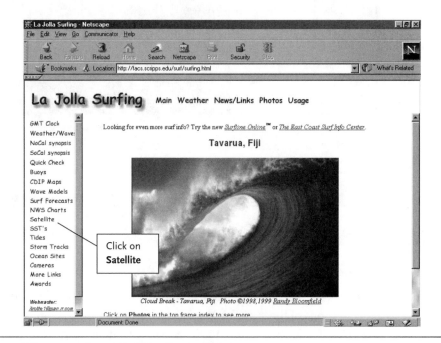

Figure 2.10   The La Jolla Surfing Weather Web Page

Now we're going to look at some maps and images from satellite photos and imaging.

☑ Do It!   Click on the hyperlink **Satellite** on the La Jolla Surfing Weather page.

Take a look at some of the satellite weather sites. When you click on some of the thumbnails of images, the image may be displayed in a new window.

That's fine, just remember to close the window by clicking on the ⊠ in the upper right corner when you're done with it.

Now we're going to go back to the satellite page and select a link to the School of Ocean and Earth Science and Technology, part of the University of Hawaii. Why? Well, after thinking about surfing and viewing this Web site, a site that deals with Hawaii seems appealing. As it turns out, this site has several links to other information about Hawaii.

6. **Visit a site with information about Hawaii.**

First, we'll get back to the page that lists satellite Web sites. If the satellite images were displayed in a new window, then close the window. If they weren't, then they were probably displayed in a frame of the La Jolla Surfing Web site. In this case, you can get to the page that lists the satellite Web sites by clicking on **Satellite** in the menu on the left.

Now we will select a site with several links to information about Hawaii. You may have to scroll down the page to see this link.

☑ Do It! Click on the hyperlink **soest: School of Ocean & Earth Science & Technology**.

This link takes you to the home page for the School of Ocean and Earth Science and Technology—the URL is **http://www.soest.hawaii.edu/** in case you want to visit the site and for some reason the path we are taking doesn't get you there. By looking at the Web page, we can see that the School of Ocean and Earth Science and Technology is part of the University of Hawaii. Several links on this page lead to some great sites about Hawaii. Some of the links are shown in Figure 2.11.

☑ Do It! Use the scroll bar to view the list of links on the **School of Ocean and Earth Science and Technology** Web page.

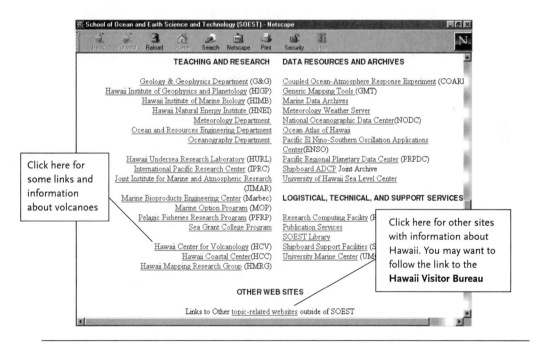

Figure 2.11   Links About Hawaii on the SOEST Web Page

☑ Do It!   Click on the hyperlink **Hawaii Center for Volcanology**.

This link will take you to a site with information about volcanoes and volcanology. The site also features several links to other sites dealing with these topics. When you're ready, come back to the page shown in Figure 2.11.

☑ Do It!   Click on **Back** as many times as needed to return to the page pictured in Figure 2.11.

You decide when to leave this section. When you're ready, we'll go through the steps of using the history list to get back to the WWW Virtual Library Sport section.

7. **Use the history list to go back to the Sport home page.**

We've traveled through several pages and now would like to get back to the home page for Sport in the WWW Virtual Library. Certainly, one way to do that is by clicking on **Back** in the navigation toolbar until the proper page appears. But we'd have to go through all the intervening pages! It's quicker to select the site from the history list. You can get to the list by pressing **Ctrl**+**H** on the keyboard.

☑ Do It!   Press **Ctrl**+**H** on the keyboard.

This displays the history list, as shown in Figure 2.12.

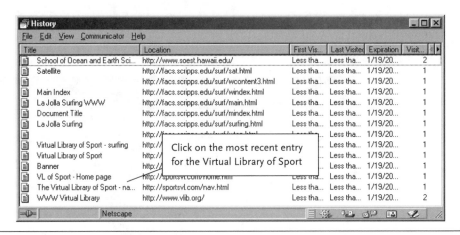

Figure 2.12   The History List

☑ Do It!   Return to the Virtual Library of Sport by double-clicking on the most recent entry for that site in the history list.

Once the Sport page appears, you may want to close the history list.

8. **Get information about golf (explore the links!).**

Now you are at the Virtual Library of Sport home page as shown in Figure 2.7. We'll follow some links for information about golf. Look for the hyperlink to golf; it's in the list of links to the right of **Ball Sports**.

▨ Do It!   Click on the hyperlink **golf**.

There's a lot to see here, and the choice is yours. An item with links to a lot of other information about golf is **GolfWeb**. Enjoy yourself and finish when you'd like.
That's it!

END OF ACTIVITY 2 ◀

In the activity above, we used some of the navigational features of the Web browser to view Web pages from a variety of sites around the world.

Summary

From a technical point of view, the Internet is a collection of thousands of networks, distributed throughout the world, that agree to communicate using certain rules or protocols.

Each site on the Internet has a unique numeric address called its IP address and usually a corresponding name called the domain name. Information is passed around the Internet in packets. The emphasis is placed on the packets, not on the connections between systems. Users generally access sites by giving a domain name; the hardware and software convert a domain name to an IP address.

Many of the services operate according to a client/server model. A program called the client is started on one system and contacts a program called the server at another computer on the Internet.

All information on the Internet is in digital format. This includes text, programs, charts, images, graphics, video, and audio. When using the WWW, you work in a hypertext or hypermedia environment. A Uniform Resource Locator (URL) specifies items, services, and resources. These are used by Web browsers to specify the type of Internet service or protocol to use and the location of the item.

The documents on the WWW are called Web pages. These are written and constructed using a language or set of rules called hypertext markup language (HTML).

A Web browser is your access point to the information and resources that make up the World Wide Web. When you click on a hyperlink or type a URL in the location field or address box, the browser requests information from a Web server. When the information is delivered, it is the browser's job to display the information or start another program to deal with it.

The commands you use to work with the Web browser are available through the menu bar, the toolbars, the keyboard, and the menus that pop up when you use the right or secondary mouse button.

Once a page is in the browser's window, you can move around the page using the keyboard, scroll bars, or mouse. You can search for words in the page.

Move the mouse to a hyperlink (the pointer turns to a hand) and click on it. You can type a URL in the location bar or address box and then press **Enter** to access it.

The browser keeps track of the sites you've visited during recent sessions. It does this so that you can backtrack and return to sites during a session.

Selected Terms Discussed in This Chapter

404 error

alternate text   Internet Protocol (IP)

bookmark list   IP address

client/server   menu bar

content area   packet-switched network

domain name system   scroll bars

favorites list   status bar

frame   thumbnail

home page   toolbars

hyperlink   Transmission Control

hypertext markup language (HTML)   Protocol (TCP)

hypertext transfer protocol (HTTP)   Uniform Resource Locator (URL)

Internet domain name

Materials on CD for This Chapter

Here is a list of items for this chapter on the CD that accompanies the text:

- ☑ "Keyboard Shortcuts"—A table that lists the keyboard shortcuts common to both Netscape and Internet Explorer
- ☑ "Details About the Internet Explorer Window"
- ☑ "Details About the Netscape Navigator Window"
- ☑ All URLs mentioned in this chapter in hypertext format
- ☑ Selected terms discussed in this chapter with hyperlinks to the glossary
- ☑ Copies of the review questions in quiz format

Review Questions

True or False?

1. In the email address **khartman@mwc.edu**, mwc.edu is the domain name.
2. The domain name **www.census.gov** indicates that it is a U.S. government site.
3. A menu bar is a row of icons or items that work like buttons; when they are pressed, a certain action takes place.
4. When you start a Web browser, the first page or document you see is called the content area.
5. The bookmark or favorites list is a collection of hyperlinks to Web pages that you want to save from session to session.

Short Answer—Completion

1. Two basic protocols used on the Internet are _____ and _____. You often seen them referred to together as _____.
2. The Internet is a _____ network.
3. The interaction in which one system requests information and another provides it is called a _____ relationship.
4. HTTP is a World Wide Web protocol that stands for _____.
5. A hyperlink is represented in a specific format called a _____, or _____.

Exercises and Projects

1. The Web site whatis.com, **http://whatis.techtarget.com/**, is sometimes useful when you need to know about technical terms. What is its definition of
   a. modem?
   b. router?
   c. protocol?
   d. domain name system?
2. Another site that can be useful when you want to define terms is TechEncyclopedia, **http://techweb.com/encyclopedia**. Using TechEncyclopedia, find definitions for the same terms as in the previous exercise.
   a. Write a description or review of each of the Web sites (whatis.com and TechEncyclopedia) using the same review format as in the exercises in Chapter 1.
   b. Decide which of the two sites you think is better for you and justify your answer.

3. **nslookup** is an Internet utility that you can use to find the IP address of a domain name or to find the domain name (if there is one) that corresponds to an IP address. Some sites that make this service available on the Web can be accessed by using these URLS: **http://dns411.com** or **http://lasaltech.com/cgi-bin/nslookup.**

   a. Use either of these URLs to find the IP addresses of the following: **skills.net.au, webliminal.com, www.library.mwc.edu,** and the Web server of your company or school.

   b. Use either of these Web services to find the domain name associated with each of these IP addresses: 216.239.37.100, 140.183.234.10, 150.203.83.3, and the IP address of the Web server for your company or school.

4. Use your browser to access the WWW Virtual Library, **http://vlib.org**, and find the Broadcasters section.

   a. Give the names of four broadcasters listed, each from a different continent. Also give the URLs of their Web sites.

   b. Visit each of the sites and write a brief description of each.

5. Use your browser to view the Web page "About the World Wide Web," **http://www.w3.org/WWW**. Follow the link **International World Wide Web Conferences.**

   a. Where and when did the first international WWW conference take place?

   b. Name the winner and honorable mention recipients in the category Best Campus-Wide Information Service at that conference.

   c. Where and when did the ninth international WWW conference take place?

   d. Name three keynote speakers and give a description of what they spoke about.

   e. Go back to "About the World Wide Web." Follow the link labeled **CERN**. What is CERN?

Searching for Information

▶ **you can** find all types of information on the World Wide Web: government statistics, fast-breaking news stories, up-to-the-minute weather reports, sales catalogs and business information, radio programs, movies, music, and virtual art galleries and museums. Searching the Web for this information can be a challenging and possibly frustrating task. The Web will not always have everything you're looking for, and sometimes the information you want is on the Web but may be difficult to find. A reference book in your library may have the information you need and may be found more quickly. But once you've decided the Web is the place to look, how do you proceed? Several major search tools are available; which one do you start with? And once you have accessed a search tool, especially a search engine, how do you formulate a search request that will provide the best results? The search tools on the Web have different rules and features that you need to be aware of before you are able to get the most out of them.

This chapter focuses on the features common to most search engine databases and will help you determine when it may be advantageous for you to use a more obscure one and how to find out if a search tool supports a particular feature. The chapter also introduces the 10-step basic search strategy. This strategy requires thinking about the type of information you need to find, determining which search features are needed to guarantee the best results, and then modifying your search as needed.

In addition to introducing you to search strategies, this chapter also gives an overview of the current content issues that Internet users should understand. These issues include pornography, free speech, censorship, and copyright.

Goals/Objectives

- ☑ Know when to use a search engine
- ☑ Know how a search engine database is constructed
- ☑ Become familiar with the search features common to search engines
- ☑ Learn how to translate a topic into a useful search expression using the search features appropriate to the search engine

Topics

- ☑ The First Step: Evaluating Your Information Needs
- ☑ Choosing the Best Search Tool to Start With
- ☑ Search Engines and Meta-Search Tools
- ☑ Search and Output Features
- ☑ 10-Step Search Strategy
- ☑ Formulating Search Expressions
- ☑ Content Issues: Pornography, Free Speech, Censorship, Filtering, and Copyright

The First Step: Evaluating Your Information Needs

Before you get online and start your search for information, think about what types of material you're looking for. Are you interested in finding facts to support an argument, authoritative opinions, statistics, research reports, descriptions of events, images, or movie reviews? Do you need current information or facts about an event that occurred 20 years ago? When is the Web a smart place to start? Keep in mind that a lot of information is on the Web, but much of it is part of proprietary or commercial services that are subscription-based. Perhaps your local library subscribes to a database that will be useful for the subject you are searching for.

Types of Information Most Likely Found on the Internet and the World Wide Web

- ☑ **Current information.** Many major newspapers, broadcasting networks, and popular magazines have Web sites that provide news updates throughout the day. Current financial and weather information also is easily accessible.
- ☑ **U.S. government information.** Most federal, state, and local government agencies provide statistics and other information freely and in a timely manner.
- ☑ **Popular culture.** It's easy to find information on the latest movie or best-selling book.
- ☑ **Full-text versions of books and other materials that are not under copyright restriction.** Works such as Shakespeare's plays, the Bible, *Canterbury Tales,* and hundreds of other full-text literary resources are available. Several of them have been made into searchable databases, which have enhanced scholarly research in the humanities.
- ☑ **Business and company information.** Not only do many companies provide their Web pages and annual reports, but several Internet-based databases also provide in-depth financial and other information about companies.
- ☑ **Consumer information.** The Internet is a virtual gold mine of information for people interested in buying a particular item and want opinions from other people about it. With access to everything from automobile reviews on the Web to Usenet newsgroups, consumers can find out about almost any item before they buy it.
- ☑ **Medical information.** In addition to the hospitals, pharmaceutical companies, and nonprofit organizations that provide excellent sources of medical information, the

National Library of Medicine has freely provided the MEDLINE database to the public since late 1997.

☑ **Entertainment.** The Web is the first place many people go to find games, audio files, and video clips.

☑ **Software.** The Web hosts software archives in which you can search for and **download** software to your computer without cost.

☑ **Unique archival sites.** The Library of Congress, for example, archives Americana in its American Memory collection.

Some Reasons Why the World Wide Web Won't Have Everything You Are Looking For

☑ Publishing companies and authors who make money by creating and providing information usually choose to use the traditional publishing marketplace and rather than make their information available for free via the Internet.

☑ Scholars most often choose to publish their research in reputable scholarly journals and university presses rather than on the Web. More academic journals are becoming Web-based, but a subscription to the online version often costs as much as the paper form. (Although many journal publishers' Web sites will provide a free article or two from an issue and include only abstracts of the other articles.)

☑ Several organizations and institutions would like to publish valuable information on the Web but don't because of a lack of staff or funding.

☑ The Web tends to include information that is in demand to a large portion of the public. The Web can't be relied on consistently for historical information, which is often not in high demand. For example, if you need today's weather data for Minneapolis, the Web will certainly have it. But if you want Minneapolis climatic data for November 1976, you perhaps would not find it on the Web.

By evaluating your goals before starting a research project, you may sometimes find that you don't need to get online at all. You may find out that your library has an excellent CD-ROM database that provides historical meteorological data for the entire United States. Perhaps your library will have a better source in paper form. Don't be shy about asking a reference librarian to help you determine whether the Internet or some other resource will have the most appropriate material to choose from on the topic you are researching.

Choosing the Best Search Tool to Start With

Once you've decided that the Web is likely to have the information you're seeking, you'll need to choose an appropriate search tool. Table 3.1 shows the major types of search tools available on the World Wide Web and their major characteristics.

Type of Search Tool	Major Characteristics
Search engines	☑ These attempt to index as much of the Web as possible.
	☑ Most are full-text databases.
	☑ Many require knowledge of search techniques to guarantee good results.
	☑ They are most often used for multifaceted topics and obscure subjects.
	☑ They search very large databases that are updated regularly.
	☑ These databases are created by computer programs.

Meta-search tools	☑ Some allow you to search several search engines simultaneously. ☑ Some supply lists of databases that can be searched directly from their pages. ☑ They provide a good way to keep up with new search engines. ☑ They may not fully exploit the features of individual search engines, so keep your search simple.
Directories and Virtual Libraries (discussed in Chapter 4)	☑ These contain topic lists of selected resources, usually hierarchically arranged. ☑ They depend on people for selection and control of the included resources. ☑ Most resources in these tools have been evaluated carefully. ☑ They can be browsed or searched by keyword. ☑ They contain links to specialized databases.

Table 3.1   Major Search Tools and Their Characteristics

A Checklist to Help You Choose the Right Tool

Search engines and meta-search tools should be consulted when looking for the following:

☑ Obscure information

☑ Multifaceted topics

☑ A large amount of information on a particular topic from different perspectives

Search engines and meta-search tools should not be used to find the following:

☑ News that happened yesterday or even last week. You'd be better off going to a specialized database that is updated daily or weekly.

☑ Information in a particular form, such as journal or newspaper articles. You'd be better off searching a specialized database that focuses on the format, and these are usually proprietary.

☑ Someone's telephone number or email address. Certain services focus specifically on this type of information. (See Chapter 4 CD items.)

☑ Maps. There are special databases for maps, too.

Directories and virtual libraries are most useful for finding the following:

☑ An overview of a topic

☑ Evaluated resources

☑ Facts such as population statistics or country information

☑ A specialized database for specific, or very recent, information

Now let's talk about the first two types of search tools: search engines and meta-search tools. In Chapter 4, "Beyond Search Engines," we'll cover directories, virtual libraries, and specialized databases.

Search Engines and Meta-Search Tools

Search engines are tools that use computer programs to gather information on the Web to create databases. These computer programs gather resources and put them into a database that you can search by using the search engine. Search engine databases were created because the number of Web documents began to increase so rapidly that people couldn't keep up with indexing them manually. Each of the major search engines attempts to do the same thing: index as much of the Web as possible. So each one of them handles a huge amount of data.

Computer-generated databases have some advantages. They are frequently updated, give access to very large collections, and are useful for providing the most comprehensive search results. If you are looking for a specific concept or phrase or if your topic is multifaceted, a search engine is the best place to start. Also, it's a good idea to use more than one search engine because each one will give different results.

These are the major search engines:

Search Engine	URL
All the Web	http://alltheweb.com
AltaVista	http://altavista.com
Direct Hit	http://directhit.com
Google	http://www.google.com
HotBot	http://hotbot.lycos.com
Lycos	http://www.lycos.com

Table 3.2   The Major Search Engines

FYI   Search Engine Information on the World Wide Web

- ☑ "Search Engine Watch" http://searchenginewatch.com

- ☑ "Search Engine Guide" http://www.searchengineguide.com

- ☑ "Search Engine Showdown" http://searchenginesshowdown.com/

Meta-Search Tools

It can be confusing and time-consuming to do your search in several databases, especially if you have to keep track of all of the resulting differences. **Meta-search tools** were created to help with some of these problems. These tools allow you to use several search engines simultaneously to collect the most relevant sites in each database. The results are compiled automatically and sent to your screen. Instead of building their own databases, meta-search tools use the major search engines and directories that already exist on the Internet and provide you with search forms or interfaces for submitting queries to these search tools. Table 3.3 shows some of the most popular meta-search tools and their URLs.

ON CD

The CD that accompanies this book includes a listing of several search engines and meta-search tools with detailed descriptions, including search and output features.

To view the listing, click on the hyperlink "Selected Search Engines and Meta-Search Tools on the World Wide Web" in the collection of items for Chapter 3.

Meta-Search Tool	URL
Dogpile	http://www.dogpile.com
IxQuick	http://ixquick.com
MetaCrawler	http://www.metacrawler.com
ProFusion	http://www.profusion.com
Search.com	http://www.search.com
Vivisimo	http://www.vivisimo.com

Table 3.3   Popular Meta-Search Tools

Search Engine Similarities and Differences

All of the major engines are similar in that you enter keywords, phrases, or proper names in a **search form**. After clicking on Search, Submit, Find, or some other command button, the database returns a collection of hyperlinks, which are usually listed according to their ***relevance*** to the keyword(s) you typed in, from most relevant to least relevant. Some search engines rank results by popularity or by how many other Web pages contain hyperlinks to those pages. All search engines have online help to get you acquainted with their search features.

The major search engines differ in several ways:

☑ Size of index

☑ Search features supported (many search engines support the same features but require different syntax to initiate them)

☑ How frequently the database is updated

☑ Ranking algorithms

It is important to know these differences because, to do an exhaustive search of the World Wide Web, you must be familiar with a few different search tools. No single search engine can be relied upon to satisfy every query.

How Search Engines Work

In search engines, a computer program called a **spider** or **robot** gathers new documents from the World Wide Web. The program retrieves hyperlinks that are attached to these documents, loads them into a database, and indexes them using a formula that differs from database to database. Then, when you consult the search engine, it searches the database looking for documents that contain the **keywords** you used in the **search expression**. Although robots have many different ways of collecting information from Web pages, the major search engines all claim to index the entire text of each Web document in their databases. This is called ***full-text indexing***. All of the major search engines are full-text databases.

Some robot programs are intuitive, which means that they know what words are important to the meaning of the entire Web page, and some of them can find synonyms of the words and add them to the index. Some search engines use robots that enable them to search for concepts as well as words. In some search engines, the robot skips over words that appear often, such as prepositions and articles. These common words are called ***stop words***.

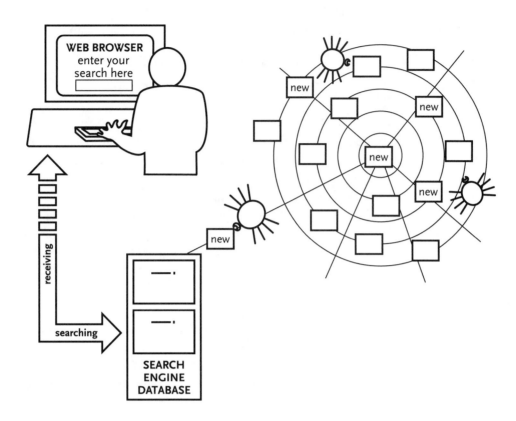

Web pages may have meta-tags inserted in the HTML code. **Meta-tags** are words that may describe the page but that don't appear on the page. They appear only in the HTML source document. You can view the HTML source code by looking at the page source. In Netscape, click on **View**, and then **Page Source**; in Internet Explorer, click on **View**, and then select **Source**. Meta-tags allow Web pages that don't have a lot of text in them to come up in a keyword search. The two most important meta-tags are the "description" and "keywords" tags. Some search engines will use the description section as the short summary that appears next to the URL in the results list.

Becoming proficient in search techniques is crucial in a full-text

---

☑ F Y I   **More About How Search Engines Work**

- ☑ "Robot-Driven Search Engine Evaluation Overview," http://lisweb .curtin.edu.au/staff/ gwpersonal/senginestudy/

- ☑ "How a Search Engine Works," http://www .infotoday.com/searcher/ may01/liddy.htm

- ☑ "The Web Robots Pages," http://www.robotstxt.org/ wc/robots.html

- ☑ "Search Engines: How Software Agents and Search Engines Work," http:// webreference.com/content/ search/how.html

indexing environment. The chance of retrieving irrelevant material is high when you can type in a word and conceivably retrieve every document that has that word in it. The following two sections define search features and can be referred to when formulating search expressions.

Search and Output Features Common to Most Search Engine Databases

It's important to understand the different search features before you begin using a search engine for research. Each search engine has its own way of interpreting and manipulating search expressions, and many search engines have *default settings* that you may need to override if you want to obtain the most precise results. Because a search can bring up so many pages, it is very easy to have a lot of hits with only a few that are relevant to your query. This is called *low precision/high recall*. You may be more satisfied with having very precise search results with a smaller set returned. This is defined as *high precision/low recall*. Ideally, using the search expression you entered, a good search engine would retrieve all of the relevant documents you need. This would be described as *high precision/high recall*.

Search Features

Search engines support many search features, though not all engines support each one. Even if they do support a feature, they may use different syntax in expressing the feature. Before you use any search features, you need to check the search engines' help pages to see how the feature is expressed in each one and whether it is supported at all. We will now list the most common search features and explain how each one is used.

Boolean Operators

Boolean logic was invented by the nineteenth century British mathematician George Boole as a way to define relationships between search terms. The three Boolean operators are AND, OR, and NOT. Using these operators, or connectors, between words and phrases focuses your search and tells the search engine how you want these separate facets of your search to relate to each other in the resulting documents. Knowing how to apply Boolean operators in search expressions is extremely important. Figures 3.1–3.4 show the different operators and how they are used.

Should Boolean Operators be Capitalized in Search Expressions?

When describing Boolean operators, we have capitalized them to distinguish them from the words that appear around them in the paragraph. Most search engines, however, recognize Boolean operators typed either way, as capital letters or lowercase. A few tools do require capitalization, so remember to check the search engine's help pages to find out which is preferred.

Use an AND between search terms when you need to narrow your search. The AND indicates that only those Web pages having both words in them will be retrieved. Most search engines automatically assume an AND relationship between two words if you don't type anything between them. This would be a default setting of the search engine.

An OR between search terms will make your resulting set larger. When you use OR, Web pages that have either term will be retrieved. Some search engines automatically place an OR between two words if there is nothing typed between them. This would be a default setting of the search engine.

The NOT operator is used when a term needs to be excluded. In the example, Web pages with *aircraft* will be retrieved, but those with the word *helicopters* in them will not be retrieved. Some search engines require an AND in front of NOT. In that case, the expression would be written like this: **aircraft AND NOT helicopters**

The example in Figure 3.4 shows **nested Boolean logic.** Use this logic when you need to include ANDs and ORs in the same search statement. For example, say that a certain term *must* appear in your results. You want to search for this term along with a concept that you can describe with synonyms. To do this, you would need to tell the search engine to find records with two or more of the synonyms and then to combine this result with the search for the first term. In the example above, the parentheses indicate that *aviation* OR *aircraft* will be processed first, and that this result will be combined with *safety.*

Implied Boolean Operators

Implied Boolean operators, or pseudo-Boolean operators, are shortcuts to typing AND and NOT. In most search engines that support this feature, you would type + before a word or phrase that must appear in the document and - before a word or phrase that must not appear in a document. For example, if you were looking for documents that must have the word

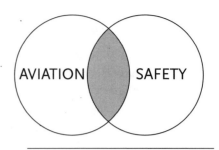

Figure 3.1 Aviation AND Safety

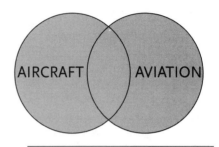

Figure 3.2 Aircraft OR Aviation

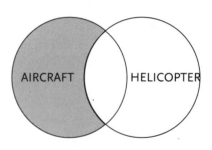

Figure 3.3 Aircraft NOT Helicopters

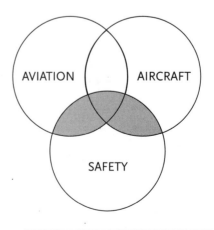

Figure 3.4 Safety AND
(Aviation OR Aircraft)

aircraft but not the word *helicopters* in them, you could state the search using implied Boolean operators like this:

+aircraft -helicopters

Natural Language Searching

Natural language searching is the capability of entering a search expression in the form of a question or a statement. For example, the following are natural language search expressions: "In what year was Martin Luther King, Jr.'s birthday made a national holiday?" and "I need a recipe for peanut butter fudge." In natural language searching, the search tool will disregard stop words and pick out the significant terms, connecting them with whatever the default feature of the search engine is—the OR connector, for example. In the examples above, the stop words in most search engines would be the following: in, what, was, a, I, for.

Phrase Searching

A phrase is a string of words that must appear next to one another. *Global warming* is a phrase, as is *chronic fatigue syndrome.* Use the phrase-searching capability when the words you are searching for *must* appear next to each other and *must* appear in the order in which you typed them. Most search engines require double quotation marks to differentiate a phrase from words searched individually. The two phrases mentioned above would often be expressed like this: "global warming" AND "chronic fatigue syndrome". In some search tools, a phrase is assumed when more than one word is typed together without a connector between them. You should read the help pages of the database you are using to find out how ***phrase searching*** is performed.

Proximity Searching

Proximity operators are words such as NEAR or WITHIN. What if, for example, you were trying to find information on the effects of chlorofluorocarbons on global warming? Maybe you would want to retrieve results that have the word *chlorofluorocarbons* very close to the phrase *global warming.* By placing the word NEAR or WITHIN between the two segments of the search expression, you would retrieve more relevant results than if the words appeared in the same document but were perhaps pages apart. (Some search tools that use this operator use a **W/#** words between the two segments, such as: **Hillary W/2 Clinton**.) This process is called ***proximity searching***.

Truncation

Truncation looks for multiple forms of a word. Some search engines refer to truncation as ***stemming***. For example, if you were researching postmodern art, you might want to retrieve all the records that had the root word *postmodern,* as well as *postmodernist* or *postmodernism*. Most search engines support truncation through the placement of an asterisk (*) at the end of the root word. For example, to retrieve all of the forms of postmodern, we would type **postmodern***. Some search engines use different symbols, however. You would need to see the help screen in the search engine you are using to find out which symbol is used. Some search engines automatically truncate words. In those databases, you could type **postmodern** and be assured that all the possible endings also would be searched for. In these cases, truncation is a default setting of the search engine, and if you don't want your search expression to be truncated, you'll need to override the default feature. You can find out how to do this by reading the search engine's help pages.

Wildcards

Using *wildcards* allows you to search for words that are very similar to one another, except for maybe a letter or two. For example, we might want to search for both *woman* and *women*. Instead of typing woman OR women, we could use a wildcard character (most often an asterisk) to replace the fourth letter. The search expression would look like this: **wom*n**.

Field Searching

Web pages can be broken down into many parts. These parts, or *fields*, include titles, URLs, text, summaries or annotations (if present), and so forth. (See Figure 3.5.) *Field searching* limits your search to certain fields. The ability to search by field can increase the relevance of the retrieved records. In AltaVista, for example, you could search for a picture of the Statue of Liberty by typing the followingin the search form: **image:"Statue of Liberty"**.

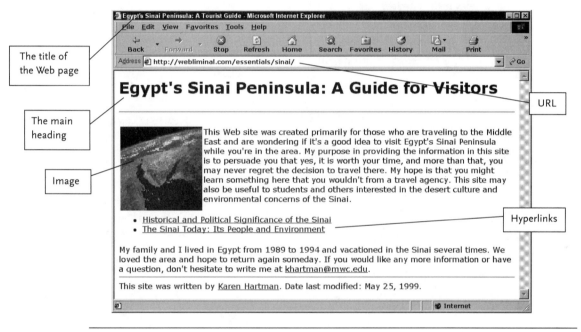

Figure 3.5   The Parts of a Web Page

Case Sensitivity

Case sensitivity is an important feature, especially if you are looking for proper names. Some search engines recognize capitalization, but most do not. If a search engine does recognize capital letters, it can lead to a much more precise search, especially if you're looking for proper names such as Sting or The Who.

Concept Searching

Concept searching is when a search engine automatically searches for Web pages that contain terms whose meanings are similar to the ones you entered in the search form.

Limiting by Date

Some search engines allow you to search the Web for pages that were modified between certain dates. In *limiting by date,* you can narrow your search to only the pages that were entered in the past month, the past year, or a particular year.

Language

The ability to limit results to a specific language can be useful. AltaVista supports this feature. AltaVista also will translate documents into many languages for you.

Output Features

The way a search engine displays results can help you decide which search engine to use. The following features are common to many engines, but as we saw earlier with the search features, the engines all have different ways of determining and showing these features.

Ranking Results

Most search engines measure each Web page's relevance to your search query and arrange the search results from the most relevant to the least relevant. This is called *relevancy ranking.* Each search engine has its own algorithm for determining relevance, but it usually involves counting how many times the words in your query appear in the Web pages. Other search tools rank results by the number of other pages that link to them (Google, **http://www.google.com**, for example) or by the most popular sites that others have chosen in the past (Direct Hit, **http://www.directhit.com**).

Sorting and Grouping Results

Some services allow you to choose how you want your results sorted—by relevance, URL, location, organization, and so forth. This feature is known as *sorting.* Some other search engines place results in subject categories.

☑ F Y I   **More Information About Search Features and Search Strategies**

- ☑ "Boolean Searching," http://exlibris.colgate.edu /web/finding/finding8.html

- ☑ "Searcher: The Magazine for Database Professionals," http://www.infotoday .com/searcher

- ☑ "How to Do Field Searching in Web Search Engines," http://www.onlineinc.com/ onlinemag/OL1998/ hock5.htm

- ☑ "Comparison of Search Engine User Interface Capabilities," http:// lisweb.curtin.edu.au/staff/ gwpersonal/compare.html

- ☑ "Search Engines Quick Guide, http://www .infopeople.org/search/ guide.html"

Annotations or Summaries

Some search engines include short descriptive paragraphs of each Web page they return to you. These annotations, or summaries, can help you decide whether to open a Web page—especially if the page has no title or if the title doesn't describe the page in detail.

Results per Page

In some search engines, the *results per page* option allows you to choose how many results you want listed per page. This can be a time saver, because it sometimes takes a while to go from page to page as you look through results. Some search engines also limit the number of results that are listed, regardless of how many actual Web pages were found during the search.

A Basic Search Strategy: The 10 Steps

The following list provides a guideline to help you formulate, view, evaluate, and modify search results. These procedures can be followed for virtually any search request, from the simplest to the most complicated. For some search requests, you may not want or need to go through a formal search strategy. If you want to save time in the long run, however, it's a good idea to follow a strategy, especially when you're new to a particular search engine. A basic search strategy can help you get used to each search engine's features and how they are expressed in a search query. Following the 10 steps also is recommended if your search is multifaceted and you want to get the most relevant results.

The 10 steps are as follows:

1. Identify the important concepts of your search.
2. Choose the keywords that describe these concepts.
3. Determine whether there are synonyms, related terms, or other variations of the keywords that should be included.
4. Determine which search features may apply, including truncation, phrase searching, Boolean operators, and so forth.
5. Choose a search engine.
6. Read the search instructions on the search engine's home page. Look for sections called "Help," "Advanced Search," "Tips," "Frequently Asked Questions," and so forth.
7. Create a search expression using syntax that is appropriate for the search engine.
8. Evaluate the results. How many hits were returned? Were the results relevant to your query?
9. Modify your search if needed. Go back to Steps 2 through 4 and revise your query accordingly.
10. Try the same search in a different search engine, following Steps 5 through 9.

Now we'll do a hands-on activity to explain these concepts in a more practical way.

ACTIVITY 3

USING THE BASIC SEARCH STRATEGY TO FIND INFORMATION IN SEARCH ENGINES

Overview

In this activity, we're going to search for resources on a multifaceted topic. We want to find World Wide Web documents that focus on how global warming and climate change can promote the spread of infectious diseases. We think that some of the research published on this topic is available on the Web.

Following the steps of the basic search strategy, we'll need to examine the facts of our search, choosing the appropriate keywords and determining which search features apply. Then, we'll go to the search engine we've chosen, All the Web, and read the search instructions. We'll formulate the search expression using All the Web's basic search capability. We'll then open a document and show you how to find the keywords in the text of the document. After performing this search in All the Web, we'll go to another search engine,

> Remember that the Web is always changing and that your results may differ from those shown here. Don't let this confuse you. The activities demonstrate fundamental skills, and these skills don't change, even though what you see when you do this activity may look different every time.

AltaVista, and look for the same topic there. We'll use AltaVista's advanced search capability, which supports full Boolean search capability.

Details

1. **Identify the important concepts of your search.**

   The most important concepts of this search are the effects of global warming and climate change on the spread of infectious diseases.

2. **Choose the keywords that describe these concepts.**

   The main terms or keywords include the following: global warming, climate change, and infectious diseases.

3. **Determine whether there are synonyms, related terms, or other variations of the keywords that should be included.**

   For global warming: ozone depletion, greenhouse effect
   For climate change: none
   For infectious diseases: none

4. **Determine which search features may apply, including truncation, phrase searching, Boolean operators, and so forth.**

   When developing a search expression, keep in mind that you will place OR between synonyms and AND between the different concepts, or facets, of the search topic. Writing down all the synonyms may help with the construction of the final search phraseology. Table 3.4 shows the three major concepts, or facets, of the search topic with their synonyms (if any) connected with the appropriate Boolean operators. Note that if we truncated the word *disease*, we would retrieve the words *disease* and *diseases.* Before you get online, take a few minutes to determine if you have used all the search features that you possibly can. It may save you a lot of time in the long run.

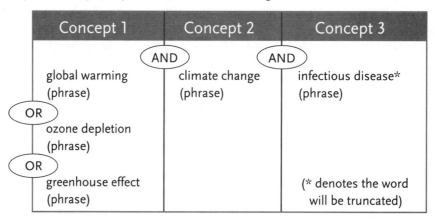

Table 3.4   Formulation of the Search Strategy

5. **Choose a search engine.**

   We've decided to use All the Web for this part of the activity. Let's discover a bit about this search engine. All the Web, **http://alltheweb.com**, is a full-text database that not only indexes World Wide Web documents, but also includes news, images, videos, MP3 files, and FTP sites. You can limit your search results to particular languages, and you can customize your search so that other related search terms are shown, offensive material may be filtered, and much more. Let's see how All the Web will handle our search request. First we need to open All the Web.

☑ Do It!   Click in the location field or address box, type **http://alltheweb.com**, and press **Enter**.

6. **Read the search instructions on the search engine's home page. Look for sections called "Help," "Advanced Search," "Frequently Asked Questions," and so forth.**

☑ Do It!   Click on **Help** on All the Web's home page.

☑ Do It!   Click on **Basic Search**.

Scroll down and read the search help. Your screen should look similar to the one pictured in Figure 3.6. Note that All the Web supports implied Boolean searching.

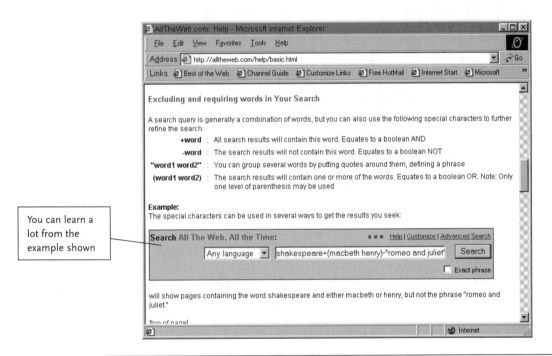

You can learn a lot from the example shown

Figure 3.6   Search Help in All the Web

z7. **Create a search expression using syntax that is appropriate for the search engine.**

After reading the help section, we have determined that All the Web, in addition to supporting implied Boolean searching, also does the following:

☑ Permits the Boolean OR in a multifaceted search expression if the user places parentheses around the terms

☑ Supports phrase searching by placing quotation marks around the words

☑ Does not support truncation

Let's see what results our search expression brings us in All the Web.

☑ Do It!   Click on the **Back** icon twice to return to All the Web's search form, or click on the **All the Web** icon on the top left of the window.

☑ Do It!   Type the following in the search form:

("global warming" "ozone depletion" "greenhouse effect") +"climate change" +"infectious diseases"

☑ Do It!   Click on **Search**.

Figure 3.7 shows the results of this search expression. Note how All the Web provides the list of results in order of relevancy.

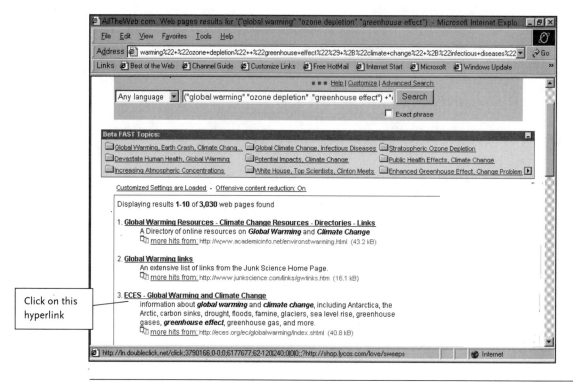

Figure 3.7   All the Web's Search Results

8. **Evaluate the results. How many hits were returned? Were the results relevant to your query?**

To begin to evaluate selected Web resources, open a few Web pages and perform a Find command to locate the keywords that were included in your search expression. This is a good way to determine the usefulness of a document by finding out where in the document your keywords appear and how they are used.

☑ Do It!   Click on the document with the hyperlink **ECES: Global Warming and Climate Change**, as shown in Figure 3.7. If you don't have this title in your results list, you can choose another hyperlink if you wish.

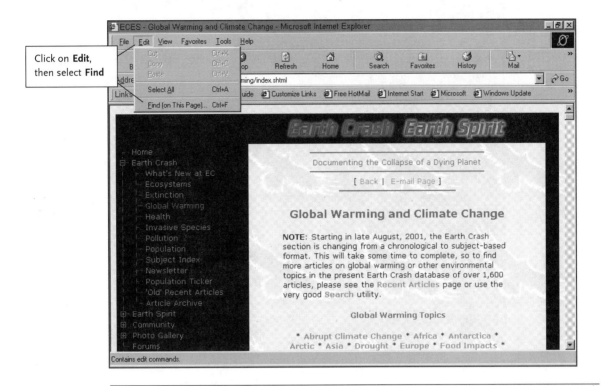

Figure 3.8   A Web Page Opened with the Find Function Activated

Let's try it!

☑ Do It! Click on **Edit** in the menu bar at the top of the screen. **Choose Find (on This Page)**, or if using Netscape, **Find in Page**.

☑ Do It! Type **infectious diseases** in the form next to **Find what**.

☑ Do It! Click on **Find Next**.

You'll be taken to that part of the page where the word or phrase you typed is found. The word or phrase will be highlighted, as shown in Figure 3.9.

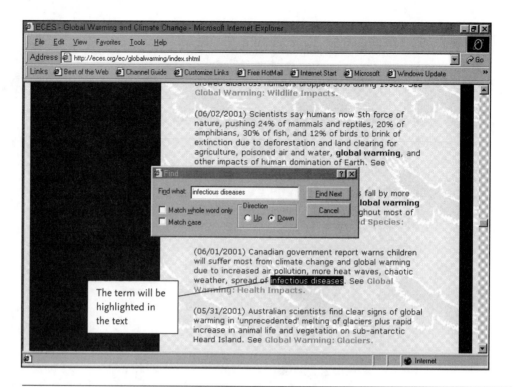

Figure 3.9   A Web Document with the Find Dialog Box Open

9. **Modify your search if needed. Go back to Steps 2 through 4 and revise your query accordingly.**

We could go back and remove *"infectious diseases"* and try searching for *epidemics* instead. We could also try searching for a specific disease, for example, malaria or dengue fever. For the purposes of this activity, and because we're quite satisfied with our search results, we'll stop here.

10. **Try the same search in a different search engine, following Steps 5 through 9.**

Let's see how a different search engine handles this topic. We're going to try AltaVista's advanced search mode.

PERFORMING THE SEARCH IN ALTAVISTA'S ADVANCED SEARCH USING BOOLEAN OPERATORS

Overview

In the next part of this activity, we will use AltaVista's advanced search mode. It supports full Boolean searching.

We'll follow these steps, which correspond to Steps 6 through 9 of the basic search strategy:

1. Read the search instructions on the search engine's home page. Look for sections called "Help," "Advanced Search," "Frequently Asked Questions," and so forth.
2. Create a search expression using syntax that is appropriate for the search engine.

3. Evaluate the results. How many hits were returned? Were the results relevant to your query?

4. Modify your search as needed. Go back and revise your query accordingly.

Details

First, we need to access AltaVista.

☑ Do It!   Click on the location field or address box, type **http://altavista.com**, and press **Enter**.

1. **Read the search instructions on the search engine's home page. Look for sections called "Help," "Advanced Search," "Frequently Asked Questions," and so forth.**

   AltaVista has two search modes: main and advanced. The main search mode only supports implied Boolean, or pseudo-Boolean, searching. This means that you could perform an AND and NOT search by typing a + before a word that has to appear in each of the resulting pages and a - before words that you don't want in the results.

   When you open AltaVista, you'll see the main search form, as shown in Figure 3.10. We want to access the Advanced Search mode.

☑ Do It!   Click on the hyperlink **Advanced Search**, as shown in Figure 3.10.

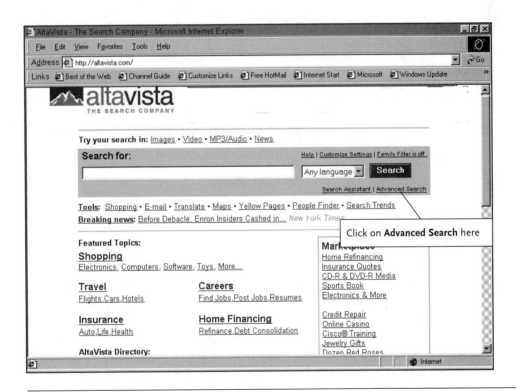

Figure 3.10   AltaVista's Home Page

Your screen will fill with information about searching AltaVista's Advanced Search mode more effectively.

See Figure 3.11 for some parts of the search help information.

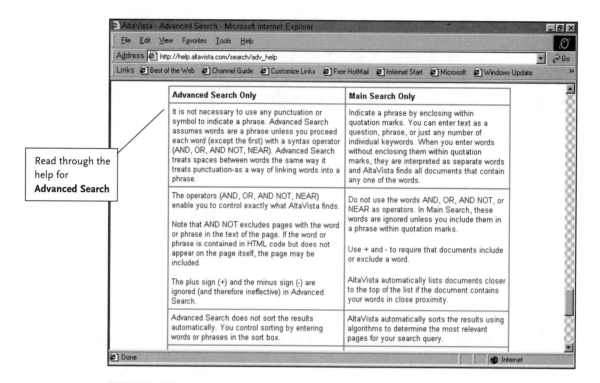

Advanced Search Only	Main Search Only
It is not necessary to use any punctuation or symbol to indicate a phrase. Advanced Search assumes words are a phrase unless you proceed each word (except the first) with a syntax operator (AND, OR, AND NOT, NEAR). Advanced Search treats spaces between words the same way it treats punctuation-as a way of linking words into a phrase.	Indicate a phrase by enclosing within quotation marks. You can enter text as a question, phrase, or just any number of individual keywords. When you enter words without enclosing them within quotation marks, they are interpreted as separate words and AltaVista finds all documents that contain any one of the words.
The operators (AND, OR, AND NOT, NEAR) enable you to control exactly what AltaVista finds. Note that AND NOT excludes pages with the word or phrase in the text of the page. If the word or phrase is contained in HTML code but does not appear on the page itself, the page may be included. The plus sign (+) and the minus sign (-) are ignored (and therefore ineffective) in Advanced Search.	Do not use the words AND, OR, AND NOT, or NEAR as operators. In Main Search, these words are ignored unless you include them in a phrase within quotation marks. Use + and - to require that documents include or exclude a word. AltaVista automatically lists documents closer to the top of the list if the document contains your words in close proximity.
Advanced Search does not sort the results automatically. You control sorting by entering words or phrases in the sort box.	AltaVista automatically sorts the results using algorithms to determine the most relevant pages for your search query.

Read through the help for **Advanced Search**

Figure 3.11   Search Help in AltaVista's Advanced Search

After reading the extensive help pages in AltaVista, you can start determining how to construct your search expression. In addition to reviewing how to combine Boolean operators with phrases and parentheses, you'll need to find out how AltaVista truncates words. When you're finished with the help section, return to the Advanced Search form.

☑ Do It!   Click on the **Back** button to return to the Advanced Search form.

2. **Create a search expression using syntax that is appropriate for the search engine.**

Now that you've read the search help, it's time to formulate the search expression. We've learned that AltaVista doesn't require quotation marks around words that should be searched as a phrase and that we can truncate a word by simply putting an asterisk after the root of the word. AltaVista also requires that a term or phrase be inserted in the **Sort by** field. This means that the results will be listed in order by how relevant documents are to the contents of this field. If a term or phrase is not entered here, the results will be listed in a random order. It will help to write the search expression out before typing it in the search form. Here is a possible way to express this search:

(global warming or ozone depletion or greenhouse effect) and climate change and infectious disease*

Note that all of the phrases will be searched as phrases because the words are next to each other with no connectors between them. Also note that *disease* is truncated so that both the word *disease* and *diseases* will be searched with the word *infectious* (as a phrase). Keep in mind that you can always modify your search later. Let's try entering it in AltaVista's Advanced Search form.

☑ Do It!   Enter the search expression in the form provided, as shown in Figure 3.12.

☑ Do It!   Insert **infectious disease*** as the Sort by term.

☑ Do It!   Click on **Search**.

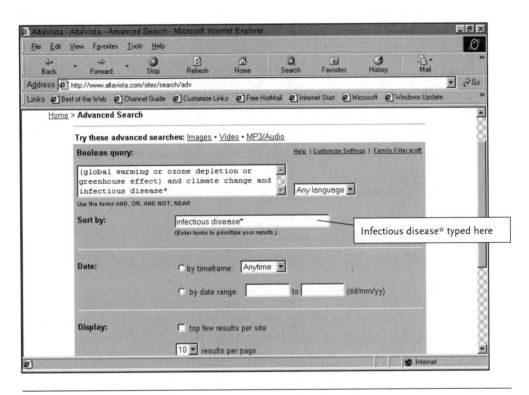

Figure 3.12   Using Boolean Operators in AltaVista's Advanced Search

3. **Evaluate the results. How many hits were returned? Were the results relevant to your query?**

Note the number of hits this search has returned to your screen. Look at a few of the titles. Do they appear to be relevant?

4. **Modify your search as needed. Go back to Steps 2 through 4 and revise your query accordingly.**

The results seem relevant, and the number of hits is an adequate set with which to work. If we wanted, we could at this point limit our search to particular domains or date ranges, or we could insert another word or phrase in the **Sort by** field, which would result in a different order of search results. But for now, we are satisfied with the results we have and will go on to the next section.

END OF ACTIVITY 3 ◀

In this activity, we searched for information on the same multifaceted topic in two different search engines, All the Web's Basic Search and AltaVista's Advanced Search. The two services had quite different search and output features. We saw the importance of reading each search engine's documentation before beginning a search. Both of the search engines provided relevant results, but they did not give the same results.

Formulating Search Expressions: Some Examples

In this section, we'll give brief overviews of topics and the search expressions that could be used for them in various search engines. These examples aren't meant to be the only correct expressions; they represent *some* of the possible ways to formulate the queries.

Topic: You need to find some information on the influence of the Koran on Islamic law. Keep in mind that the word "Koran" may be translated from the Arabic as Qur'an.

Possible Search Expressions

- ☑ (Koran or Qur'an) and "Islamic law"
- ☑ Koran Qur'an + "Islamic law"

Topic: You're looking for Web documents on teenage girls and how their likelihood to develop eating disorders is related to their self-esteem.

Possible Search Expressions

- ☑ "teenage girls" and ("eating disorders" or "anorexia nervosa" or bulimia) and "self-esteem"
- ☑ +"teenage girls" +"eating disorders" "anorexia nervosa" bulimia +"self-esteem"

Topic: You are searching for information that supports your thesis that gender bias has affected career choices for women, starting when they are schoolgirls.

Possible Search Expressions

- ☑ (girls or women or female) and "gender bias" and ("computer science" or comput* or engineering) and stereotyp*
- ☑ +girls women female +"gender bias" +"computer science" comput* engineering +stereotyp*

Topic: You're looking for information on the Shining Path, a revolutionary group in Peru. You don't want information on Tupac Amaru, which is another group there. Keep in mind that Shining Path is Sendero Luminoso in Spanish (and Spanish is the official language of Peru).

Possible Search Expressions:

- ☑ (("shining path" or "sendero luminoso") not "tupac amaru") and peru
- ☑ +"shining path" "sendero luminoso" +peru -"tupac amaru"

Topic: You want to find out what poem contains the line "Till human voices wake us, and we drown."

Search Expression

- ☑ "till human voices wake us and we drown"

Note: There is no need to type in the comma.

Topic: You are looking for information on how mad cow disease causes Creutzfeldt-Jakob disease in humans. Keep in mind that mad cow disease is also known as Bovine Spongiform Encephalopathy.

Possible Search Expressions

- ☑ ("mad cow disease" or "bovine spongiform encephalopathy") and "creutzfeldt-jakob disease"
- ☑ "mad cow disease" "bovine spongiform encephalopathy" +"creutzfeldt-jakob disease"

Topic: You are looking for an image of a bird common in the Middle East and Africa called the hoopoe.

☑ In AltaVista, **http://altavista.com**	From AltaVista's home page, simply click on the **images** link next to **Try your search in:** In the search form, type **hoopoe**. You can indicate whether you want photos, graphics, color, black and white, and more. From the results, you can choose to view the image in a new window, and the Web page where the image exists will appear. If you click on the thumbnail image, the Web page that includes the image will fill the entire window.
☑ In Lycos, **http://www.lycos.com**	From the Lycos home page, click on **multimedia**, and select **pictures**. Enter **hoopoe** in the search form, and view the results. Lycos does not refer you to the Web pages where the images are located.
☑ In Google, **http://www.google.com**	You can select the **Images** tab from Google's home page or visit **http://images.google.com**. Enter the word **hoopoe** and click the **Search** button. Click on the thumbnail to see a larger version, and the Web page in which the image is located will appear in a lower frame.

Content Issues: Pornography, Free Speech, Censorship, Filtering, and Copyright

Because any individual or organization can publish information on the Internet easily without editorial and other content control, you can expect to come across material that mirrors the wide range of preferences and interests of people throughout the world. A small proportion of the material found may be offensive to some people or inappropriate for children. Sexually explicit or pornographic material may exist as text, pictures, or chat and can be accessed deliberately or unintentionally. Most pornographic sites require a fee for access. Seldom does one encounter explicit material in a casual way—usually there is an introductory page that warns the user that the material linked to it is for adult viewing only. The focus of the debate about this so-called "cyberporn" has been whether the material be readily available to children and whether it's appropriate to pass laws that restrict the content of the Internet.

Free Speech vs. Censorship

The debate regarding civil liberties, free speech, and sexually explicit material led to the United States Congress approving and the President of the United States signing legislation called the **Communications Decency Act of 1996**. On June 27, 1997, in Reno vs. the American Civil Liberties Union, the U.S. Supreme Court ruled that this act abridged the freedom of speech that is protected by the First Amendment. The court stated, "The interest in encouraging freedom of expression in a democratic society outweighs any theoretical but unproven benefit of censorship." You can read this opinion by going to **http://supct.law.cornell.edu/ supct/html/96-511.ZO.html**. This opinion held that the Internet should not be viewed as a broadcast medium like television or radi,o but as a medium in which individuals are guaranteed free speech.

Filtering and Blocking Devices

Parents and others concerned about what children may be viewing on the Web can install computer programs that restrict access to certain material. These programs are referred to as **filters** or **blocking devices**. These programs control access to information in a number of possible ways.

While filters may be helpful, keep in mind that they may screen some sites with useful material. For example, when using filters, Web pages for gay teens, safe sex information, or information about drug legalization or other controversial issues may not appear in the results list because certain words have been filtered out and therefore made inaccessible. Certain medical topics such as breast cancer may also be avoided because the words that describe these medical conditions and body parts may be on the filter list. It is for this reason that the American Library Association has stated in "Access to Electronic Information, Services, and Networks: An Interpretation of the Library Bill of Rights," **http://www.ala.org/alaorg/oif/ electacc.html**, that by using filters, a library would be restricting access to information when it's a library's role to provide access to information and let users choose what they want to read, hear, or see. Opponents of this view say that libraries don't generally collect pornography in book or magazine form, so why should they allow this material to be accessed on the Internet? In the future, filtering or blocking software may be developed that could be turned on or off, so that individuals could choose whether or not to have restrictions placed on their searches.

Intellectual Property and Copyright

Intellectual property has been defined as:

> The ownership of ideas and control over the tangible or virtual representation of those ideas. Use of another person's intellectual property may or may not involve royalty payments or permission, but should always include proper credit to the source.
>
> —*The Free On-line Dictionary of Computing*
> **http://foldoc.doc.ic.ac.uk/foldoc/index.html**

Much of what you find on the Internet can be viewed, copied, printed, saved, and distributed to others quite easily. Anyone with a Web browser can make exact digital copies of documents, images, recorded music, and just about anything that is available. Unauthorized copying and distribution of this information may be illegal. Only the owners of the information can grant the right to copy or duplicate it. This is called the **copyright**. Some documents on the Internet contain a statement asserting the copyright and giving the permission for distributing the document. For example, here is a section from **http://www.ibiblio.org/expo/vatican.exhibit/exhibit/About.html**, describing limitations on the use of the materials in the exhibit "Rome Reborn" offered by the Library of Congress:

> The text and images in the Online Exhibit ROME REBORN: THE VATICAN LIBRARY AND RENAISSANCE CULTURE are for the personal use of students, scholars, and the public. Any commercial use or publication of them is strictly forbidden.

Regardless of whether a Web page is accompanied by a copyright statement, it is still protected by the copyright laws of the country where it was produced, the Universal Copyright Convention, and the Berne Convention. Most copyright conventions or statutes include a provision that makes it possible for individuals to copy portions of a document for short-term use. This is known as *fair use*. If there is no charge to access the information, it can often be shared in electronic form. This doesn't mean that you can freely copy images or documents and make them available on the Internet, share them in printed form, or distribute them to people using email attachments. Quite naturally, people who create or provide material in any format expect and deserve to get credit for their work. Remember that anything available on the Internet and World Wide Web is a copyrighted work, and you need to treat it in the same way as you would a book, an article in a journal, artwork, a play, or a piece of recorded music.

Speaking of recorded music, you may have heard of the MP3 controversy in the news. People have been copying music from CDs, creating files in MP3 format, and making these files available on the Web for other people to download without charge. MP3 is a standard technology and a format for compressing sound into a very small file without sacrificing quality. MP3 files sound as good as the originals, so people are tempted to download the music they like without buying the CDs. Almost all of the music recorded by musicians is copyrighted. This means that the musicians or the recording companies that recorded the music have the right to determine how the music is distributed and how much it will cost. Copyright laws apply to MP3 just as they do to other formats. Because artists frequently place portions of their work on the Web, making it freely available so that people can get a preview of their music, not all MP3 downloads are illegal. We will show you how to download legal MP3 music and play it on an MP3 player in Chapter 8.

To put it simply, just because something is available on the Internet doesn't mean that you can use it as your own. You are generally allowed to copy the material for personal use, but in almost every case, you cannot use it for commercial purposes or distribute it freely without written permission from the copyright holder. And if you do use someone else's ideas in your work, you should give the author credit by citing the information properly. We will discuss citing information in Appendix B, "Evaluating and Citing Information from the Internet."

Summary

Search engines are tools that search databases created by computer programs commonly referred to as spiders or robots. These spiders comb the World Wide Web, select every single word of every Web page they find, and put all of these words in a database that the search engine then searches for us, with the help of our search request. Each of these full-text databases accesses its database differently. Even though many search engine databases attempt to cover the entire Web, none of them actually do. The Web is getting too large for any one database to index all of it. In addition to this, the same search performed in more than one database never returns the same exact results. If you want to do a thorough search, it is wise to become familiar with a few of the different search engines. To understand search engines, it is important to become familiar with the major search features, such as Boolean logic, phrase searching, truncation, and others, before you get online. It is also necessary to read each individual search engine's documentation before typing the search request in the search form. It is also a good idea to get in the habit of checking the documentation often because search engines are constantly changing their search and output features.

Meta-search tools allow you to search several search engines simultaneously and can save you time if you're not sure which search engine to use.

In this chapter, we introduced the basic search strategy, a 10-step procedure that can help you formulate search requests, submit them to search engines, and modify the results retrieved. We have focused on the major search engines on the World Wide Web, but several hundred smaller search engines are also on the Web that search smaller databases. We'll discuss these in some detail in Chapter 4, "Beyond Search Engines." In addition, other search engines are not free to the public, but require a subscription. Our intent in this chapter is to give you a foundation for searching any database, no matter if it is fee-based or not, large or small. All of the steps in the basic search strategy apply to any online database.

The information found on the World Wide Web is diverse and some of it may be offensive to some people or inappropriate for children. There are software programs that have been designed to block or filter Web sites that have certain words in them. There was a movement to force the government to control the content on the Web and the Internet. The U.S. Supreme Court ruled in 1997 that the Communications Decency Act of 1996 was unconstitutional in that it abridged the freedom of speech upheld by the First Amendment.

Selected Terms Discussed in This Chapter

blocking device

case sensitivity

Communications Decency Act of 1996

concept searching

copyright

default setting

download

fair use

field

field searching

filter

full-text indexing

high precision/high recall

high precision/low recall

implied Boolean operators

keywords

limiting by date

low precision/high recall

meta-search tool

meta-tags

natural language searching

nested Boolean logic

phrase searching

proximity searching

relevance

relevancy ranking

results per page

robot

search engine

search expression

search form

spider

stemming

stop words

truncation

wildcard

Materials on CD for This Chapter

Here is a list of items for this chapter on the CD that accompanies the text:

- ☑ Basic Search Strategy: The 10 Steps (Practice Activity)
- ☑ Selected Search Engines and Meta-Search Tools on the World Wide Web
- ☑ All URLs mentioned in this chapter in hypertext format
- ☑ Selected terms discussed in this chapter with hyperlinks to the glossary
- ☑ Copies of the review questions in quiz format

Review Questions

True or False?

1. Search engines and meta-search tools should be consulted when you are searching for obscure information.
2. Search engines and meta-search tools should not be used when you need news that happened yesterday.
3. All search engines list results using the same type of relevance-ranking algorithm.
4. Boolean operators should always be capitalized in search expressions.
5. Most information on the Internet is not protected by copyright laws.

Short Answer—Completion

1. Search engine databases are created by computer programs called _____ or _____.

2. Common words that a search engine skips over, such as *of* or *the*, are known as _____.

3. Typing a search expression with one character that stands in for a group of characters, such as **m*n**, is making use of a(n) _____.

4. _____ means that a search engine recognizes capital and lower-case letters.

5. Searching for the term **colleg*** is an example of _____.

Exercises and Projects

1. Using All the Web's Advanced Search, **http://alltheweb.com**, search for government Web sites that have dealt with the subject of *school violence*. Limit your search to resources that have been added to the database in the past six months. Describe in detail which categories you chose and how you limited your search by date.

2. Using AltaVista's simple search mode at **http://altavista.com**, look for Web pages on *total quality management*. How many did you find? Now modify your search to also include the word *benchmarking* (note how AltaVista does this). Now how many results did you find? Refine your search further by limiting your results to those published by IBM Corp. (Hint: You're looking for a host.) How many pages do you have now?

3. What did Persephone have to do with pomegranate seeds? Go to All the Web at **http://alltheweb.com**, and see if you can find the answer. Give the title and URL of the page, and also see if you can find the number of seeds that were involved.

4. Go to Google, **http://www.google.com**, and search for the phrase *"global warming"* (don't forget to surround the phrase in quotes). Note the first few resources on the list. Now go to Alta Vista, **http://altavista.com**, and enter the very same search. Note the first few resources listed from this service. What can you conclude about the difference in results, knowing what you do about Google's and Alta Vista's output features?

5. Using AltaVista, **http://altavista.com**, and Google, **http://www.google.com**, find images of the Shroud of Turin. Describe the steps you took to find these images in each search engine.

Beyond
Search Engines

▶ there are two basic ways to find information on the World Wide Web: You can search databases,

or search engines, by keyword as we discussed in the last chapter; or you can browse topical lists of

resources, commonly referred to as directories. The main difference between search engines and directo-

ries is that search engines are computer programs that look for information on the Internet, while directo-

ries are created and maintained by people. Because directories rely on people to select, maintain, and

update their resource lists, they contain fewer resources than search engine databases. Having this smaller

collection of resources to look through can be an advantage. Virtual libraries are directories with resources

that information professionals, including librarians, have organized in a logical way. It is helpful to think of

these directories as similar to libraries; people who are committed to finding the very best resources on the

Internet have carefully selected the information, much as they would for a library's collection. The portal,

another type of information resource, is a blend of directory and search engine—along with other various

services and resources—on a single page. Some portals may be modified to fit an individual's needs.

The Web also includes a growing number of specialized databases. These databases can be searched

much like the search engines explored in Chapter 3. Using a specialized database that covers the subject

you are researching can save you time and give you reliable and relevant information.

Other databases on the Web require a subscription fee. These are commonly referred to as commercial or

proprietary databases. You can sometimes access these databases at libraries that subscribe to them, or

you can subscribe to them yourself. In this chapter, we'll show you how to find information by using some

of the special databases freely accessible on the Web.

Goals/Objectives:

- ☑ Learn how directories and virtual libraries differ from search engines
- ☑ Know when it's advantageous to use a directory or virtual library
- ☑ Know the reasons why some Web information is not indexed in the major search engines
- ☑ Know how to find specialized databases and become familiar with a few different types

Topics:

- ☑ Directories
- ☑ Virtual Libraries
- ☑ Specialized Databases
- ☑ How to Find Specialized Databases
- ☑ Using Specialized Databases to Find Company Information
- ☑ Portals
- ☑ Proprietary Databases

Directories

Directories, sometimes referred to as "subject catalogs," are topical lists of selected Web resources arranged in a hierarchical way. By "hierarchical" we mean that the *subject categories* are arranged from broadest to most specific. For example, the figure to the left shows a *hierarchy*.

In this example, **management** is a subcategory of **business**, **human resources** is a subcategory of **management**, and **wages and benefits** is a subcategory of **human resources**. In a hypertext environment such as the World Wide Web, browsing from one subject to a more detailed part of that subject is quite simple. If you click on **business**, which is the *top-level category* or heading, the computer screen will fill with a list of subject categories narrower than **business** including, in our example, **management**. Clicking on **management** will cause the screen to fill with even more subject categories. You can choose whatever subject you want—say, **human resources**. Then, from there, you can click on one of the items in the last subcategory, such as **wages and benefits**. After you choose each subcategory, the screen will fill with a list of Web page titles that you can pick from by clicking on the one you are interested in.

The following are the most well-known directories on the World Wide Web:

Directory	URL
Galaxy	http://galaxy.com
HotBot Directory	http://hotbot.lycos.com
LookSmart	http://www.looksmart.com
Open Directory Project	http://dmoz.org
Yahoo!	http://www.yahoo.com

Table 4.1   Major Directories on the World Wide Web

Many of the major search tools contain a directory and a search engine. This enables you to try both methods in one service. Many search engines use other established directories at their sites. For example, AltaVista, **http:// altavista.com**, has contracted with LookSmart, while Google, **http://www.google.com**, and HotBot, **http:// hotbot.lycos.com**, use the Open Directory Project for their directory listings.

Characteristics of Directories

While all directories rely upon people to select, maintain, and update their resource lists, each one differs from the others mainly by the level of quality control involved in the management of the directory.

For example, some directories function with very little management; instead, Web page submitters are allowed to provide annotations and decisions about where their resource should be placed in the directory's hierarchy. Other directories are much more selective about not only which resources are included but also about where in the subject hierarchy the pages will be located. In addition, the managers of this kind of directory often write detailed annotations of the submitted Web pages, which can be evaluative, descriptive, or both. Many annotated directories also rate Web resources using criteria that vary from one directory to another. Some of the inherent strengths of directories also can be weaknesses and vice versa. We'll examine some of these strengths and weaknesses here.

☑ F Y I   **Information on the Web About Directories**

☑ "Searching by Means of Subject Directories," http:// www.monash.com/ spidap1.html#directories

☑ "Comparing Internet Subject Directories," http:// www.notess.com/search/dir

☑ "Using Subject Directories: A Tutorial," http:// home.sprintmail .com/~debflanagan/ subject.html

Strengths of Directories

Because directories are maintained by people, they contain fewer resources than search engine databases. This can be a plus, especially when you are looking for information on a general topic. In addition, many directories rate, annotate, analyze, evaluate, and categorize the resources that are included, so you can quickly access the information that is most useful. With thousands of resources appearing on the Web each day, it is important that people are determining which sites and pages on the World Wide Web have the highest quality.

For example, if we wanted to find some language translation services on the Web, we could try Yahoo!, **http://www.yahoo.com.** Yahoo! contains one of the most comprehensive directories on the World Wide Web. Yahoo! relies on Web page submitters to annotate and categorize the resources that are included, so some sites have a brief descriptive note, and others do not. Some sites in Yahoo! will link to a review, but most will not. Yahoo! strives to be extensive; consequently, there is minimal filtering of resources. You can browse Yahoo! or search it by keyword. When you perform a search in Yahoo!, the first results are from the directory, listed by relevance to the search topics. At the same time, a search engine powered by Google will automatically perform an Internet search for you. Figure 4.1 shows the top-level categories of the Yahoo! directory. We'll click on **Social Science** for our example.

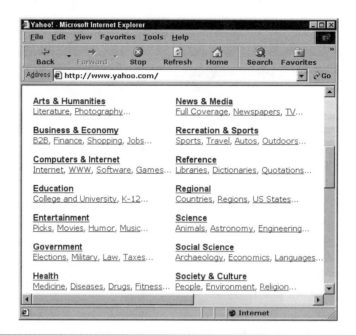

Figure 4.1   Yahoo!

After you choose **Social Science**, your browser window shows subcategories that you can choose from. A logical choice is **Linguistics and Human Languages**. After clicking on this category and then selecting **Translation and Interpretation** from the subsequent page, you are given a list of resources to choose from as well as more subcategories to select from, as shown in Figure 4.2.

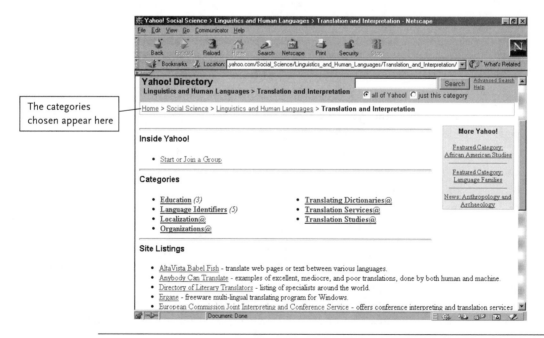

Figure 4.2   Language Translation Materials Found by Browsing Yahoo!

Weaknesses of Directories

It may be helpful to think of browsing a directory by subject like going through subjects in a card catalog. You may find exactly what you are looking for by browsing through many pages or cards filled with information, but then again, you may miss some related information because your subject may appear in many different categories. For example, we found translation services in the Social Science category in Yahoo!, but there may be information on this topic in the Business & Economy category as well, because businesspeople often have a need for translation services. Browsing a directory requires that you think categorically about the subject you are looking for. Many directories have simple keyword searching ability for just this reason. Keyword searching was created to help you find information without having to know which category the information may be in. A well-designed directory with keyword searching ability can help alleviate the problem of arbitrary hierarchical arrangements.

Another potential drawback, especially in those directories that rate and review resources, is the fact that someone else has selected, rated, and possibly reviewed a resource. This subjectivity, by its very nature, restricts your choices. You may not agree with the selections or ratings that the directory administrators have made. What seems to be a good resource to one person may not seem that way to the next. Thus, it is important for the directory management to have well-stated criteria for its selection and rating of resources.

Virtual Libraries

Virtual libraries are directories that contain collections of resources that librarians and information specialists have carefully chosen and organized in a logical way. The Web pages listed in virtual libraries are usually evaluated by someone knowledgeable in that particular field. Virtual libraries typically provide an organizational hierarchy with subject categories to facilitate browsing. Most include query interfaces for performing simple searches. Virtual libraries are great places to begin a research project. The following is a list of some of the most well-known virtual libraries on the Web:

Virtual Library	URL
Academic Info: Your Gateway to Quality Educational Resources	http://www.academicinfo.net
The Argus Clearinghouse	http://www.clearinghouse.net
Infomine	http://infomine.ucr.edu
The Internet Public Library	http://www.ipl.org
Librarians' Index to the Internet	http://lii.org
Library Spot	http://libraryspot.com
World Wide Web Virtual Library	http://vlib.org

Table 4.2   Virtual Libraries

The main difference between virtual libraries and the directories we talked about earlier in the chapter is that virtual libraries are much smaller because the resources included are very carefully selected. The people who organize virtual libraries are usually on the lookout for three major types of information: *subject guides*, *reference works*, and *specialized databases.*

Subject Guides

A subject guide is a World Wide Web resource that includes the hyperlinks of several Web pages on a particular subject. For example, the resource pictured in Figure 4.3 is a subject guide that lists Web pages on environmental ethics.

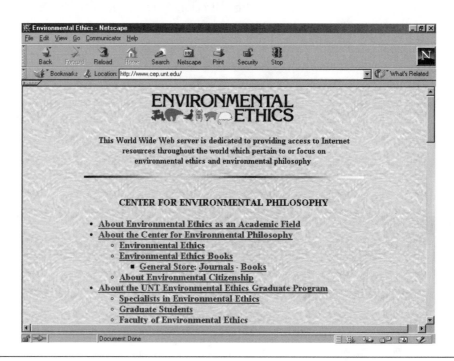

Figure 4.3   The Environmental Ethics Subject Guide, **http://www.cep.unt.edu**

Reference Works

Another common type of resource that is collected by virtual libraries is a reference work. A reference work is a full-text document with self-contained information. In other words, it doesn't necessarily contain hyperlinks to other resources. A reference work on the World Wide Web is very similar to its print counterpart in the way it looks; however, you can move around the document by clicking hyperlinks instead of turning pages and looking in the index for related topics. There are encyclopedias, handbooks, dictionaries, directories, and many other types of reference works on the World Wide Web. For example, "The World Factbook," **http://www.odci.gov/cia/publications/factbook/index.html**, is a reference work.

Specialized Databases

Virtual libraries are useful for finding specialized databases as well. A specialized database is an index that catalogs specific material such as patent literature, journal article citations, company financial data, court decisions, and so forth. Specialized databases can usually be searched by keyword and often support a myriad of sophisticated search features and capabilities. Figure 4.4 shows the home page of PubMed, the National Library of Medicine's search service. PubMed includes MEDLINE, a database of the premier medical journal article citations and abstracts that covers thousands of international journal titles.

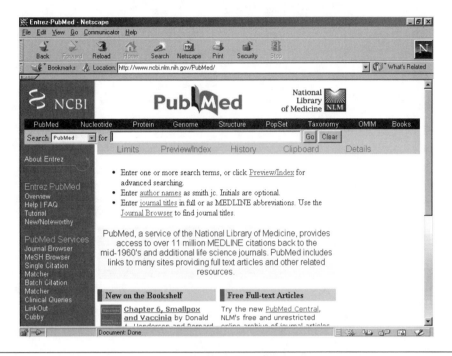

Figure 4.4   PubMed: The National Library of Medicine's Search Service
for the MEDLINE Database, **http://www.ncbi.nlm.nih.gov/PubMed**

The following example shows you how useful a virtual library can be.

Example: Using a Virtual Library to Find Information

Let's say we are looking for information on the country Azerbaijan. We hope to find a reference work; for example, an almanac-type publication that will give a brief history of the country, statistics, and other general information. A virtual library is an excellent place to start looking for information of this kind. We'll use the virtual library developed by librarians at the Berkeley, Calif., public library—the Librarians' Index to the Internet.

1. **Go to the home page for the Librarians' Index to the Internet,** http://lii.org.

   The home page is shown in Figure 4.5. Note that it looks very similar to Yahoo!, with the alphabetical list of top-level subject categories on the first page and the search form at the top.

2. **Browse the subject categories for country information.**

   Again, we have to make an educated guess when browsing subject categories in a directory. Because we think that an almanac-type reference work would include the type of information we're looking for, we'll try the Reference Desk.

Figure 4.5   The Librarians' Index to the Internet Home Page

After clicking on the Reference Desk link as shown in Figure 4.5, a list of several reference topics is provided. One link is called **Almanacs**. We'll try that first.

3. Access the Information Please Almanac.

Notice in Figure 4.6 that the first almanac listed is *Information Please.* This resource may be the one we're looking for.

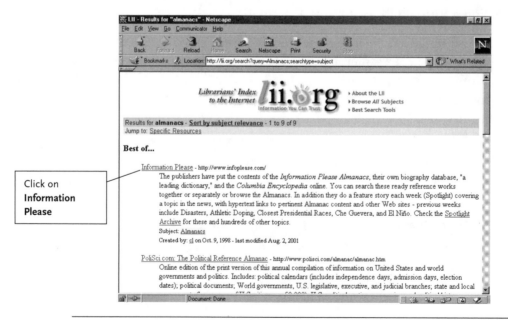

Figure 4.6   List of Almanacs in the Reference Desk Category in the Librarians' Index to the Internet

On the Information Please home page, there is a hyperlink called **Countries** in the **World** category. If we click on this link, our window will look much like the one pictured in Figure 4.7.

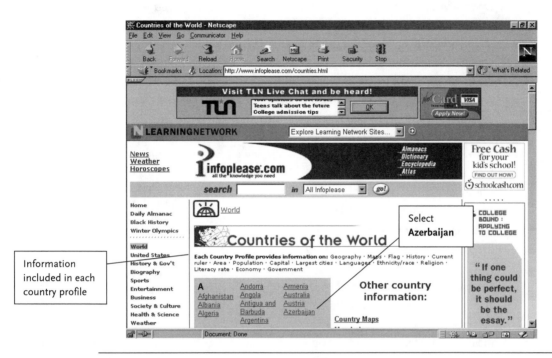

Figure 4.7   A List of the Country Profiles Available

We could choose **Azerbaijan** to retrieve a profile, which would include the geography of the country, a map, flag, history, current government, population, and more.

END OF EXAMPLE ◀

Directories and virtual libraries can be useful if you have a broad subject and aren't sure how to narrow it down. They are also helpful if you want to get a general idea about what resources are available to help you focus your topic. Virtual libraries are especially useful as a starting point for research on a particular topic or as a place to find subject guides, reference works, and specialized databases. In the next section, we'll focus on specialized databases and why they are so important.

Specialized Databases

Information on the World Wide Web that is not accessible from the major search engines or directories can generally be found in specialized databases. Some folks describe this group of resources as the "invisible Web" or the "hidden Internet." Specialized databases are indexes that can be searched, much like the search engines explored in Chapter 3. The main difference is that specialized databases are collections that cover particular subjects, such as government data files, census information, news and magazine archives, email address directories, company financial information, medical information, and so forth. You can often find information in specialized databases that you would not locate by simply using a general search engine.

Why Information in Specialized Databases Is Often Not Accessible via Search Engines

The major search engines discussed in Chapter 3 build their databases by collecting URLs that exist on the World Wide Web. The Web pages attached to the URLs are then indexed. When you type a word or words in a search engine's search form, you retrieve a list of URLs that already exist in the search engine's database. To put it simply, a search engine typically cannot search a specialized database for the following reasons:

☑ One database usually cannot search another database without some very special programming. Think about it. The search engine you are using may come across a specialized database but then may be stopped from going any further because the specialized database has a search form that requests information from the user. For example, you wouldn't look in AltaVista to see what books are in your library; you'd look at your library's Web-based catalog.

☑ F Y I   Read More About It

Researchers Steve Lawrence and Lee Giles have shown that search engines are not indexing even half of the information available on the Web. Their research is published in Nature, Vol. 400, July 1999, p. 107–109. You can read about the results of this recent study at **http://www.wwwmetrics.com.**

☑ Many specialized databases contain information that is retrieved dynamically every time a request is made, and the URLs that are generated are different each time. A search engine usually can't build its database with URLs that may work today and not tomorrow. (Although we have seen that occasionally a search engine picks up information from a dynamic Web site and indexes the unstable URL. If you retrieved that page from your results list, your keywords wouldn't appear.)

☑ Most search engines are unable to index content from specially formatted files. For example, the content in Adobe PDF (portable document format) files is inaccessible to many search engines because the text is formatted in such a way as to be unindexable. Google, **http://www.google.com**, has made great progress with its attempts to reach the invisible Web. It now indexes PDF files and has been able to include some dynamically generated Web pages in its search results. Other Web search engines are likely to start improving their ability to reach more content on the Internet as well.

How to Find Specialized Databases

By some accounts, more than 7,000 specialized databases are on the World Wide Web. How do you find them? Sometimes you'll stumble across specialized databases while doing a keyword search in a search engine. Occasionally, a Web page will have a hyperlink to a database, or a friend or colleague will tell you about a particular site. There are more precise ways to find them, but even these are not always foolproof.

☑ You can go to a search engine and type in the kind of database you're searching for along with the word **database**. For example, each of these search expressions typed in Google's search form provided excellent databases in the areas requested:

☑ medical database

☑ flags database

☑ "zip codes" database

☑ Virtual libraries, meta-search tools that include lists of databases, and directories are often the best sources to use when looking for specialized databases. Here is a list of some of the most popular ones:

Tool	URL and Description
Beaucoup	**http://www.beaucoup.com** Beaucoup lists more than 2,500 specialized databases and directories and also serves as a meta-search tool.
Digital Librarian: a Librarian's Choice of the Best of the Web	**http://www.digital-librarian.com** The Digital Librarian is maintained by Cortland, N.Y., librarian Margaret Vail Anderson.
Direct Search	**http://gwis2.circ.gwu.edu/~gprice/direct.htm** Direct Search is a collection of links to specialized databases compiled by Gary Price, a librarian at George Washington University.
Internet Public Library (IPL) Reference Center	**http://www.ipl.org/ref** The IPL is a virtual library that provides a good starting point for finding reference works, subject guides, and specialized databases.
Fossick.com	**http://www.fossick.com** This meta-search tool contains links to hundreds of specialized databases.
The InvisibleWeb	**http:// invisibleweb.com** Produced by IntelliSeek Inc., the InvisibleWeb is a well-organized, comprehensive directory of thousands of specialized databases.
LibrarySpot	**http://libraryspot.com/** LibrarySpot collects links to quality reference resources and provides links to more than 2,500 libraries around the world.
Librarians' Index to the Internet	**http://lii.org** A virtual library that is both searchable and browsable, this is an excellent source for specialized databases.
The Scout Report	**http://scout.cs.wisc.edu/** The Scout Report is a good way to keep up with new search tools, especially specialized databases. You can view its weekly report and its archive of previous Scout Reports on the Web. You also can have the report delivered to you via email by subscribing through a listserv. Send an email message to **listserv@hypatia.cs.wisc.edu**. Type **subscribe scout-report** in the body of the message.

Table 4.3   Some Tools That List Specialized Databases

Now we'll talk about using specialized databases to find information about companies.

Using Specialized Databases to Find Company Information

The World Wide Web has become a useful place to conduct business research. Most companies use their home pages as marketing or communications tools. These home pages might include annual reports, press releases, or biographies of the people in top-level management. The home pages also might include information about companies' products and services, including catalogs.

If you want to do industry research, you can use business-related subject guides. These contain hyperlinks to businesses within the particular industry that interests you. You can easily find subject guides in virtual libraries and major directories.

You also can find business directories on the Web by using one of the virtual libraries or meta-search tools

ON CD

The CD that accompanies this book includes a listing of several directories and virtual libraries with detailed descriptions.

To view the listing, click on the hyperlink "Selected Directories and Virtual Libraries" in the collection of items for Chapter 4.

listed at the beginning of this chapter. Keep in mind that companies providing the most financial information on the Web are usually publicly traded. Public companies are required to provide very detailed information to the U.S. government, whereas privately held companies are not. If a private company is listed in a nonproprietary (open to the public) database, some financial information will be available, but not nearly as much as if it were a public company. In the following activity, the company we'll be researching is Apple Computer, a publicly traded company.

ACTIVITY 4

FINDING COMPANY INFORMATION

Overview

In this activity, we'll find information about a specific company: Apple Computer, Inc. Suppose you need to find a home page, an address, an annual report, a 10-K report, and recent newspaper articles about this company. Several company directories on the Web might provide a starting place for this type of research. Virtual libraries and meta-search tools list databases by subject. You'll need to use one of these tools to find company databases. In this activity, we'll go to the InvisibleWeb, **http://invisibleweb.com**, which is a directory that provides hyperlinks to specialized databases. After we find a company directory that gives

Remember that the Web is always changing and your results may differ from those shown here. Don't let this confuse you. The activities demonstrate fundamental skills. These skills don't change, even though what you see when you do this activity may look different every time.

general information, we'll search it to find basic information about Apple Computer. Then we'll return to the InvisibleWeb to find a database that indexes newspaper articles and search it for information on Apple Computer. Apple's headquarters is near San Francisco, so it makes sense for us to search that city's newspapers.

We're assuming that you have a browser program set up on your computer, you have a way of connecting to the Internet, and the browser is started.

We'll follow these steps:

1. Go to the InvisibleWeb and find a company directory.
2. Search Hoover's Online to find the company's address, home page, and other basic information.
3. Find newspaper articles about the company.

Details

1. Go to the InvisibleWeb and find a company directory.

☑ Do It!   Click on the location field, type **http://invisibleweb.com**, and press **Enter**.

Note the directory structure of the InvisibleWeb in Figure 4.8. Under the top-level category, **Business**, you'll find the subcategory **Company Research**. It makes sense that this subcategory would have databases listed to help us locate information about a company.

☑ Do It!   Click on **Company Research**.

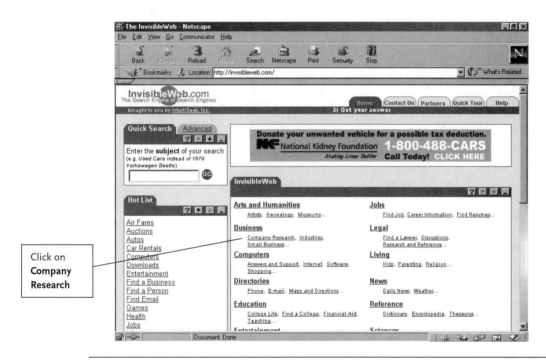

Figure 4.8   The InvisibleWeb, **http://invisibleweb.com**

Figure 4.9 shows the list of resources in this category. Because we are looking for general information about a company, **Company Profiles** may be the best category to choose.

☑ Do It!   Click on **Company Profiles.**

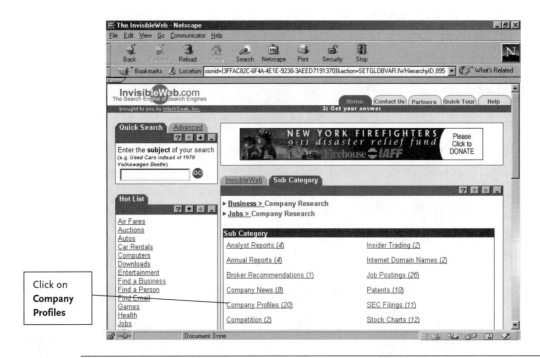

Figure 4.9   Categories in the Company Research Section of the InvisibleWeb

A list of databases will appear in the window. One of them is Hoover's Online. This is the database we want to access.

☑ Do It!   Click on **Hoover's Company Capsule Search**.

   2. Search Hoover's Online to find the company's address, home page, and other basic information.

   Figure 4.10 shows the home page of Hoover's Online.

☑ Do It!   Type **apple computer** in the **by Company Name** field, and click on **GO**.

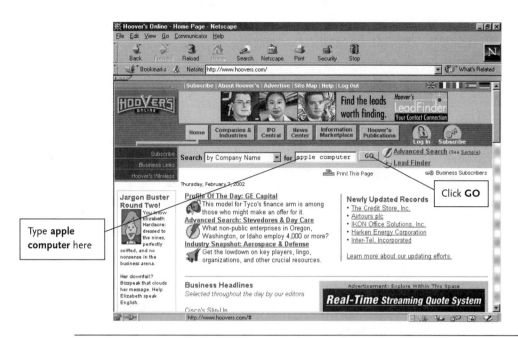

Figure 4.10   Hoover's Online with **apple computer** Typed in the **by Company Name** Field

Several links will appear in your window. Links with a key icon next to them indicate that the information provided at that link is proprietary and is available only to people who have a subscription to Hoover's. The best link for us to choose is the **Company Capsule**.

☑ Do It!   Click on **Company Capsule.**

Figure 4.11 shows a portion of the capsule for Apple Computer, Inc.

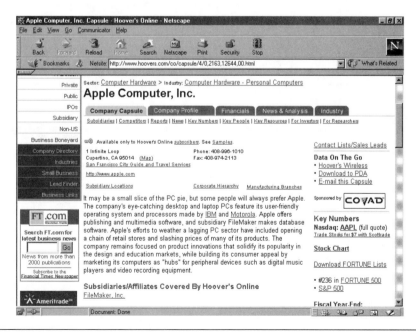

Figure 4.11   A Portion of the Capsule for Apple Computer, Inc.

Note the information provided by Hoover's Online. If you scroll down the page, you will find a lot more information about Apple, including hyperlinks to its Web pages and some primary financial information.

3. Find newspaper articles about the company.

The best place to look for articles about a company is in a newspaper near its headquarters. Because the headquarters for Apple Computer is located near San Francisco, it would be a good idea to search one of that city's newspapers. To locate a database that indexes such resources, let's go back to the InvisibleWeb and see if there are newspaper databases listed.

☑ Do It!   Type the URL for the InvisibleWeb in the location field or address bar: **http://invisibleweb.com.**

☑ Do It!   Click on the following hyperlinks:
News » Daily News » Regional » National (USA) » California » News

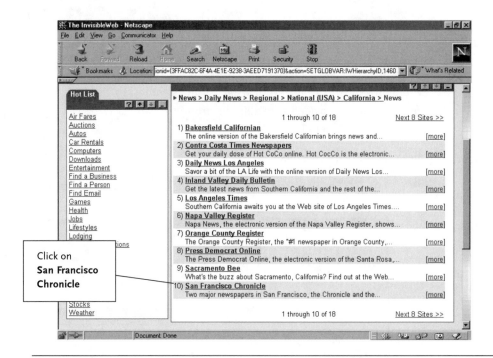

Figure 4.12   Listing of California Newspapers in the InvisibleWeb

Note in Figure 4.12 that the San Francisco Chronicle is listed. Let's access this database.

☑ Do It!   Click on **San Francisco Chronicle**.

Note in Figure 4.13 that you can search the *Chronicle* and the *Examiner* at the same time by using the "All Sources" selection from this Web site.

You'll notice a hyperlink titled **Search Tips**. It's always a good idea to read the search tips before you start searching a database. Note that we can search headlines and bylines or the entire text of an article using keywords. Let's do a simple search, retrieving articles with the word **Apple** in the headline and both of the words **computer** and **industry** in the text of the article. Note that to search for both words, we need to combine the terms with an "AND." In this database, the Boolean operators need to be typed in all caps. We'll also limit our search to articles that were published in 2001.

☑ Do It!   Type **apple** in the search form **Headline:**.

☑ Do It!   Type **computer AND industry** in the search form **Keywords:**.

☑ Do It!   Click on **Begin Search**.

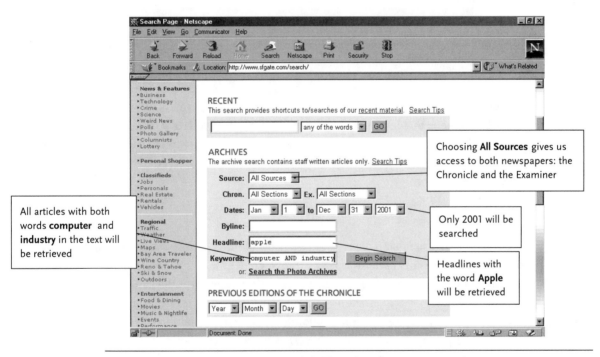

Figure 4.13   Searching the San Francisco Chronicle and Examiner

Figure 4.14 shows the results of this search. Note that the results are displayed by the most recent article first.

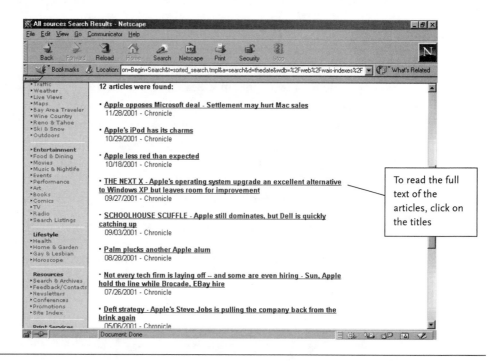

Figure 4.14   The Results of Searching the Archive

END OF ACTIVITY 4 ◀

Although this activity skimmed the surface of the types of business information available on the Web, we hope that it gave you an overview of what's involved with searching for information about a company. Using specialized databases for information like this is much more effective than using global search engines because they allow researchers to focus on specific types of information.

Portals

A portal is a Web site that pulls together a variety of information sources and offers them from one location, making it easier for people to find content that is of great interest to them. Many portals contain dynamic information, such as current news, weather, and stock exchange reports, in addition to free email services and chat groups. Many other portals offer Web search engines, directories, online shopping, map services, and links to travel information.

An example of a portal is Excite, **http://www.excite.com**. Figure 4.15 shows Excite's home page and several of the services it provides. You will have to scroll down the screen to see some of the options. Lycos, **http://www.lycos.com**, and Yahoo!, **http://www.yahoo.com**, listed previously in this book as a search engine and a directory, also offer many other services at their sites and may be more accurately referred to as portals.

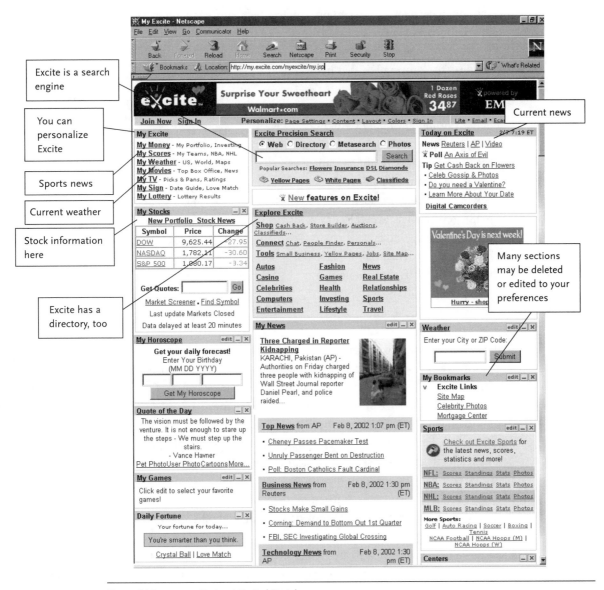

Figure 4.15   Excite: A Typical Portal

Many portal sites allow users to personalize their pages with content and layout preferences. This approach allows you to organize your Web space with favorite Web sites, services, online stores, search resources, and other sources tailored to your special needs. It may be convenient for you to create your own portal and set the page to be your browser's home page. This page would then appear on the screen when your browser starts up, and it would be the place where you go "home."

Proprietary Databases

Hundreds of *proprietary* or *commercial databases* exist on the World Wide Web, but these are available only if you or your organization has purchased access to them. For example, FirstSearch, **http://www.ref.oclc.org**; DialogWeb, **http://www.dialogweb.com**; STN, **http://www.cas.org/stn.html**; and Lexis-Nexis, **http://lexisnexis.com**, all provide proprietary databases.

Proprietary databases have certain value-added features that databases in the public domain do not have. Here are some examples of that enhanced content:

☑ Proprietary databases are likely to include extra information that helps the researcher. For example, most of the databases in FirstSearch, the Online Computer Library Center's (OCLC) proprietary database system, have links to library holdings. This means that if you find an article or book in a database provided by FirstSearch, such as MEDLINE, you can immediately find out which libraries own the material. Even though MEDLINE is available free to the public from the National Library of Medicine, you might prefer to use the FirstSearch version if you want to know who has the listed journal articles.

ON CD

The CD that accompanies this book includes information about using specialized databases to find information about people, which includes a detailed activity on how to use specialized databases to find a person's email address, phone number, and mailing address.

To view this set of resources, click on the hyperlink "Using Specialized Databases to Find Information About People" in the collection of items for Chapter 4.

☑ Proprietary databases also allow you to download information easily. For instance, some of these databases include financial information that is commonly free to the public, but they charge for the use of their databases because they have made it much easier for the user to download the information to a spreadsheet program.

☑ Proprietary databases often index material that others do not. The information is distinguished by its uniqueness, its historical value, or its competitive value (for example, private company financial information).

☑ Proprietary database systems are more responsible to their users. Because there is a fee, these databases are more apt to provide training and other user support information, such as newsletters that update their services.

☑ Some databases on the Web are free to the public but charge for the full-text version of the articles indexed. The Electric Library, **http://ask.elibrary.com**, is an example of this type of database. Many newspaper archives work the same way. You can search the archive, but if you want a copy of the newspaper article, there is a fee involved. For all of these fee-based databases, the fees can be paid with a credit card on an article-by-article basis, through an account, or through a monthly charge.

Accessing Fee-based Databases

If you want to know the proprietary databases available for you to use, you can always ask a librarian at your local public or academic library. The library may have several databases on CD-ROM or may have purchased access to databases via the Internet. The specialized databases covered in this chapter are free and open to anyone.

Summary

This chapter introduced different types of resources that help us find information on the World Wide Web. Directories, sometimes referred to as subject catalogs, are topical lists of selected Web resources, arranged in a hierarchical way. Directories differ from search engines in one major way: the human element involved in collecting the information and maintaining it. While search engine databases are created by computer programs, directories are created and maintained by people. Browsing directories can be a very effective way to find the resources you need, especially if you're sure where the information is located, but you're not quite sure how to narrow down a topic.

Virtual libraries are directories that contain collections of resources that librarians or information specialists have carefully chosen and organized in a logical way. Virtual libraries typically provide an organizational hierarchy with subject categories to facilitate browsing. The main difference between virtual libraries and directories is that virtual libraries are much smaller because the resources included are very carefully selected. The people who organize virtual libraries are usually on the lookout for three major types of information resources: subject guides, reference works, and specialized databases.

Specialized databases are searchable collections on particular subjects. The U.S. government and nonprofit organizations maintain many of the free, nonproprietary databases on the Web, but commercial databases are also starting to appear with greater frequency. You can usually find specialized databases by accessing virtual libraries and meta-search tools as well as by conducting a search in a search engine. These databases are like search engines in that they support different search features. Most databases have search instruction pages that you should read before you start searching.

Selected Terms Discussed in This Chapter

commercial database	specialized database
directory	subject category
hierarchy	subject guide
proprietary database	top-level category
reference work	virtual library

Materials on CD for This Chapter

Here is a list of items for this chapter on the CD that accompanies the text:

- ☑ Selected Directories and Virtual Libraries
- ☑ Using Specialized Databases to Find Information About People
    1. Email and Telephone Directories
    2. Activity: Finding an Individual's Email Address, Phone Number, and Mailing Address
    3. Privacy and Ethical Issues of Personal Records on the Web
    4. Searching for Experts and People Who Share Your Interests
- ☑ All URLs mentioned in this chapter in hypertext format
- ☑ Selected terms discussed in this chapter with hyperlinks to the glossary
- ☑ Copies of the review questions in quiz format

Review Questions

True or False?

1. Directories list resources in categories that are arranged from the most specific to the broadest subjects.
2. Directories and virtual libraries are created and maintained by computer programs.
3. Yahoo! is one of the most comprehensive directories on the Web.
4. All specialized databases are fee-based.
5. Almost everything that is indexed in specialized databases can be found by searching a global search engine.

Short Answer—Completion

1. _____ can be searched, much like the search engines explored in Chapter 3.
2. Three major types of resources most often found in virtual libraries are _____, _____, and _____.
3. Some folks refer to the resources found in specialized databases as the _____ or the _____.
4. A strength of many directories and all virtual libraries is that _____.
5. A weakness of some directories and virtual libraries is _____.

Exercises and Projects

1. Browse Yahoo!, **http://www.yahoo.com**, for a list of zip code directories. Write down the top-level category and all the subcategories that you clicked on to reach the list.
2. Using the Librarians' Index to the Internet, **http://lii.org**, find a Web site devoted to the writings and teachings of philosopher George Gurdjieff. Find the site by searching with keywords and browsing the subject categories. Provide the strategies that you used for each method.
3. Go to LibrarySpot, **http://libraryspot.com**, and locate a genealogy database by clicking on the **Genealogy** hyperlink. Do a search on your family name. Did you find any historical information on your family? Which databases did you try?
4. Go to the Internet Public Library, **http://www.ipl.org**, and find the Web site "Foreign Languages for Travelers." Describe the steps you took to find this database. While you are here, find Arabic words for numbers. Describe the steps you took to find these words. What happens when you click on one of the Arabic words?
5. Use the Open Directory Project, **http://dmoz.org**, to find the Internet Movie Database. Explain the procedure you followed to locate this database. Once you have accessed it, find out who played Boo Radley in the 1962 film *To Kill a Mockingbird.* What are three other movies he or she had a role in?

CHAPTER 5

Communication
on the Internet

▶ the most popular use of the Internet? Communication! It's been that way almost since the Internet began. Soon after the introduction of electronic mail, it became apparent that email was the most popular and one of the most important Internet services.

People enjoy, value, and appreciate being able to communicate with others. The communication isn't only chitchat, either. The Internet has become a medium for professional communications, distributing and sharing information related to education, research, business, and other professional areas.

There are other types or forms of communication on the Internet too. These include discussion groups and Usenet newsgroups, as well as realtime communication such as chat groups and virtual worlds. Each of these has characteristics that make it more appropriate to use in certain situations. The majority use only text (typed words and symbols) for communication, but some allow for audio, video, or images to be part of the communication.

Goals/Objectives

☑ Understand the concepts associated with communication on the Internet

☑ Know some of the prevalent technologies used for communication on the Internet

☑ Be able to decide, based on specific requirements, which communication technology is appropriate

☑ Know how to communicate effectively on the Internet

☑ Be aware of legal and ethical issues related to the use of communication technologies

Topics:

☑ Communication Technologies

☑ Effective Internet Communication

☑ Behavior and Etiquette Guidelines

☑ Legal and Ethical Issues

Communication Technologies

The Internet is accessed by hundreds of millions of people throughout the world, and communication is one of its most popular uses. Using the Internet is an accepted (if not preferred) means of personal and professional communication. Furthermore, the Internet supports a variety of ways for people to communicate, each form differing from the others in terms of the technologies employed and the type of social interaction it supports. Some forms of communication are between individuals, and others are used for group communication. Some of the technologies or ways of communicating are unique to the Internet—email, Usenet, and chat groups, for example. These forms of communication have come about because information is transmitted on the Internet in digital format. The Internet connects people without regard for distance.

Asynchronous and Synchronous Communication

Internet communication can be characterized in other ways, too. Some forms of communication, such as sending email messages, is **asynchronous**. A message is sent or read without the sender and the recipient participating in the communications system simultaneously.

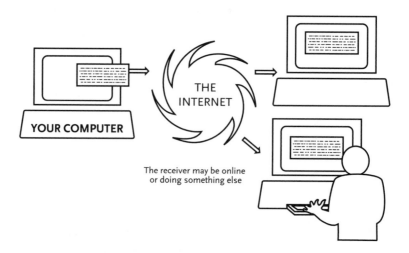

Figure 5.1   Asynchronous Communication

For example, let's say you send a message to Chris. Chris may or may not be connected to the Internet when the message is sent. But the message can be read when Chris connects to the Internet.

Synchronous communication, on the other hand, requires all parties involved to be present at the same time. An example of this type of communication on the Internet is through the use of an online *chat room*.

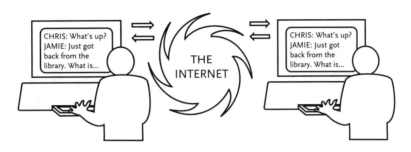

Figure 5.2   Synchronous Communication

In synchronous communication, you and Chris both would be connected to the Internet and using communications software at the same time or you might be at a Web site that lets each of you send and receive messages in real time (as it's happening).

Here we'll list, briefly characterize, and describe some of the major forms of Internet communication. We'll do this in two groups. The first group uses the most established Internet communications technologies and includes email, discussion groups, and Usenet news. We discuss them in greater detail in the next chapters. They're used for personal communications, business uses, and the exchange of scholarly research.

Electronic Mail (Email)

This is a basic Internet service that allows individuals or groups to communicate. People use email programs to read, send, and manage their email. The program is sometimes called an email client or mail user agent. Most email programs make it easy to work with text, images, and other types of files that are part of or attached to an email message. Others work best with messages that are only text.

Email is an example of asynchronous communication. It's good for individual or group communication. You can communicate with groups either by including a list of recipients in the address of the email or by sending email to an email discussion group. Email is well-suited for personal or professional communication.

Discussion Groups

Discussion groups also are called *interest groups*, *listservs*, or *mailing lists*. Internet users join, contribute to, and read messages to the entire group through email or a similar technology. An individual group may keep archives of the postings to the group. In many cases, it's more appropriate to think of a group's members rather than a group's archives as a good resource for information.

A discussion group is an example of asynchronous communication. It's designed for group communication. You communicate by sending email to the address for the group, and the message is automatically distributed to everyone in the group. You also can post messages using a Web browser. Some discussion groups focus on professional or research issues, while others are recreational, dealing with personal interests.

Usenet News

Usenet news is a collection of messages called "articles" grouped into categories called "newsgroups." There are thousands of newsgroups, with tens of thousands of articles posted daily. Rather than exchanging messages or articles among individuals, the articles are sent from one computer system, acting as a Usenet host, to another. The tool that an individual uses to read, post, reply to, and manage articles is called a newsreader. Several different newsreaders are available. Usenet has a long history, in Internet terms, of supporting uncensored free speech with little or no central control.

Usenet news is an example of asynchronous communication. It's designed for group communication. An article posted by an individual to a newsgroup is likely to be available throughout the world within a few hours. The topics for newsgroups run the gamut from professional or research issues to a wide variety of recreational topics dealing with special interests.

Realtime, Synchronous Communication on the Internet

Realtime or synchronous communications on the Internet are a lot like the conversations and meetings we have in real space, as part of our daily lives when we're not using the Internet. They're like two or more people talking in a classroom, in the mall, in a meeting, at a sporting event, or at a party. There may be one or several conversations going on at once. Everyone is in the same place and participating in some way or other; one or more people are talking, some people are listening, and somebody else is waving to get another person's attention. All of this can be happening at the same time.

The same kinds of interactions can occur with the Internet being used as a communications medium. The environment where the communication takes place is called a virtual meeting place, a virtual room, or a virtual world.

We'll discuss these types of communication in some detail here.

Internet Relay Chat (IRC), Web-Based Chat Rooms, MOOs, MUDs, and Instant Messaging Systems

Each of these services has its own characteristics, but they operate essentially in the same way. Usually several people participate simultaneously. People meet on channels that, depending on the service, can be called either chat rooms, *MUDs* (multiuser dimensions or multiuser dungeons), *MOOs* (multiuser dimensions that are object-oriented), or Instant Messaging Systems. There are thousands of channels covering a wide range of topics. Think of these as virtual meeting places or even virtual communities. People usually converse through text, each person typing a message that's displayed in real time to the computer screens of all participants. Some of these virtual communities are elaborate three-dimensional environments where participants may construct objects, houses, buildings, and cities.

These synchronous communication forms are designed for group communication but can be used for individual communication. Communication is immediate and lends itself to brief informal comments similar to what one would use in a conversation. The topics run the gamut from business or technical issues to a wide variety of recreational topics dealing with special interests. Some of these technologies, most notably MOOs, have been used for educational purposes.

To use any of these services you need to be connected to the Internet, as they all involve realtime communication. Because of the nature of this communication, you can't always be certain with whom you're communicating, so you have to be careful about giving out personal information.

IRC

IRC (Internet Relay Chat) is a popular chat system that was developed in the late 1980s by Jarkko Oikarinen in Finland. It operates using a client/server model. You use an IRC client on your computer to contact one of several IRC servers throughout the world. You then connect to a channel or chat area provided by the server. Some servers support thousands of channels, and there are different channels or chat areas on each network. Each channel has an operator who can be contacted if you need help dealing with someone else in the channel or chat room.

Individuals are known by nicknames that they choose. They also control the amount of information that they make public about themselves.

Everyone on a channel can communicate simultaneously. Whatever one person types is broadcast to everyone in the channel. As you might imagine, this can get hectic or confusing. If a large number of people are communicating, the text of the conversations moves too fast to follow. IRC, similar to other chat technologies, allows users to set up exclusive conversations.

Once you connect to a server, you use IRC commands to work with the server. There are lots of commands available. Most folks start with a small set of commands and learn more as they need them.

Web-based Chat

Web-based chat is usually easier to use and more closely moderated than IRC. Most of the Web's major news sources, including CNN.com and the New York Times on the Web; portals, including Excite, Lycos, and Yahoo!; and many other types of Web sites provide chat capabilities. Some sites specialize in providing chat services, and others sponsor chat events with celebrities.

In many cases, you can use a Web-based chat site without needing any special software. Sometimes, though, you can download software that makes working with the chat group easier to manage. Some chat sites require that you download particular chat software to participate in the discussions. At Yahoo! Chat, **http://chat.yahoo.com**, for example, you have a choice of not using any special software or using Java-enhanced chat. The chat rooms at ivillage.com, **http://www.ivillage.com/chat**, also let you use other chat software such as ichat, a popular chat client. (For more information, take a look at the ichat home page by using the URL **http://ichat.com**.)

☑ F Y I   **Where Are the Chat Sites?**

☑ "The Webarrow Chat Directory," http://webarrow .net/chatindex/list.html

☑ "The Ultimate Chat Links Page," http://cyberdrive .net/~mredding/chat/ chat.html

The chat groups or chat rooms, as they're called, all operate essentially the same way. You register at a site, and then you can participate in the chat rooms available at that site. In most cases, you need to supply your name and email address. Then you choose a login name or nickname and a password. You'll want to be very careful about making personal information public. This will help you avoid, at the least, unsolicited email or, worse, strangers knowing your home address. Many chat sites also let you include a picture, a link to your home page, and other ways to let people know about you. The sites also give you ways of keeping all of that information private. You may want to check out a Web chat site's privacy policy before you submit any information. For an example, take a look at "Yahoo! Privacy," **http://privacy.yahoo .com/privacy/us/**.

Most of the Web-based chats are text-based, but some allow you to include image files and some allow for audio files and avatars. An avatar is an icon, image, or figure that you can use to represent yourself in a chat. Some of the avatars are quite elaborate, with three-dimensional attributes and animation. To use these more sophisticated and complex avatars, you'll have to select one from a collection at the site or, in some cases, you can create your own. You'll also have to download or purchase software to enable an avatar, and if the chat involves audio or video, then you may also have to get the hardware and software necessary for that. Some Web sites that host chats with avatars or other exceptional features are:

- ☑ "Alpha World"   **http://activeworlds.com/tour/alpha.html**
- ☑ "The Cybertown Palace" **http://cybertown.com/palace.html**
- ☑ "Worlds.com 3D Portal" **http://worlds.net/3dcd/index.html**

Now we'll take a look at a specific Web-based chat site, Yahoo! Chat. We'll start with the home page that lists some of the chat rooms or groups, and then we'll take a look at the Web page you would use to register at Yahoo! Chat. We'll talk about what you can expect at this popular type of chat site and some of the issues related to using a Web-based chat site, and then we'll leave it to you to explore. This chat site, like many other Web-based chat sites, has lots of help available.

The home page for Yahoo! Chat is shown in Figure 5.3. Its URL is **http://chat.yahoo.com**. You will follow steps similar to those from activities in earlier chapters to access this page.

- ☑ Start your browser.
- ☑ Click on the location field.
- ☑ Type **http://chat.yahoo.com** and press Enter.

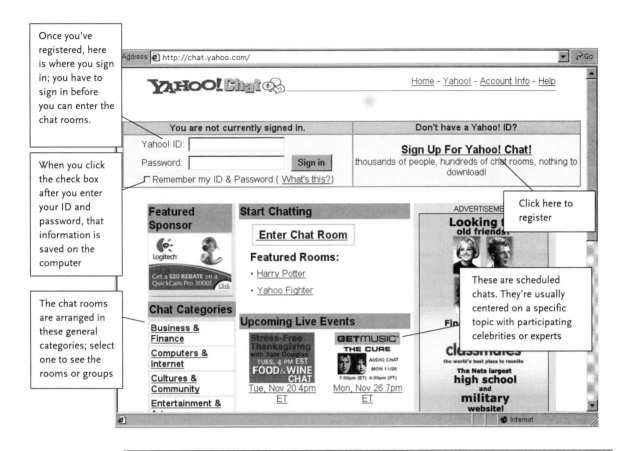

Once you've registered, here is where you sign in; you have to sign in before you can enter the chat rooms.

When you click the check box after you enter your ID and password, that information is saved on the computer

The chat rooms are arranged in these general categories; select one to see the rooms or groups

Click here to register

These are scheduled chats. They're usually centered on a specific topic with participating celebrities or experts

Figure 5.3   The Yahoo! Chat Home Page

If you're interested in using chat technology, the most important things on the Yahoo! Chat home page may be the hyperlinks to the categories of chat rooms, the specific chat rooms themselves, and the chat events. Before you can enter any of the chat rooms, you have to sign on as a registered member. When you register, you'll choose a user name and may give other information about yourself—in other words, you can create your persona at Yahoo! Chat. By allowing only registered users to access the chat rooms, this server (Yahoo! Chat) can exercise some control over who can use the service. Two reasons for registering are that the service may deny access to a user who doesn't follow agreed-upon rules or is causing a problem for others, and the service can collect information about its users for marketing purposes. We'll look at registering in more detail shortly.

When you type your ID and password, you can request that the browser remember that information when you click on the button labeled "Sign in." Clicking the check box labeled "Remember my ID & Password" means the browser will write your ID and password to the computer. To do this, the browser writes what's called a *cookie*, so that a Web server at yahoo.com can access the information. A cookie is a relatively small amount of information, about as long as a sentence, that a server uses to instruct a browser to write to the client computer. Only a server from the same domain as the server that deposited the cookie can read it. This "remembering" is convenient if you're the only person who uses the computer, but you shouldn't select that option if you're using a public computer. If the computer is public, another person could use it and possibly access Yahoo! Chat using your ID and password, because when you ask the browser to remember your information, it is stored on the computer. Yahoo! uses cookies for other parts of the chat session, but these don't contain sensitive information. Yahoo! claims that the ID and password cookie is erased when you click on the hyperlink **Sign Out** or when you exit the browser.

Now let's take a look at what we need to do to register at Yahoo! Chat.

☑ To register or sign up for the service, click on the hyperlink **Sign Up for Yahoo! Chat!**, as in Figure 5.3.

This opens another Web page where you type and submit the required information to sign up for Yahoo! Chat (and other services that Yahoo! offers). Yahoo!, like most services, also asks for information that it would like to have but doesn't require. A portion of that page is shown in Figure 5.4.

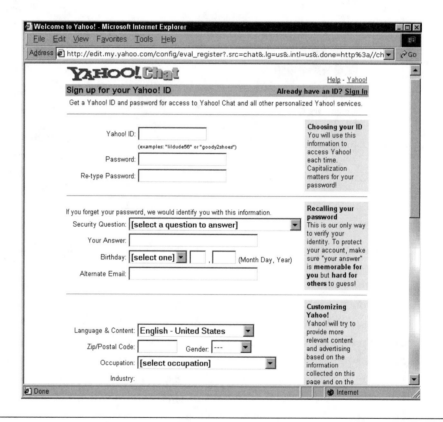

Figure 5.4   The Yahoo! Registration Page

Figure 5.4 shows the registration page for Yahoo! Chat. It is similar the type of registration page you'll find at other chat services. The ID and password are used to log in as a registered member. You can choose them to be whatever you'd like, but you may have to make more than one choice for an ID if the one you choose is already taken. You must give your email address, gender, and zip code. Most sites require at least that much so that members aren't completely anonymous. You can choose what information you'll reveal to other people who've registered. You do that after registering—click on **Add/Create Profiles**. Be sure to

Why Register?

You'll want to register if you're interested in taking advantage of the services Yahoo! offers, such as chat and access to Web-based email. In exchange for these services, you give up information about yourself. Some say it's an exchange of your privacy for the services. It's really less simple than that; you have a choice about some of the information you disclose, and you can make choices about some of the ways you prefer the information to be used.

check the privacy policy before you register so you know how this service will use the information you give it. Yahoo! also might use your email address to send you information, but you can choose to request that it not do this. The last portion of the page contains a link to "Terms of Service." You will have to read and agree to it before you are registered. Take the time to read it so you know what you may or may not do with this service. Also read the Yahoo! Privacy Policy by clicking on the hyperlink at the bottom of the Web page.

Once you've filled in the necessary and perhaps some of the optional information, a confirmation will be sent to the email address you gave.

Once you're registered, you can enter a chat session.

Figure 5.5 shows the home page for Yahoo! Chat after you've signed in. You can see that there are several hyperlinks for selecting a chat room. Once a group is selected, a page pops up showing the ID of each person currently in the chat room with a message displayed every few seconds. You also can invite friends who have registered for Yahoo! Messenger—an instant messaging service—to join in a chat room. We'll leave looking at individual chat rooms up to you because it wouldn't be appropriate to show actual conversations here.

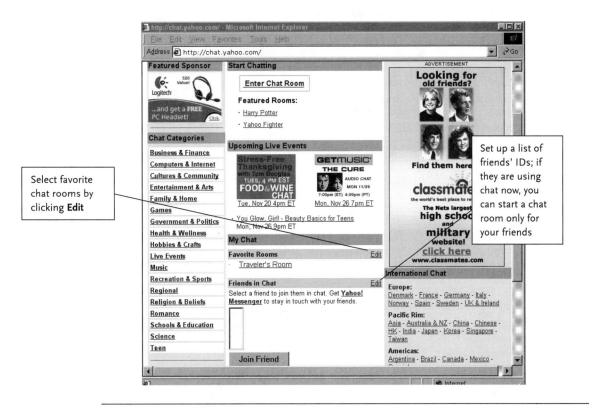

Figure 5.5   The Yahoo! Chat Web Page After You Sign In

Some people visit chat rooms regularly and make friends or acquaintances with other frequent visitors. It is natural to call a group of people who regularly get together to communicate using the Internet a *virtual community*.

MUDs

The term MUD, or multiuser dungeon, was first applied to a multiuser role-playing game or environment developed in the early 1980s by Richard Bartle and Roy Trubshaw at the University of Essex, in England. Now the term is used as an acronym for any multiuser domain as well as to describe any of a class of virtual environments based on some theme (such as a castle or a world) with several participants communicating using (usually) only text in real time.

Some of these environments are based on competition or (virtual) combat, while more recent versions, such as TinyMUD, are built around cooperation, world-building, and socialization. People usually access a MUD by using Telnet to log onto a server or by using a MUD client. Using a MUD, or MUDding, can be addictive and can consume a great deal of time. (We personally know students who have essentially dropped out of several of their classes and spent most of their time MUDding.) A good place to start to learn about MUDs and how to connect to them is the Web site "The MUD Connector," **http://mudconnect.com**.

Blocked by a Firewall?

Some networks use a firewall system, usually a combination of hardware and software, as a security measure. All packets to and from the Internet have to go through the firewall system, but certain packets are not permitted to pass through. This filtering of packets is often done based on the port number associated with the packet. The port number is used to identify the type of Internet service, such as HTTP with standard port number 80. Many of the MUDs and MOOs use nonstandard port numbers, and the firewall on the network you use may not let you contact a MUD or a MOO.

What to do?

You can ask the network administrator if some ports may be opened up, permitting packets for services that support MUDs and MOOs. If that's not possible, then you'll probably have to find another Internet service provider.

MOOs

In 1990, Pavel Curtis, a researcher at Xerox PARC, became interested in a programming language developed by Stephen White, a student at the University of Waterloo. This language, called MOO (MUD Object-Oriented), helped enable the easy construction of MUDs. Curtis worked to develop the concepts further so that people who were not experienced programmers could develop MUDs customized for a specific purpose. These are called MOOs and have become popular with educators and others involved in computer-mediated communications, training, and distance learning. Curtis developed a well-regarded MOO called Lambda MOO.

A good straightforward introduction to the value and purpose of MOOs is "MOOs, Not Just Cows," available at **http://www.lib.usf.edu/~ifrank/lis5937/moo.html**, by Ilene Frank. She also describes some of the basic commands in MOOs and gives links to other resources.

Internet Instant Messaging Systems

Several services available on the Internet and the Web will notify you when someone you know also connects to the same service. You can then send a message directly to that person through the service instead of using email. These services are somewhat like paging or messenger services. You also can use these services to set up chat sessions with one or more people who use the service.

Three popular messenger and paging services are AOL Instant Messenger, ICQ (an acronym meant to represent "I seek you") from Mirabilis LTD, and Microsoft MSN Messenger Service. Other software companies are releasing similar products.

The services are very similar and, like some of the other software we've been discussing in this chapter, are free, have good documentation and help, and are relatively easy to install.

☑ You can get AOL Instant Messenger (AIM) through the AIM home page with the URL **http://www.aol.com/aim/homenew.adp**. The online help is part of the software you install on your computer.

☑ ICQ is available through the ICQ home page with the URL **http://www.icq.com/index**. Online help is available through that Web page and also through the ICQ FAQ, **http:// www.icq.com/support**.

☑ Go to the home page for MSN Messenger Service, **http://messenger.msn.com**, to download the software. You can get help by using the URL **http://messenger.msn.com/ support/helphome.asp**.

After you get the software and follow the instructions to install it, you're led through a registration process.

☑ With each of the services, you select an online name, screen name, or nickname—the name people will use to contact you. You'll have to supply an email address and other information, as well. You can take steps to protect your privacy by keeping that information hidden from other users of the service. However, you can choose to make information public to all or just to selected registered users.

☑ With each service, you can construct one or more lists of friends, colleagues, or work groups. Then whenever you sign on, the service checks to see which of the people in your groups is online.

These services offer convenient ways to keep in touch with other people on the Internet. Take a look at the home page for each service. The services are usually not compatible, though. A person registered on one isn't always accessible from another. These services are popular and becoming more so.

Having introduced some of the technologies that are used to communicate on the Internet, now we'll go over some guidelines for effective Internet communication.

Effective Internet Communication

We'll discuss effective Internet communication as it relates to the communication technologies that are unique to the Internet—email, discussion groups, Usenet news, and synchronous communication such as chat. Most of the communication in these technologies is done through text.

Differences and Similarities Between Spoken and Traditional Written Communication

Because messages are sent electronically, it is possible to get a response in a matter of minutes or seconds. When we're using synchronous communication, the response is immediate. When we're trading comments separated by only a few seconds, Internet communication is similar to spoken communication. It tends to get informal and personal, and that's probably just the way we want it to be. On the other hand, when we're communicating using the written word, we can't show our facial expressions or gestures or express intonation the same ways we would when speaking.

Internet communication is, of course, a form of written communication, but it's a different medium from traditional written communication. It isn't bound by the physical limitations of a page of paper; it can be transmitted and received very quickly, and a single message can be sent to a group of thousands of people as easily as it can be sent to one or two people. Because the communication is written, we have to do what we can to make it easy to read and easy to comprehend.

There's no substitute for a well-thought-out and well-expressed message. To make your communication most effective, you need to write clearly, take into account that people will most likely be reading your message on a computer screen, and take full advantage of the medium itself.

> ☑ T I P ! You'll have to take full advantage of your writing ability, the jargon and acronyms available, and the generally accepted rules for effective communication in a text-based electronic environment.
>
> Remember the difference between casual communication and business or professional communication. Using the Internet for communication doesn't mean you can be more or less casual than when you're face to face.

Here are some guidelines for effective Internet communication using text:

- ☑ Be careful about spelling and punctuation. Follow the same rules you'd use if you were writing a letter or a memo.
- ☑ If you want to state something strongly, surround it with asterisks (*) or write it in uppercase, but don't take this too far. Some folks equate items in uppercase letters with shouting. **Emoticons** or **smileys** were developed to express facial expressions or gestures

as part of text-based communication. Take a look at the Web page "Common Emoticons and Acronyms," **http://pb.org/emoticon.html.**

☑ Use a subject header or tag that gets the reader's attention and accurately characterizes what's in the message.

☑ Make your message as short as possible, but don't make it cryptic or unclear. Most users have to deal with limits on the amount of information they can receive. Keep the body of the message succinct. If you're using email or posting a message to a discussion group or Usenet, limit the message to one or two screens. In some cases—such as using chat—you need to capture someone's attention quickly, and you may be limited to the amount of text you can send in one message.

☑ Write relatively short paragraphs and limit lines to 75 characters. Some email and Usenet programs wrap long lines at whatever the window margin is set. Others don't do this. Give your readers a break and wrap the lines for them.

☑ Include part—but not all—of an original message when you are writing a reply. Include only the portions pertinent to your reply. You do this to set a context for

---

☑ F Y I **Tips on Writing Effective Email**

You can also use the tips in these resources for other forms of Internet communication.

☑ "A Beginner's Guide to Effective Email," http://webfoot.com/advice/estyle.html

☑ "BUSINESS NETIQUETTE INTERNATIONAL," http://bspage.com/1netiq/Netiq.html

---

your message. This takes advantage of a unique feature of Internet communication: It's relatively easy to include your reply within the context of the original message.

Figure 5.6 shows some of the features of using the Internet for communication and demonstrates some of the guides to effective communication. The example pertains to email, but it could be another type of communication. The figure shows how to use email within Outlook Express, the email program included with Internet Explorer.

Here are a few things to note about the message:

☑ It is a message to a group. Multiple copies are sent by including multiple addresses in the header.

☑ The subject header is to the point and will get the reader's attention.

☑ The message uses the same tone of voice as you would find in an interoffice business memo. The spelling and grammar are correct, but not formal.

☑ The message uses an asterisk (*) to emphasize a word in the text.

☑ The message discloses business information such as email address and office phone and fax numbers, but it doesn't contain other personal information.

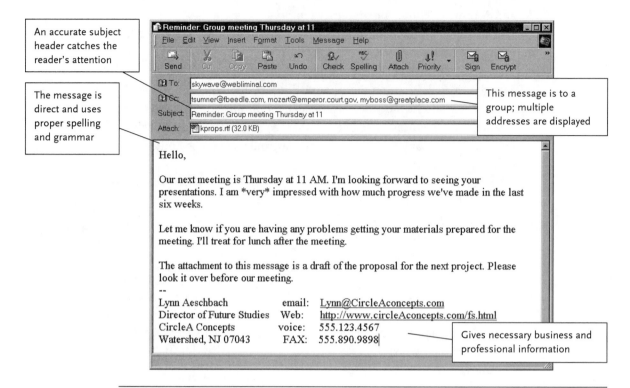

Figure 5.6   An Email Communication to a Group

☑ Any of the recipients of the message shown in Figure 5.6 may send a reply. When they do, they'll need to decide whether to reply to the original sender only, Lynn Aeschbach, or to the group.

Next, we'll consider some accepted and appropriate ways to behave or act when you're communicating on the Internet.

Behavior and Etiquette Guidelines

Using the special technologies for communicating on the Internet carries its own set of rules of etiquette and proper behavior. In most cases, your communication will be using only text. You need to remember that the recipient will read it without the benefit of being with you, seeing your expressions, or getting your immediate and considerate reactions. You need to say what you mean in a clear, direct, and thoughtful way. In some cases, you may not know the person you're communicating with. What follows is a list of guidelines to follow.

Be aware of the risks involved with giving out personal information.

Common sense tells us not to give out personal information, home phone numbers, or home addresses to people we don't know.

Because it may be difficult to know with whom you're communicating, you particularly need to be careful about disclosing personal information. Children especially need to be informed of the risks and dangers involved with using the Internet. Parents should discuss these issues with their children so that they clearly understand not to give out any personal information or tell someone where they go to school or play. The Web page "Staying Street Smart on the Web!" **http://www.yahooligans.com/docs/safety**, is a good place to find information about Internet safety issues for children and parents.

Dangerous situations can arise when we develop a relationship with someone through email or a chat group. Most of the communication is through text; we don't get to hear the person's voice or see them. We may see a picture or get a description, but we may never have certain knowledge. You may, for example, be involved in a long series of email messages or have several conversations in a chat room with a person who claims to be your age and gender. The person may even send a photograph. It could be that the person is totally misrepresenting his or her true self. So we need to be very careful about giving out any personal information, and we certainly wouldn't make arrangements to meet the person without having the meeting take place in a public location and without taking other precautions.

The Internet gives us lots of opportunities for learning, recreation, and communication. We don't need to be rude or unfriendly, but we do need to be very careful.

Take time to consider what you will write.

You'll find you can usually give a better response if you take some time to think about it. Also, if someone writes something that upsets you, don't react immediately. Perhaps you've misinterpreted the original message. Treat others with dignity and respect, as if you were communicating face to face.

Be careful when using humor and sarcasm.

The person reading your message may misinterpret your remarks, and you won't be able to immediately clear up a misunderstanding. When you use the Internet, you have the chance to communicate with people throughout the world. The person with whom you are communicating may be from a different culture, may not be familiar with your language, and may have views and values that are different from yours.

Don't assume the communication is private.

You can never be sure where a copy of the email you write will end up. It's easy to forward email, so the message you send could be shared with others. When you're participating in a group discussion, remember that everyone in the group is likely to see your messages. Everyone in the group has the chance to read, save, print, or forward your message.

Check the address when you compose a message or reply to a message you've received.

Be sure your message is going to the person(s) you want to receive it. If the original message was sent to a group of people, such as a discussion group or Usenet newsgroup, double check the address you reply to, so you can make sure that it is going to an individual or the entire group as necessary. It's embarrassing when email is sent to a group but was meant for an individual.

The guidelines above should help in dealing with some of the issues related to using the Internet for communication. We've mentioned that Internet communication isn't necessarily private, and we'll take a more detailed look at that issue in the next section.

Legal and Ethical Issues

Communication on the Internet has spawned a number of social, ethical, and legal issues. Some of these are related to important personal concerns, such as privacy; some are related to ensuring confidential communications, such as encryption; and others are related to appropriate business practices. In this section, we'll discuss the following:

- ☑ Privacy
- ☑ The Electronic Communications Privacy Act
- ☑ Encryption
- ☑ Offensive and Abusive Email
- ☑ Libel
- ☑ Unsolicited and Inappropriate Email—Spam

Privacy

What's reasonable to expect in terms of privacy when you use the Internet for communication?

Your initial response might be that you would expect the same level of privacy on the Internet as you have in other areas of communication. Codes of behavior or rules of etiquette related to privacy have developed on the Internet over the years. Some of these rules are informal, and others have been codified into policy statements for network use in a company, organization, or school.

In some cases, laws have been adopted to provide the same level of protection of privacy for working with electronic media as with any other media. An important point is that privacy, as it relates to communication, is sometimes defined in terms of the medium. The laws in the United States dealing with communications in printed form, i.e., on paper, have had to be changed to suit electronic communications. We'll cover a few of the important issues related to privacy.

Privacy in the Workplace: Can Your Employer Monitor Your Electronic Communications?

Yes! If you're using an email system owned by your employer, then any email message—or other communication—transmitted by or received by that system belongs to your employer. Decisions in several court cases support the concept that your employer owns and may monitor email or other communications. It's a good idea to check with your employer to learn the company policy and see what practices are followed.

One site to visit for more information about privacy in the workplace is the *Privacy Rights Clearinghouse*. Specifically take a look at "Fact Sheet # 7: Employee Monitoring: Is There Privacy in the Workplace?" **http://privacyrights .org/fs/fs7-work.htm**

The manner in which communication is implemented on the Internet makes it susceptible to monitoring. We can't assume that our Internet communications are private.

When you send a message, the message is broken into packets and the packets are sent out over the Internet. Packets from a single message may take different routes to the destination or may take different routes at different times. This works well for the Internet and for you. Packets are generally sent through the best path, depending on the traffic load on the Internet. The packets making up a message may pass through several different systems before reaching their destination. This means there may be some places between you and the destination where the packets could be intercepted and examined.

Some say that sending email is like sending a message on a postcard.

If you're using a computer system shared by others or if the system at the destination is shared by others, there is usually someone (a system administrator) capable of examining all the messages. So, in the absence of codes of ethics or the protection of law, Internet communications could be very public. Most system administrators adopt a code of ethics under which they will not examine email unless they feel it's important to support the system(s) they administer. The truth of the matter is that they are often too busy to bother with reading other people's mail.

The Electronic Communications Privacy Act

One example of a law that helps ensure the privacy of email is the *Electronic Communications Privacy Act (ECPA)*, which was passed in 1986 by Congress. It prohibits anyone from intentionally intercepting, using, or disclosing email messages without the sender's permission. The ECPA was passed to protect individuals from having their private messages accessed by government officers or others without legal permission. That bill extended the protections that existed for voice communications to nonvoice communications conveyed through wires or over the airwaves. You can, of course, give your permission for someone to access your email. However, law enforcement officials or others cannot access your email in stored form (on a disk or tape) without a warrant, and electronic transmission of your email can't be intercepted or "tapped" without a court order. The ECPA does allow a system administrator to access users' email on a computer system if it's necessary for the operation or security of the system. The ECPA gives the system administrator the authority to allow no access to email passing within or through a system without a court order or warrant. The administrator can and indeed should refuse any requests to examine email unless the proper legal steps are followed.

Although the ECPA makes it illegal for someone else to read your email, the law has been rarely applied.

Encryption

When you send a message by email, it's often transmitted in the same form you typed it. Even though it's unethical and illegal for someone else to read it, the message is in a form that's easy to read. Deleting email from your mailbox doesn't necessarily mean that it's gone. On many computer systems, email is routinely backed up or saved to tape in case it's necessary to retrieve a "lost" message.

A better way to prevent others from reading your email is to use *encryption* to put a message into an unreadable form. The characters in the message can be changed by substitution or scrambling, usually based on some code. The message can't be read unless the code and method of encryption are known. The code is called a key. A popular and effective way of encoding messages is called **public key encryption.**

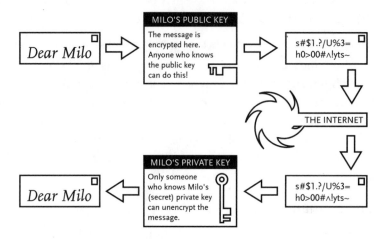

Figure 5.7   Using Public and Private Keys to Encrypt Messages

With public key encryption, there are two types of key, one public and the other private. The public key needs to be known by the sender to send a message. You use someone's public key to encrypt the message, and the receiver then uses her or his private key to decode the message after receiving it. Suppose you want to send an encrypted message to your friend Milo. He tells you his public key (in fact, there's no harm if he tells everybody). You write the message and then encrypt it using Milo's public key. He receives the message and then uses his private key to decode it. It doesn't matter who sent the message to Milo as long as it was encrypted with his public key. Also, even

☑ F Y I   **More Information About Electronic Privacy**

☑ "6.805/STS085: Readings on Privacy Implications of Computer Networks," http://www-swiss.ai.mit.edu/6095/readings-privacy.html

☑ "EPIC Online Guide to Privacy Resources," http://epic.org/privacy/privacy_resources_faq.html

if the message was intercepted, it couldn't be read without knowing Milo's private key. It's up to him to keep that secret. By the same token, if he wanted to respond, he would use your public key to encrypt the message. You would use your private key to decode it.

What we've said so far still allows someone to forge an email message. Someone using your name could encrypt a message and send it to Milo. He might think it came from you! Some encryption techniques using private and public keys are used to virtually eliminate the possibility of forgery. When you send a message, you use your private key to create an encrypted digital signature. When Milo gets your message, he can apply your public key to the signature to verify that it was sent by you and that the message hasn't been altered.

You can obtain a version of public key encryption software called *PGP*, for Pretty Good Privacy. It's freely available to individuals and may be purchased for commercial use as well.

There are some restrictions on the use of the encryption software developed in the United States. At the time of this writing, State Department regulations prohibit the export of most encryption methods, while other countries allow the export of encryption methods and algorithms. Some people feel strongly that these policies should be changed for the sake of sharing information and for the sake of allowing common encryption of sensitive and business-related messages, but others don't agree.

One issue that needs to be resolved is whether it should be possible for law enforcement or other government officials to decode encrypted messages.

Some argue that because of the need to detect criminal action or in the interests of national security, the means to decode any message should be available to the appropriate authorities. Others argue that individuals have the right to privacy in their communications. In the United States, the issue has been decided in favor of government access in the case of digital telephone communications. The issue hasn't been settled yet for email or other forms of electronic communications.

☑ F Y I **More Information About PGP**

- ☑ "Introduction to PGP," http://web.bham.ac.uk /N.M.Queen/pgp/pgp.html

- ☑ "MIT distribution site for PGP," http://web.mit.edu /network/pgp.html

- ☑ "The comp.security.pgp FAQ," http://www.cam .ac.uk.pgp.net/pgpnet /pgp-faq

Offensive and Abusive Email

Virtually all codes of etiquette, ethics, and policies for acceptable use of networked computer facilities include statements that prohibit sending offensive or abusive messages by email. This is, naturally, similar to the codes of behavior and laws we adhere to in other kinds of everyday communications. One difference between dealing with this sort of behavior on the Internet and other forms of communication, such as the telephone or postal service, is that no one is in charge of the Internet—it is a cooperative organization.

If you have a problem with someone at your site, talk with your supervisor, his supervisor, your system administrator, or your Internet service provider about it. If the problem comes from another site, send email to the address postmaster@the.other.site, **and talk with the system administrator at your site or your supervisor about it. (Be sure to substitute the Internet domain name of the site in question for** the.other.site.)

Individuals have been arrested and prosecuted for making threatening remarks by email. Civil suits and charges have been filed against individuals in cases of harassment, abuse, and stalking.

It may be that someone gets upset about what another has written and sends a message that insults, scolds, berates, or is downright nasty about the author of the original message. This type of message is called a *flame*.

When you get a message like this, take some time to think about it before replying. To reply with a similarly rude or angry message really doesn't help the situation.

Libel

Some libel suits have been filed based on postings to the Internet. This happens when one person or company feels that another has slandered them or falsely attempted to damage their reputation. Once again, you would expect the same laws or rules for libel in the society at large to be applied to network communications. That's generally the case, but an interesting issue comes up, centering around whether the company or organization that maintains a computer telecommunication system is responsible for libelous or even illegal messages posted there. In the United States, the courts have generally drawn an analogy between these systems and a bookstore. The owner of a bookstore is not responsible for the contents of all the books in the store, and likewise, the management of commercial networked systems on the Internet have not been held responsible for all messages on their systems. On the other hand, some commercial network systems claim to screen all messages before they're posted. In that case, they may be held accountable for libelous messages. Also, consider that telephone companies aren't held responsible for the speech on their equipment since they fall into the category of a "common carrier." However, television and radio stations are responsible for the content of their broadcasts.

Unsolicited and Inappropriate Advertising—Spam

There was a time—before the late 1980s—when commercial traffic was not allowed on the Internet. Now the use of the Internet for commercial activities is commonplace. It's not unusual for Web pages to carry advertisements. Usenet and email discussion groups developed on the Internet in the late 1970s and early 1980s in an atmosphere free from marketing and advertising. While some (relatively few) Usenet newsgroups and discussion groups tolerate commercial announcements, most are adamantly opposed to any selling or advertising, and unsolicited marketing is met with strong resistance. This resistance has included attempts to have the advertiser dropped by its ISP and flooding the advertiser's mailbox with email messages.

Most users prefer that advertising and commerce be done in clearly identified newsgroups, discussion groups, or Web pages.

Unsolicited commercial email is called *spam*. That term is also applied to inappropriate commercial postings to newsgroups. Because email is composed and sent by a computer, it's relatively easy to send several thousand messages in less than an hour. Naturally, it's annoying to get this "junk" email or posting to groups. It's also costly to the person receiving the spam, and, unfairly, not very costly to the person sending the email. Some estimates put the cost of spam at over $30 million per year.

Spam is more than an annoyance; it slows other traffic on the Internet and imposes a cost on the receiver through dealing with the unsolicited commercial email or newsgroup postings, with little cost to the sender.

Some legislation dealing with spam is pending in the U.S. Congress, and several states have passed anti-spam laws. Identifying spammers and notifying their Internet service provider is sometimes helpful in dealing with the problem. Several major ISPs have instituted policies that attempt to prohibit spam from their servers (but still it's the ISP's customers that have to eventually pay the bill for that). In 1997, one ISP—EarthLink—successfully mounted a legal challenge against Cyber Promotions Inc. to stop the company from sending unsolicited email to its customers or using the ISP's networks for distributing unsolicited email. In 1998, Cyber Promotions was ordered to pay EarthLink $2 million.

The Coalition Against Unsolicited Commercial Email (CAUCE) is an all-volunteer organization that supports legislative and technical solutions to eliminating spam. Visit its Web site "Join the Fight Against Spam," **http://www.cauce.org**, for more information. The Web site "Get that spammer!" **http://triode.net.au/~forever/gspam.html**, by Julian Byrne, contains lots of information about ways to track down and stop spammers.

People who send out spam use various methods to get email addresses, including harvesting addresses from postings to Usenet newsgroups, discussion groups, and mailing lists. Some use tricks such as collecting email addresses from what may seem like legitimate services that require registration. Unfortunately, you can't eliminate the possibility of getting spam, but here are some steps you can follow to cut down on the amount of spam you receive:

- ☑ Be careful about giving out your email address, and only register for services that agree not to share your address.
- ☑ When posting messages to Usenet newsgroups use a From: or Reply To: address such as **ernie_REMOVE THIS TO REPLY@mwc.edu**.
- ☑ Include a note at the end of your email messages warning people that spam will be read and forwarded to the appropriate authorities.
- ☑ When you receive spam, *don't* respond or click on a hyperlink that promises to remove you from a mailing list.
- ☑ Take a look at the techniques for reducing spam in the section titled "Suggestions" at the site "Get that spammer!" mentioned above.

Summary

Communication is the most popular use of the Internet, with email topping the list of all the technologies used. Some of the other types of communication technologies used include email discussion groups, Usenet news, chat groups, and IRC. These technologies are unique to networked computer environments and have come into wide popularity because of the Internet.

Most of the communication technologies used on the Internet require communication to be done using text—letters with some symbols and punctuation. Communicating effectively involves taking the time—except in truly informal communications—to use correct grammar, spelling, and punctuation as well as writing an appropriate message. When replying to a message, include the pertinent parts of the message and use an appropriate and interesting subject header.

When you're communicating on the Internet, take special care not to give out personal information to strangers and to treat others with respect. Be aware of the risks involved in communicating with people you cannot see and may never meet in person. Take time to consider what you write to others, and be careful to avoid humor and sarcasm except with the best of friends. You can't assume that your messages are private, so be careful about what you write.

Several ethical and legal considerations arise from using the Internet for communication. The manner in which communication is implemented on the Internet makes it susceptible to monitoring. You can't assume that communications are private. Some people believe that sending email is like sending a message on a postcard. Some laws have been enacted to help protect privacy during electronic communications. These, however, have been difficult to enforce and are rarely applied. One way to protect privacy is to encrypt or code a message. A common way of encrypting messages is through the use of public and private keys. Although software for encryption is readily available, current policies and laws prohibit its export.

Another area of concern is dealing with abusive or offensive communications. Laws that apply to libel, harassment, and abuse have been applied to cases where the offending behavior has occurred on the Internet. Unsolicited email or other forms of communication is called spam. Spam definitely is an annoyance, but it also can be quite costly to the people who receive it. It's relatively inexpensive to produce spam because most of the cost of transporting the email is shifted to the receiver and all the people who use the networks supporting the Internet.

Selected Terms Discussed in This Chapter

asynchronous communication	listserv
chat room	mailing list
cookie	MOO
discussion group	MUD
Electronic Communications Privacy Act (ECPA)	PGP (Pretty Good Privacy) public key encryption
emoticon	smiley
encryption	spam
flame	synchronous communication
interest group	
Internet Relay Chat (IRC)	virtual community

Materials on CD for This Chapter

Here is a list of items for this chapter on the CD that accompanies the text:

- ☑ All URLs mentioned in this chapter in hypertext format
- ☑ Selected terms discussed in this chapter with hyperlinks to the glossary
- ☑ Copies of the review questions in quiz format

Review Questions

True or False?

1. A chat room is an example of synchronous communication.
2. Discussion groups also are called interest groups, listservs, or mailing lists.
3. It really doesn't matter if your electronic messages are in uppercase or lowercase letters.
4. It is illegal for an employer to monitor employees' email messages.
5. Email is the most popular communication technology on the Internet.

Short Answer—Completion

1. A popular and effective way of encoding messages is called _____.
2. Unsolicited and inappropriate advertising using email is called _____.
3. Chat, MOOs, MUDs, and instant messaging systems are all examples of _____ communication.
4. _____ or _____ were developed to express facial expressions or gestures as part of text-based communication.
5. Individuals may obtain a free version of public key encryption software called _____.

Exercises and Projects

1. Take some time to explore two Web sites that deal with effective email, "A Beginner's Guide to Effective Email" by Kaitlin Duck Sherwood, **http://webfoot.com/advice/estyle.html**, and "Business Netiquette International" by Frederick Pearce, **http://bspage.com/1netiq/Netiq.html**.
   a. Each site lists several tips about writing effective email. Pick the three most important tips and explain why they are important.
   b. Describe each site and list the major points covered at each.
   c. Which of the two sites gives tips that are more appropriate to your professional or academic tasks? Explain your choice.
2. Do you know what an autoresponder is? Send email to **autoreponder@webliminal.com** to see an example of how an autoresponder works. For more details, take a look at the Web page "Auto Responder Comparison," **http://makura.com/auto/autocomp.html**. Now write answers to the following questions:
   a. What is an autoresponder?
   b. How should you prepare information for an autoresponder?
   c. Explain how a business or organization of your choice could use and benefit from an autoresponder.
3. Take a look at the home page for the Electronic Privacy Information Center (EPIC), **http://epic.org**.
   a. Select two items from the section "Latest News." Give a synopsis and a URL to use for more details about each item.
   b. Follow the hyperlink to the EPIC Online Guide to Privacy Resources. List the names of five international privacy sites. Follow a hyperlink to one of the sites and describe what's available at that site.
4. Let's explore Yahoo! Chat.
   a. You can see what chat topics are available at Yahoo! Follow some of the hyperlinks on "Yahoo! Chat," **http://chat.yahoo.com** to see what rooms are available. What's available under the topics "Recreation and Sports" and "Computers & Internet"?

b. Want to try a chat session? Follow the steps in this chapter to sign up for a Yahoo! ID. You may want to create an ID that you'll use only for this purpose. After you have an ID, you can take a look at what's going on in some of the chat rooms. Try one that looks interesting, visit it, and after you've been able to observe what's going on, write an opinion or rating for the chat room. Give it a rating of 1 to 5, with 5 being the most positive and 1 being the most negative, and explain why you gave it that rating.

5. Suppose you're in the real estate business. Describe ways to use the different modes of communication mentioned in this chapter in a meaningful way. For each type of activity, note its advantages, disadvantages, and significance.

Electronic Mail

▶ electronic mail, or email, was one of the first Internet services available. People enjoy, value, and appreciate being able to communicate with others. Email has special features that make it different and more useful in some cases than other forms of communication such as writing letters on paper, talking on a telephone, or sending a fax. Because it is asynchronous communication, when you send an email, the receiver doesn't have to be connected to the Internet at the same time. It's just as easy to send a message to many people as it is to send it to one person. You can reply to email at your convenience—receiving it doesn't necessarily interrupt your work or recreation. With most modern email programs, you can include text, images, and sound within a single message. Because email is fast becoming a preferred method of communication, you'll want to learn about how it works and how you can use it effectively.

Goals/Objectives:

- ☑ Understand the concepts associated with electronic mail
- ☑ Gain a working knowledge of an email system to read, send, and otherwise manipulate electronic mail folders
- ☑ Be aware of common features of modern email systems
- ☑ Learn how to work with email in text and nontext formats
- ☑ Learn the basic features of an email system

Topics:

- ☑ How Email Works
- ☑ Advantages and Limitations of Email
- ☑ Email Programs and Their Features
- ☑ Email Addresses
- ☑ Dissecting a Piece of Email—Headers, Message Body, and Signature
- ☑ Attachments and Nontext Email
- ☑ Using Email Filters to Organize or Block Email

How Email Works

Electronic mail, or email, lets you communicate with other people on the Internet. It's used for all types of communications: personal, business, scholarly, and professional. You can send messages to anyone with an Internet address, and likewise, you can receive email from anywhere on the Internet. With more than 200 million people having some sort of connection to the Internet and the increasing use of the Internet in all aspects of our society, email gives you an opportunity to communicate with people nearby and around the world in a relatively quick and efficient manner.

Email programs are called **mail user agents** because they act on the user's behalf. The email program acts as a go-between for you and the computer systems, and the computer systems handle the details of delivering and receiving mail.

When you compose your message, it's all in one piece, but when it's sent out to the Internet, it's divided into several pieces called "packets."

The packets can travel and arrive at their destination in any order, and they don't all have to take the same path. When you communicate with a remote site, you may think you have a direct connection, but that's not always the case. At the destination, the packets are collected and put in order so the email is back in its original form. If a packet contains an error or is missing, the destination sends a request back to the source asking for the message to be resent. All of this takes place according to **SMTP, Simple Mail Transfer Protocol**, the standard protocol used on the Internet to transport email between computer systems.

Advantages and Limitations of Email

Advantages

Email has a number of advantages over some other forms of communication. It's quick, convenient, asynchronous, and nonintrusive.

☑ Email usually reaches its destination in a matter of minutes or seconds.

☑ You can send letters, notes, files, data, or reports all using the same techniques.

☑ You don't have to worry about interrupting someone when you send email. The email is sent and delivered by one computer system communicating with another across the Internet. Although it is put into someone's mailbox, the recipient isn't interrupted by the arrival of email.

☑ You can deal with your email at your convenience, reading it and working with it when you have the time.

☑ You don't have to be shy about using email to communicate with anyone. You can write to anyone with an Internet email address. But remember that email isn't anonymous— each message carries the return address of the sender.

☑ The cost to you for email has nothing to do with distance, and in many cases, the cost doesn't depend on the size of the message. Most Internet access charges either are based on the number of hours per month you access the Internet or are a flat monthly fee.

☑ FYI **The Essential Information Is:**

You use an email program on your computer to compose, send, read, and manage email. Once you compose (write) a message, you can send it on the Internet in electronic form, where it usually passes through several other sites before reaching its destination. Once there, it is held until the person to whom it's addressed reads it, saves it in a file, or deletes it. The recipient does not have to be logged in or using a computer for the email to be delivered. When she does use her computer and checks for email, it will be delivered to her.

Email messages can arrive at any time. They're added to a file, your mailbox or inbox, which is part of a directory that holds all the email for the system. The mailbox holds the messages on the server addressed to you, and only you (or the system administrator) can read your mail. On many systems, the maximum size of the mailbox is limited, and the amount of time email is held is limited as well. It's important that you delete old email so new mail won't be rejected because your mailbox is full.

Limitations

Although email is an effective and popular way to communicate, there are some drawbacks to its use.

☑ Email isn't necessarily private. Since messages are passed from one system to another, and sometimes through several systems or networks, there are many opportunities for someone to intercept or read email.

☑ It's possible to forge email. This is not common, but it is possible to forge the address of the sender. You may want to take steps to confirm the source of some email you receive.

☑ Some email systems can send or receive text files only. Even though you can send and receive images, programs, files produced by word-processing programs, or multimedia messages, some folks may not be able to view them.

Email Programs and Their Features

Email Programs

If you read your email using a microcomputer, then you probably contact a computer system that acts as a mail server. That computer system is the one that receives the email for you from others on the Internet. The mail is held for you until you check it. The program you use to work with your email, the mail user agent, is also called an **email client**. It works directly with the email server.

There are several different types of email programs or systems.

☑ **Mail systems designed for proprietary networks.** These email systems were originally designed for use on private or proprietary networks that used protocols different from the Internet protocols. They have been extended to work with Internet mail. Examples of these are GroupWise and AOL Mail.

☑ **Mail clients designed for text-based mainframe or minicomputer systems.** These are designed for use on a computer terminal. The terminal can be physically connected to a computer or a network, or it can be a virtual terminal that's accessed through Telnet (an Internet protocol for setting up a terminal session). Until the mid-1990s, these email systems were the prevalent Internet email clients, and they are still common on Unix, VAX, and IBM mainframe systems. Elm, Pine, and Mailx are examples of this type of email program.

☑ **Mail clients designed for microcomputer systems.** Your computer acts as a client and sends a request to the mail server to see if there is mail and to bring it to your computer. This exchange between the two computer systems is usually done using *POP*,

---

ON CD

The CD that accompanies this book includes detailed instructions for setting up Outlook Express and Netscape Messenger. Setting up other email clients is similar.

To view them, choose the hyperlinks "Configuring Outlook Express for Email and Usenet News" and "Configuring Netscape Messenger for Email and Usenet News" in the collection of items for Chapter 6.

Post Office Protocol, or *IMAP, Internet Message Address Protocol*. You or someone else has to set the Internet addresses on your computer for the outgoing and incoming mail servers. With these common types of clients, the email is delivered to the microcomputer you're using from the mail server. That way you can work in an offline mode if you'd like, connecting to the Internet only to retrieve and send email. In order to use these clients, you may have to go through some steps for setting the Internet addresses for the servers and other information.

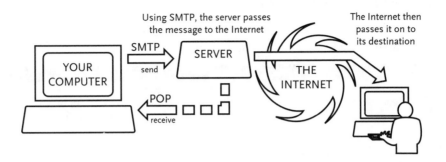

These clients are designed to work on a microcomputer, so they have features that take advantage of the available graphical interface, text formatting, and file management facilities. Many of these email clients allow for including multimedia elements and Web page elements using HTML as part of a message. Some popular email clients are Eudora, Netscape Messenger, and Microsoft Outlook Express.

☑ **Web-based email services.** You use these mail systems, sometimes called free email systems, through a Web page. Some examples are:
Angelfire, **http://email.angelfire.mailcity.lycos.com/**
Hotmail, **http://hotmail.com**
Yahoo! Mail, **http://mail.yahoo.com**

These Web-based email services allow you to retrieve your email using a Web browser. They offer several advantages:

☑ Using one of these services, you can use your email from any location that has access to the Web—your office, your home, a public computer lab, or a public library.

☑ These services let you check email from one or more POP email servers. This is useful if you have more than one email account or if you change your ISP.

☑ If your employer provides you with an email account, you may be able to access these systems without having your messages monitored.

You register at one of these sites to get a login name and password. In exchange, you give up some information about yourself, and advertisements are displayed when you use these services for email.

Take a look at the Web site "Free Web-based Email Services," http://emailaddresses.com/email_web.htm, for more information and links to several of these services.

☑ F Y I   **Comparing Email Clients**

If you've got a choice of email clients then you'll want to know what features each client supports and how they would fit your needs. These two Web pages compare features of popular email clients.

☑ "Comparing HTML-aware Email Clients," http://webreview.com/1998/01_16/strategists/01_16_98_3.shtml

☑ "Email Client Comparison," http://www.brandeis.edu/its/resources/standards/emailcomparison.html

---

Common Features of Email Systems

No matter which email system or program you happen to be using, there are certain features that are common to all modern email systems. Here's a list:

Feature	Comments
Read	Naturally, you expect to use the email program to check your mailbox and read messages. Usually, you'll be able to choose which message to read from a list of messages. Some email programs can be set to notify you when new mail arrives.
Delete	To delete a message from a list of messages, you make a specific request to do so, such as pressing the **Delete** key. Some email systems keep these deleted messages in a folder named **Trash** so you can change your mind and recall them. In those cases, you'll have to be sure to occasionally delete messages from your Trash—and then they're gone for good!
File	With this feature you can save email in different folders or mailboxes. This helps manage your email.
Print	Sometimes you'll want a hard copy of a message. This lets you send the current message to the printer.
Save	This feature lets you save a message from the mailbox to a file on your computer. This way, you can keep messages around without clogging your mailbox.
Compose	Composing a message means writing a message or putting a message together by copying text from other programs. You can expect the email program to include a way to check spelling in the message. Some email programs allow you to use HTML to compose messages.
Attachments	You can include nontext items such as images, data, programs, documents, or spreadsheets with a message.
Signature	This feature automatically adds some information—usually your name, address, phone number, and so on—to all outgoing email.
Reply	You use this feature to reply to the current message. Usually, the original message is included as part of the reply. Recall the tip for effective email communication that said to only include portions that are pertinent to your reply. You'll be able to choose whether to reply to the sender of the message or to everyone who was on the address list of the message.
Forward	The current message is passed on to another email address. The forwarded mail is email that you send, so at that point your address is used for the return address.
Mark	You'll be able to mark a group of messages, so you can apply most of the features above to the group all at once.
Sort	You can sort a list of messages by subject, sender, date sent, and so on.
Address Book	This lets you keep a list of addresses so you don't have to remember them all. You'll also be able to use nicknames or aliases with the addresses, for example, **karen** for **khartman@mwc.edu**.
Online Help	This can answer your questions or let you know how to use the features of the email system.

Some mail programs also allow you to encrypt a message and include a digital signature to help protect your privacy.

Email Addresses

The Format of an Internet Email Address

An email address on the Internet usually has the form:

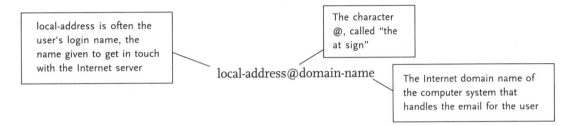

Sometimes the domain-name portion is the name of a specific computer, such as **oregano.mwc.edu**. It could be more general, such as **earthlink.net**. In this case, the systems at the site **earthlink.net** handle delivering mail to the computer that acts as the incoming mail server for the addressee. The portions or fields making up the domain name are separated by periods (the periods are called dots).

Here's an example:

ernie@paprika.mwc.edu

If you were going to tell someone the address, you would say "ernie at paprika dot mwc dot edu." *Ernie* and *paprika* are pronounced as words, but *mwc* (em double-u see) and *edu* (e dee you) are pronounced as individual letters.

ON CD

The CD that accompanies this book includes an activity that deals with finding email addresses.

To view it, click on the hyperlink "Using Specialized Databases to Find information About People" in the collection of items for Chapter 4.

Finding Someone's Email Address

Once you get the bug of communicating by email, you'll probably start to want the email addresses of your friends and others you'll want to communicate with by email. There are some methods and services to help find email addresses, but none of them are guaranteed to always give satisfactory results.

The problem with finding someone's email address is that there is no central directory or any central agency that registers each user. Users are added and deleted by individual Internet sites; the decisions are made locally. It might be helpful to have a directory of all Internet users and their email addresses, but such a directory just doesn't exist.

Here are a few ways to find someone's email address:

☑ Call or write (using paper mail) to ask for an email address.
☑ Check for an email address on a resume, a business card, stationery, or a Web page.
☑ Look at the return address in the From:, Return-Path:, or Reply-To: email header.
☑ If you know the school the person attends or an organization with which he or she is

affiliated, check the Web page for the school or organization for ways to find the email addresses of students, faculty, or employees.

☑ Try a Web-based "white pages" service to search for an address. Some examples are InfoSpace, **http://infospace.com**, and Switchboard, **http://switchboard.com**.

☑ Consult some directories for collections or lists of email addresses. One site is "Finding Email Addresses," **http://emailaddresses.com/email_find.htm**.

☑ Read and use "FAQ: How to Find People's Email Addresses," **http://www.qucis.queensu.ca/ FAQs/email/finding.html**, maintained by David Alex Lamb (**dalamb@cs.queensu.ca**). It contains many resources and tips for finding email addresses.

Dissecting a Piece of Email— Headers, Message Body, and Signature

A piece of email has three main parts:

1. Headers
2. Message body
3. Signature

Some messages also include other files called *attachments*. We'll deal with those in a later section.

Headers

Headers are pieces of information that tell you and the email system several important things about a piece of email. Each header has a specific name and a specific purpose. They're all generated and put in the proper form by the email program used to compose the message. Some headers are typed in, and others, such as the date, are entered automatically.

Working Online and Offline

Most email systems let you choose whether to work online or offline. That way you can do your work but not have to be connected to the Internet. You go online to get and send messages, and work offline when you're replying to messages or composing new ones.

Initially you connect to the Internet and go online. You contact your mail server and retrieve any messages. Then you disconnect from the Internet. This takes you to offline mode. You can reply to any messages or create new ones in offline mode. The email program will save the messages you'll want to send in a list. When you're ready to send the messages, go to online mode. Give the command to send off the messages you've written and to download any new ones.

When you read an email message, you're likely to see these common headers:

Subject:	The subject of the email
Date:	When the email was sent
From:	The email address of the sender
To:	The email address of the recipient

Message Body

The message body is the content of the email—what you send and what you receive. Most of the time you'll probably be writing email for another human to read, and in that case there aren't any special rules for the format of the message body. Sometimes, though, you may be sending email to a computer system where your message will be interpreted by a computer program. In that case you'll be given instructions to use specific words or phrases in the message body.

Signature

The *signature* isn't a signed name but a sequence of lines, usually giving some information about the person who sent the email. It is made up of anything the user wants to include. Typically, a signature has the full name of the sender and some information about how to contact the sender by email, phone, or fax. A signature is optional, but you'll want to be sure that one is included with professional or business communications. Some signatures also contain a favorite quotation or some graphics created by typing characters from the keyboard. Try to keep yours brief. The longer it is, the more bytes or characters that have to be sent, and so the more traffic to be carried on the Internet. It's fun to be creative and come up with a clever signature, but try to limit it to five lines.

Here's an example:

```
Ernest Ackermann              http://www.mwc.edu/ernie
Department of Computer Science   Mary Washington College
Fredericksburg, VA 22401-5358    VOICE 540 - 654 - 1320
ernie@paprika.mwc.edu           FAX   540 - 654 - 1068
```

You don't have to type in the signature each time. The email program automatically appends it to each outgoing message. The way you create a signature may differ from one email program to another.

Figure 6.1 shows an email message with several of its parts labeled.

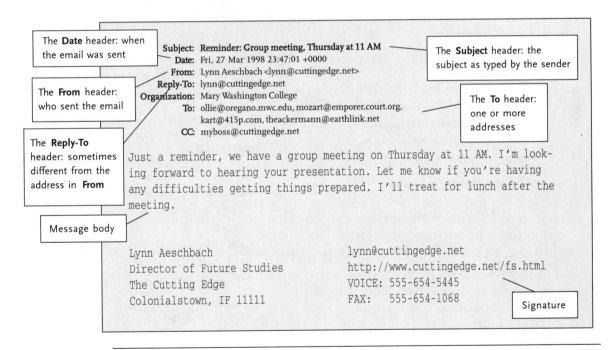

Figure 6.1   An Email Message

Dissected Attachments and Nontext Email

An *attachment* is a file that's sent along with email and is usually viewed separately from the message body. People often use attachments to send along other types of files such as ones that contain an image, multimedia, a program, a document written using a word-processing program, or a spreadsheet.

The protocols used to exchange mail between computer systems were originally written to handle only text, so-called *ASCII (American Standard Code for Information Interchange)* files. Files containing information in other formats are called *binary files*. To send information in binary files, the files have to be *encoded* into ASCII. When the message is received, the attachment holding the encoded file has to be *decoded* from ASCII back to binary.

Many email systems take care of the encoding or decoding, but there are different schemes used. *BinHex* has been used on Macintosh systems; uuencode and uudecode have been typically used on Unix computer systems. Many email programs now handle the encoding and decoding using *MIME (multipurpose Internet mail extensions)* types. MIME is the standard way to work with nontext files as part of email or Usenet articles.

If you're dealing with an email program that doesn't automatically decode attachments, then a message containing attachments might look like the following. We show only the first two lines of the encoded image.

Can My Computer Get a Virus from Reading an Email Message?

It's not possible to get a computer virus from ordinary text email messages. But it is possible for a virus to be part of an attachment. To protect your computer system, don't open any attachment without scanning it first for a virus, and don't use a word-processing or spreadsheet program to read your email, unless you can check it for macro-type viruses.

A computer virus needs to be attached to or part of an executing or running program. This is similar to a biological virus that needs to be part of a living host. It is possible to include a program as an attachment to an email message. The program that's been encoded and attached may have a virus that could infect your computer system, but only if you open the attachment or decode the program. The sensible thing to do is to scan any attachment for a virus.

Word-processing programs and spreadsheet programs sometimes allow a document to contain macros, a way of combining several commands, instructions, or steps into one command. The macros are like programs in that they contain a set of instructions that are executed by the computer. Some mischievous and (perhaps) malicious people have found ways to include a virus in a macro. When you open an email using a word-processing program or a spreadsheet program, you run the risk of your computer getting a virus.

Every once in a while a new hoax pops up about a virus being spread by opening or reading an email message. Take a look at the Web site "Vmyths.com - The Truth About Computer Virus Myths & Hoaxes," **http://vmyths.com**, for more information about these hoaxes. You'll also want to check that page before repeating a message you've received about a virus.

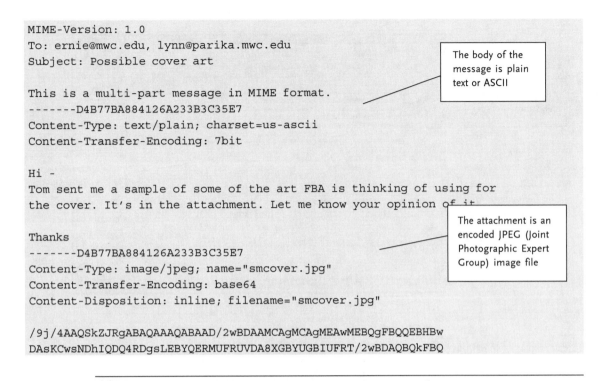

```
MIME-Version: 1.0
To: ernie@mwc.edu, lynn@parika.mwc.edu
Subject: Possible cover art

This is a multi-part message in MIME format.
-------D4B77BA884126A233B3C35E7
Content-Type: text/plain; charset=us-ascii
Content-Transfer-Encoding: 7bit


Hi -
Tom sent me a sample of some of the art FBA is thinking of using for
the cover. It's in the attachment. Let me know your opinion of it


Thanks
-------D4B77BA884126A233B3C35E7
Content-Type: image/jpeg; name="smcover.jpg"
Content-Transfer-Encoding: base64
Content-Disposition: inline; filename="smcover.jpg"


/9j/4AAQSkZJRgABAQAAAQABAAD/2wBDAAMCAgMCAgMEAwMEBQgFBQQQEBHBw
DAsKCwsNDhIQDQ4RDgsLEBYQERMUFRUVDA8XGBYUGBIUFRT/2wBDAQBQkFBQ
```

The body of the message is plain text or ASCII

The attachment is an encoded JPEG (Joint Photographic Expert Group) image file

Figure 6.2   An Email with an Encoded Attachment

Adding and Viewing Attachments

When you work with an email program that automatically encodes and decodes binary files, you can sometimes view the attachment when you're viewing the message. If the image can't be viewed or the attachment is a file of another type (a word-processing document, a spreadsheet, a database, or a program), then you'll likely be able to save the file or open an application to work with it. Here's how we sent the image mentioned in Figure 6.2, using Outlook Express.

1. **Compose the message.**

☑ Do It!   Click **File** in the menu bar, select **New**, and then select **Mail Message**. You can send email from Internet Explorer too; click on **File** in the menu bar, select **New**, and then select **Message**. In any case, a window like the one in Figure 6.3 appears. In Figure 6.3, we've filled in the addresses, the subject, and the body of the message. We've left out the signature to save space here.

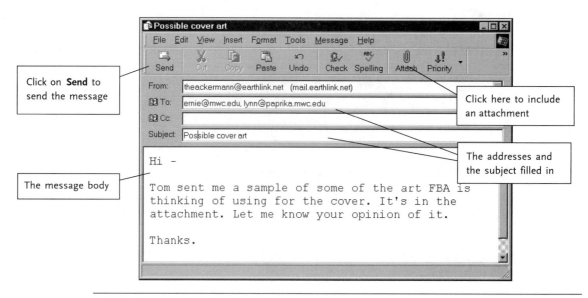

Click on **Send** to send the message

Click here to include an attachment

The addresses and the subject filled in

The message body

Figure 6.3   Composing a Message

2. Include the attachment.

☑ Do It!   Click **Attach** as shown in Figure 6.3. A dialog box appears, and we can choose to attach a file.

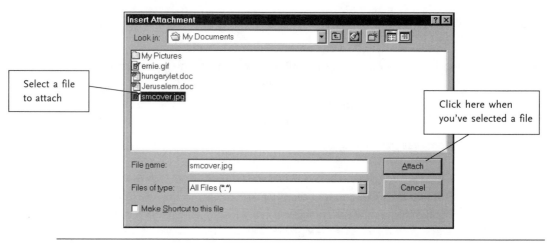

Select a file to attach

Click here when you've selected a file

Figure 6.4   The Dialog Box for Selecting an Attachment

3. Send the message.

☑ Do It!   **Send** as shown in Figure 6.3.

When the message arrives, we can view it by clicking on the entry in Inbox (the folder that holds incoming messages). Figure 6.5 shows a portion of the email when viewed using Outlook Express.

The paperclip indicates there's an attachment

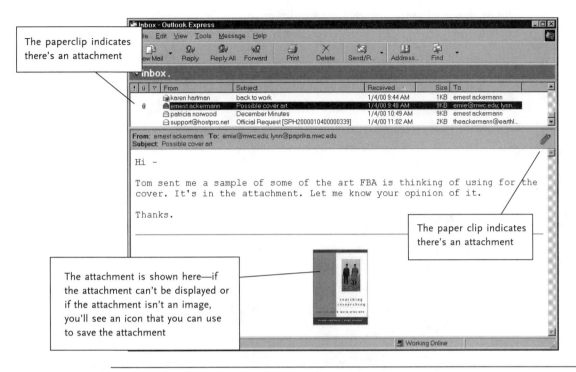

The paper clip indicates there's an attachment

The attachment is shown here—if the attachment can't be displayed or if the attachment isn't an image, you'll see an icon that you can use to save the attachment

Figure 6.5   An Email Message with a Decoded Attachment

Email with HTML

Some email programs such as Eudora, Outlook Express, and Netscape Messenger can work with messages that contain HTML. They can display a message that's written the same way as a Web page. CNET, **http://www.cnet.com/subscription/0-16335.html**, for example, provides subscriptions to a variety of email newsletters that can be delivered in HTML or text format.

Outlook Express and other email clients make it relatively easy to compose email that includes HTML. You can choose fonts, colors, and images for your email. We go over some of the basics of HTML in Chapter 9. If you choose to send email in that form you need to be sure the person you're sending it to can read email in HTML format. If they can't then they may not be able to read it at all. We only use plain text and attachments for the examples in this book so the messages can be read by anyone.

Using Email Filters or Rules to Organize or Block Email

Most email programs contain ways of filtering email so that messages can be put into specific folders based on the subject, sender, or other information. It's smart to use an email program this way. What you're doing is setting certain rules that the program can follow so that it automatically puts incoming email that matches those rules into existing folders for you. You can check the folders anytime to read, answer, or delete your mail. You're using the (limited) intelligence of the email user agent to help organize your mail!

For example, you may want to put all the email from your family members into a folder that keeps it separate from your professional mail. Consider this as an another example: It may be that you don't want to waste your time reading email from a specific individual or that has a particular subject. In this case you can have that email put directly in the trash.

These methods are called filters if you're using Netscape email or Hotmail, and they are called rules if you're using Outlook Express or GroupWise. The details for setting filters or rules differ depending on which email client or user agent you're using. Here's a brief example for setting a rule using Outlook Express. You can use it as a guide for the email system you use.

We're going to set a rule in Outlook Express so that email from family members gets put into a folder named **family**. After that's set, then all the incoming email from the email addresses we specify are put into the folder named **family**. To read the email, just select the folder **family**. Here are the steps to follow:

1. **Start Outlook Express.**

   Look for the icon for Outlook Express on your desktop and double-click on it.

2. **Click on Tools in the menu bar, select Message Rules, and then select Mail as shown in Figure 6.6.**

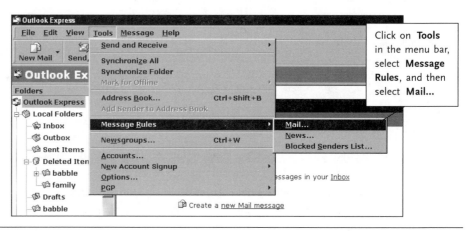

Figure 6.6   Selecting Mail Rules in Outlook Express

3. **Select options to set rules.**

   We're setting a rule so that all email from specific people is put into a folder. Those options are shown in Figure 6.7. After you make those selections you need to click on "Where the From line contains people," as shown in Figure 6.7, to specify the email address(es). When mail is received from those email address, the rule will automatically put it into the folder you specify.

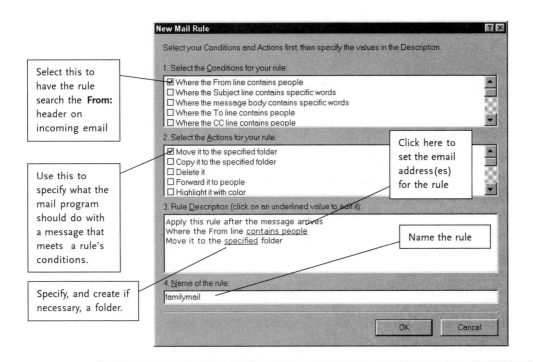

Select this to have the rule search the **From:** header on incoming email

Use this to specify what the mail program should do with a message that meets a rule's conditions.

Specify, and create if necessary, a folder.

Click here to set the email address(es) for the rule

Name the rule

Figure 6.7   Setting Options for a Rule in Outlook Express.

4. Name the rule.

We gave the name **familymail** to this rule. You can set several rules or filters. You can delete or modify a rule, and you can set a rule to be inactive or activate it.

5. Test the rule.

Ask someone on your list of addresses for the rule to send you a message. Alternatively, you could include your own email address in the list of addresses for the rule and send yourself some email. If you didn't include your address, add it now. Follow Step 2 above. Then select the rule **familymail**, and click on **Modify**. Then add your address in the same way you added addresses when you created the rule.

There is another way to set a rule or a filter with the conditions based on a specific message. First select the message, then click on Message in the menu bar and select Create Rule from Message… It's a relatively easy way to set a rule for messages that contain the same word(s) in the **Subject** header.

ON CD

The CD that accompanies this book includes details for using Outlook Express and Netscape Messenger.

To view them, choose the hyperlinks "Using Outlook Express" and "Using Netscape Messenger" in the collection of items for Chapter 6.

We've looked at some general ways of using an email system. The concepts are similar, but details differ between specific email systems.

Summary

Electronic mail allows users on the Internet to communicate with each other electronically. Using the email program with Netscape Communicator, you can compose messages and then send them to any other Internet address. You can read the messages you've received, save them to a file, print them, or delete them. You can also reply to a message or forward one to another Internet address. There are several other email clients available and other ways to work with email on the Internet.

An email message consists of three main parts: the header, which contains information about the address of the sender, the address of the recipient, when the message was sent, and other items; the message body, which holds the text portion of the email; and an optional signature, which holds information about the sender such as their full name, mailing address, phone number, and so on. The signature, which should be limited to four or five lines, is put into a file that can be automatically included with each message.

In order to send email, you give the Internet address of the recipient, compose or write the message, and then give a command to send it on its way. The message is broken up into packets, each containing the address of the sender and the address of the recipient, and the packets are routed through several sites on the Internet to the destination. The computer systems on the Internet handle the transmission and delivery of the email. Once email arrives at a site, it is put into a system mailbox for an individual user. The user can read the email on the system by using an email program such as the one available with Microsoft Outlook Express.

Email is a convenient and efficient means of communication. However, most communication is done by the text of messages, so you have to be considerate and careful to communicate effectively, without misunderstandings. Since you probably have a limited amount of space for your email, be sure to get rid of unwanted or unnecessary email and also be sure to send concise, appropriate messages to others. Email isn't necessarily private. Because it's transmitted electronically, there are several opportunities for someone to read your messages. It's relatively easy to forward copies of email so a message sent to one person can be easily transmitted to others.

Email or Internet addresses usually have the form of **local-name@domain-name**. *Local-name* is often the login or user name of the person receiving the email, and *domain-name* is the Internet name of the site or computer system receiving the messages. It's possible to send email to addresses on networks not on the Internet. You need to know the proper form of an address to communicate with users on these networks.

Finding someone's email address isn't always easy. There is no central directory keeping a list of the email address for everyone on the Internet. If you want to find someone's address, one of the best things to do is to call or write that person and ask for their email address. There are a number of automated services to use to search for an email address.

Selected Terms Discussed in This Chapter

American Standard Code for
   Information Interchange (ASCII)
attachment
binary file
BinHex
decoded
email client
encoded

Internet Message
   Address Protocol (IMAP)
mail user agents
multipurpose Internet
   mail extensions (MIME)
Post Office Protocol (POP)
signature
Simple Mail Transfer Protocol (SMTP)

Materials on CD for This Chapter

Here is a list of items for this chapter on the CD that accompanies the text:

- ☑ "Configuring Outlook Express for Email and Usenet News," Has detailed instructions for setting up Outlook Express.
- ☑ "Using Outlook Express," Has details about using Outlook Express for email.
- ☑ "Configuring Netscape Messenger for Email and Usenet News," Has detailed instructions for setting up Netscape Messenger.
- ☑ "Using Netscape Messenger," Has details about using Netscape Messenger, the email system that comes with Netscape Communicator.
- ☑ All URLs mentioned in this chapter in hypertext format.
- ☑ Selected terms discussed in this chapter with hyperlinks to the glossary.
- ☑ Copies of the review questions in quiz format.

Review Questions

True or False?

1. Email is an example of asynchronous communication.
2. An email signature provides information about the sender of an email message.
3. It is not possible for a computer to get a virus from an email attachment.
4. It's extremely easy to find someone's email address because all addresses are kept in a central directory.
5. An email message is broken up into packets as it is sent out over the Internet to its destination.

Short Answer—Completion

1. Email programs are called _____ because they act on the user's behalf.
2. The standard protocol used on the Internet to transport email between computer systems is _____.
3. The protocols used to exchange mail between computer systems were originally written to handle only text, or _____ files.

4. Email addresses usually have the form of **local-name**@_____.

5. _____ contain information that tell you and the email system several important things about a piece of mail.

Exercises and Projects

1. Using your email program, save a message to a folder and print the same message.
2. Create a signature for yourself and test it by sending yourself a short message.
3. Do the following:
   a. Find a picture of Salvador Dali on the Internet and send it as an attachment to an email message.
   b. Find an image of a piece of work by Salvador Dali on the Internet and send it as an attachment to an email message.
4. Learn how to create a filter or rule for your email system. For each of the parts below, send yourself a message with the subject "testing filters" to demonstrate that you've completed the exercise.
   a. Create a filter or rule that automatically puts all email with the subject "testing filters" in the **Deleted Items** or **Trash** folder.
   b. Create a folder named **testing** and create a filter or rule that automatically puts all incoming messages with the subject "testing filters" in the folder named **testing**.
5. The Web page "Different Types of Free Email," **http://emailaddresses.com/ guide_types2.htm**, gives pros and cons of POP email systems and Web-based email systems. Considering your needs, decide whether POP or Web-based email is better for you. Write a paragraph supporting your choice using some of the points made in the Web page.

CHAPTER 7

Discussion Groups and Usenet Newsgroups

▶ fan out: to send one message to a group and have it automatically distributed or made available to every member of the group. That is one of the important features of discussion groups on the Internet and Usenet newsgroups. These groups are a great way to share information, and there are thousands of them, focusing on all sorts of topics. Some of the people who participate in the discussions are novices, and others are experts. One person posts a message, and others can read it and respond at their convenience. Another characteristic of this kind of communication is called "fan-in." This means that an individual in the group receives all the messages sent to the group. With this type of communication, a person might ask a question to the group and the replies could come from anywhere in the world. We'll take a further look at Internet discussion groups and Usenet newsgroups in this chapter.

Reading and writing the news—that's what Usenet is about. Started in 1979 so that people on one computer system could share news (announcements, information, comments, and discussions) with people at another site, Usenet news was developed using technology different from the Internet. Now it is available to everyone and is an important part of the way people communicate with each other on the Internet.

Goals/Objectives:

- ☑ Understand the nature of email discussion groups
- ☑ Know what resources are available through these groups
- ☑ Learn how to work with email discussion groups
- ☑ Understand netiquette issues related to participating in email discussion groups
- ☑ Understand the nature of Usenet news
- ☑ Know the resources available through Usenet
- ☑ Learn how to work with Usenet news through a specific newsreader
- ☑ Understand issues related to participating in Usenet newsgroups

Topics:

- ☑ Overview and Essential Information About Discussion Groups
- ☑ Details of Working With a Discussion Group
- ☑ Finding the Discussion Groups You'd Like to Join
- ☑ Proper Etiquette and Behavior Within a Group
- ☑ Overview and Essential Information About Usenet News
- ☑ Details of Working With Usenet News
- ☑ Using FAQs, Finding Newsgroups, and Searching Archives
- ☑ Usenet News Etiquette

Overview and Essential Information About Discussion Groups

People have been using email since the beginning of the Internet, and individuals with common interests have formed **email discussion groups**—also called **interest groups**, **mailing lists**, or **listservs**—based on specific topics.

Other types of discussion groups are frequently accessed and used through a Web page interface. These are called discussion groups, Web boards, or bulletin boards. These types of discussion groups or boards have similarities with email discussion groups. You might need to register—provide a login name, password, your real name, and email address—to read the messages, and you'll almost always have to register to post messages to the group. Messages are displayed and accessed through the Web rather than through email. To get an idea of how these groups work, take a look at any of the discussion boards listed at "The New York Times: Readers' Opinions," **http://forums.nytimes.com/comment.**

We'll use the terms *discussion group* and *list* to refer to any of these groups—email discussion groups and Web-based groups or message boards. These groups foster discussions as individuals compose and post messages, answer questions, and respond to other people's statements.

The groups operate and discuss topics in a truly asynchronous, "any place, any time" manner. When an individual posts or sends a message, it's distributed or made available to the group. The message is delivered through email, and individuals participate at their convenience. They don't have to participate at a fixed time or in the same real or virtual space.

All the advantages, disadvantages, and tips for effective communication that we listed in the previous chapter on email and Internet communication apply here. Take a moment to review them while you're reading and working with this chapter.

Discussion groups give you valuable resources when you're searching for information on specific topics or seeking answers to questions. Here are a few reasons that these resources are so helpful:

- **The group itself.** Replying to messages, giving help, and supplying accurate information when possible are part of Internet culture. Although it's unreasonable to expect group members to do your research for you, the group can be very helpful.
- **The discussions.** The messages or articles are often archived and can be searched and retrieved.

Essential Information

Discussion groups are made up of people anywhere on the Internet who agree to communicate as a group to share messages related to a certain topic. The group named "Gardens," for example, is a group where people use email to discuss aspects of home gardening. Anyone can join or *subscribe* to the group. Usually, discussions are on the main topic, but messages on other topics are tolerated or redirected to other groups.

The communication in these groups is two-way, but each member chooses his or her level of participation. The groups also serve as a means of fostering virtual communities because they are collections of people with an interest in communicating with each other.

When someone types a message and sends it to an email group, the message is routed, virtually immediately, through email, to all members of the group. When someone posts a message to a Web-based message board, the message can be read by any member of the group. This is what we mean by the term *fan-out*. Anyone in the group can respond to the message, either by replying to the group or sending email to the individual who sent the original message—this is *fan-in*. Responses can come from around the world or next door. Members of the group don't all have to be using their computers at the same time to participate in the discussion.

Table 7.1 lists the essential features and concepts connected with using an email discussion group.

Feature/Concept	Explanation
It's all done by email.	All communication in a discussion group is carried on by email. A user joins or subscribes to a group (the request to join is made by email) and then shares in the discussions of the group. A message sent to the group is broadcast via email to all members of the group, so these discussions are public.
You decide how much you want to participate.	You don't have to respond to every message. It's usually a good idea to only read messages when you first join a group so you can get an idea of the general tone and level of the discussion. Some folks use the term *lurking* to describe the behavior of observing the discussions. Lurking is just fine; it may be exactly what you want.

A group or list is managed (when everything goes well) by software.	Most of the management of a list, such as adding new members or subscribers and removing members who choose to leave—or **unsubscribe** from—a list, is handled automatically by software on the computer that serves as the host system for the list. Requests for service are handled by commands sent to an email address, called the ***administrative address***. A computer program processes messages to the administrative address, so they have to be in a format that follows very strict and specific rules.
There are two addresses associated with a discussion group: the administrative address and the ***group address***.	When you're a member of a list, you need to know two addresses and you need to know when to use them: ☑ **The administrative address.** That's the address you use to join or subscribe to the group. It's used for administrative requests, such as subscribing to the group or getting a list of the members. ☑ **The group address.** That's the address you use to communicate with the group. Once you've joined the group, you send email to the group address and it gets sent to all the other members of the group.
Each group has a name.	The name of a discussion group is usually part of the group address. These are some examples: ☑ **C-opera**—a list about contemporary opera and music theater; the group address is **c-opera@listserv.unb.ca**. ☑ **Net-happenings**—a list used for announcing new or changed Web sites and other Internet resources; the group address is **net-happenings@cs.wisc.edu**. ☑ **Net-Essentials-L**—a list for learning to use a discussion group; the group address is **Net-Essentials-L@listproc.mwc.edu**.
Your messages are public.	Your original messages and your replies to messages from other group members are sent to all members of the group. Think twice about what you write, and check your message for spelling and grammar.
The membership list may be available to everyone in the group.	Some discussion groups make their membership list (names and email addresses) available to any member of the group. Any member can retrieve the list by sending a command to the administrative address.
It's easy to get help.	Send a simple message (HELP) to the administrative address, and you'll receive by email a list of all the commands you can use with the list. This works for any type of software managing a list.

Table 7.1   Essential Features and Concepts of Email Discussion Groups

Details of Working with a Discussion Group

Working with Web-based discussion groups or bulletin boards is fairly easy once you've decided which group you want to use. You register for the group by giving your real name and email address and selecting a login name and password. Then, when you want to access a group's messages, you go to the Web site or Web page for the group, type in your login name and password, and select a category or single message that you want to read.

How do you join and participate in an email discussion group? To put things in context, we'll give an overview of working with a discussion group that we've set up: **Net-Essentials-L**. We'll use this group for examples throughout this chapter. Don't worry if some of the terms we use here are unfamiliar. Read on, and you'll see they're explained later.

Table 7.2 shows a list of steps you are likely to go through when working with a discussion group.

Be Prepared for More Email

If you join a group that has lots of members, you might be flooded with email, so be prepared if you join a popular group or one with lots of messages per day. In some groups or lists, you can request that messages arrive in digest format. A digest is one email message that contains several other messages (to cut down on the clutter in your mailbox).

1.	Identify or choose a group.	You'll find out about groups by reading about them on the Internet, getting recommendations from friends, or searching a collection of lists. Below, we'll point out some ways of finding the name and administrative address for a list.
2.	Join the group by sending email to the **administrative address**.	You'll send email to the administrative address with the body of the message reading as follows: subscribe *list-name your-name* The address used to join the group **Net-Essentials-L** is **listproc@listproc.mwc.edu**. Check the section later in this chapter that gives the proper form to use for the type of list or group you're working with.
3.	Communicate with members of the group by sending email to the **group address**.	The group address for **Net-Essentials-L** is **Net-Essentials-L@listproc.mwc.edu.** If you want to post a question, make a statement, or help someone out, simply send an email to **Net-Essentials-L@listproc.mwc.edu**.
4.	Use services available from the list.	The services available and the ways to access them will most likely be contained in the reply you get from the administrative address when you join the list. Save that reply because you may need it later. Services can include access to a list of members, archives of previous discussions, and so forth.
5.	Unsubscribe or leave a group.	To unsubscribe, send email to the administrative address, not to the group address. In most cases, the body of the email message should read as follows: unsubscribe *list-name your-name*. Check the section in this chapter that gives the proper form to use for the type of list or group you're working with.

Table 7.2   Steps in Working with a Discussion Group

The commands you use to join a group and to request certain services are often cryptic and have to be stated precisely in a specific format. A computer program, not a human, usually interprets them. Email sent to an administrative address is passed on to a computer program. The program acts as an intelligent agent or helper.

When you join the group, you'll get an email message about the commands you'll need to use. For example, it will tell you how to get help and information about other commands. Be sure to save that email because it contains important information.

☑ T I P ! Remember never to send a message to join (subscribe) or leave (sign off) to a group or list address. You use the administrative address for that.

It's easy to make a mistake. If you send a request to the wrong address, a member of the list will usually remind you of the correct address. If you send a message that's passed on to the managing software but was meant for the members of the list, you'll usually get a reply indicating an error.

How to Join, Contribute to, and Leave an Email Discussion Group

In this section, we'll go over the commands used to join and access other services of an email discussion group. We already know that you send email to the administrative address for group services. The specific commands depend on the type of software that's used to manage the group. The common ones are Listserv, Listproc, and Majordomo.

A Description of the List "Net-Essentials-L"

List name:
Net-Essentials-L

Administrative address:
listproc@listproc.mwc.edu

Group address:
Net-Essentials-L@listproc.mwc.edu

Brief description:
Discussions related to the topics, activities, exercises, and projects in the textbooks by Ackermann & Hartman

To join:
Send email to
Listproc@Listproc.mwc.edu
with the message

subscribe Net-Essentials-L *your-full-name*

For example:
subscribe Net-Essentials-L Chris Athana

You can usually tell which software manages the list by looking at the administrative address. For example, if the address is **listproc@coco.great.edu** (a fictitious address), Listproc is being used.

The type of software maintaining the group is chosen when the group is created; it isn't a decision each member can make. When you join the group, you'll get information about the commands to use, and you can usually get help from other members of the list.

How to Join a List

To join a list, you need to send email to the administrative address for the list. The email should contain the word SUBSCRIBE (usually SUB will do) and the name of the list. For most lists, you will also need to include your full name (first name and last name), but the software that manages some lists doesn't allow you to include your name. Be sure to follow the instructions.

Regardless of the type of list, the command to subscribe to the list has to be in a specific format. You're not writing something for another person to read, you're giving a command to a software program. Also, you don't have to supply your email

Be Persistent!

It's easy to make a mistake when you're beginning to work with email discussion groups. Sometimes you'll send a message to the wrong address or in an improper form. It seems that these things happen to everyone. If a message doesn't go through or you get email that your message wasn't in the proper form, try again.

address in the body of the message. The software that manages the list automatically adds your name and address to the list of members.

What Happens Next?

You'll receive a response from the software managing the list within a few minutes or hours. That is, of course, provided you've used the proper address and commands and that the list still exists.

In some cases, you'll be asked to confirm your request to subscribe, but in many cases, you'll receive an immediate email message welcoming you to the list. **Save the welcome message!** It usually contains important information about communicating with the group and how to get help and more information. You might need to know about commands to leave the group and to request other services from the software that manages the list. Once again, **save that message!** You'll probably need it in the future.

Figure 7.1 is an excerpt from a sample welcome message. The message is from Listproc and is for **Net-Essentials-L**.

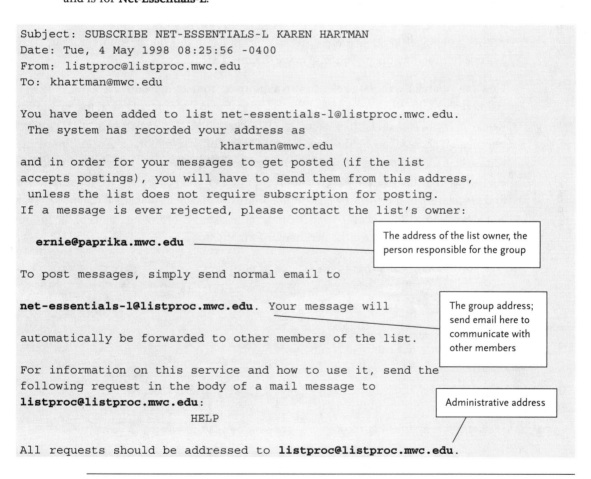

```
Subject: SUBSCRIBE NET-ESSENTIALS-L KAREN HARTMAN
Date: Tue, 4 May 1998 08:25:56 -0400
From: listproc@listproc.mwc.edu
To: khartman@mwc.edu


You have been added to list net-essentials-l@listproc.mwc.edu.
 The system has recorded your address as
                        khartman@mwc.edu
and in order for your messages to get posted (if the list
accepts postings), you will have to send them from this address,
 unless the list does not require subscription for posting.
If a message is ever rejected, please contact the list's owner:


  ernie@paprika.mwc.edu ────────────────    The address of the list owner, the
                                            person responsible for the group

To post messages, simply send normal email to


net-essentials-l@listproc.mwc.edu. Your message will            The group address;
                                                                send email here to
                                                                communicate with
automatically be forwarded to other members of the list.        other members


For information on this service and how to use it, send the
following request in the body of a mail message to
listproc@listproc.mwc.edu:                                      Administrative address
                        HELP


All requests should be addressed to listproc@listproc.mwc.edu.
```

Figure 7.1   A Welcome Message from Listproc—Very Important!

How to Communicate with and Contribute to an Email Discussion Group

☑ Any message that you want to go to all the members of the group should be sent to the group address. Email that's sent to the group address is either sent to all members of the group or sent to a moderator who decides whether to distribute the message to the rest of the group.

☑ Write to the list owner or moderator when you have questions about the nature of the group, if you think something is wrong with the list's operation, or to volunteer to help the moderator. If you're having technical problems, first try to solve them yourself. You'll probably get the moderator's address with your "welcome to the group" email. We've marked it in Figure 7.1.

☑ If you have problems sending or posting a message to a group, try posting a message from the address you used to subscribe to the group. Many groups allow you to send a message to the group only from the same address you used to join or subscribe to the group.

Communicate with a Single Member or the Whole Group?

You can send email either to everyone in the group or to only the person who originated a message. Usually, if you use the reply feature of your email program, a message will be sent to the group. You shouldn't respond to the group when you mean to respond to the individual. If you see a public message that was obviously meant for an individual, you might want to send a gentle reminder to the person who made the mistake.

How can you tell if a message came from a group or from an individual?

Using **reply** in the email program will send a message to the group. Look at the email headers **Reply-To**, **From**, and **To**. Each email message carries with it a collection of headers that include information about who would receive a reply (**Reply-To**), who sent the message (**From**), and to whom the message was sent (**To**). If an email message has the header **Reply-To**, the address after **Reply-To** is the address your email program uses when you choose the reply option. You find the address of the person who sent the original message by looking at the header **From**. You also can look at the header **To** to see if the email was sent to all members of the group or just to you. Figure 7.2 shows the pertinent information.

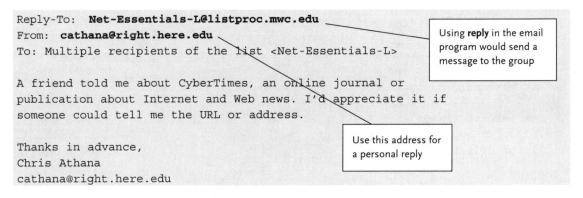

Figure 7.2   An Example Message to an Email Group

Here are two responses to this message. The first is the type of response that could properly go to just the individual sending the original message (**cathana@right.here.edu**) or to the entire group. Because the response might benefit everyone on the list, it's appropriate to reply to the group.

```
The URL for CyberTimes is http://www.nytimes.com/yr/mo/day/cyber/.
It's published by the NY Times. Another source for similar news is
Wired News, http://www.wired.com/news/.
```

The next response should be sent only to the person who sent the original message (**cathana@right.here.edu**), definitely not to the entire group. Chris may appreciate the message, but other members won't.

```
Chris,
How are you? I haven't heard from you in a while. Send me some
email and I'll give you the answers to all your questions.

J. Richmond - richster@far.away.com
```

Figure 7.3 can help you decide which email address to use for the different types of communication with an email discussion group.

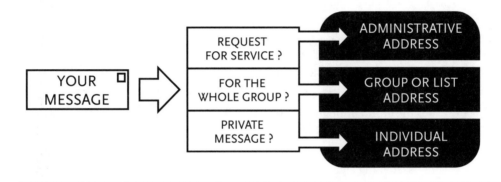

Figure 7.3   Which Address to Use for Discussion Group Messages

Leaving or Unsubscribing from a Group

The name of the group is represented by *GROUP-NAME* below. In most cases, you'll need to send the email message for leaving or unsubscribing from the same Internet address that you used to join the group. If you have difficulty leaving a group, write to the group owner or moderator.

In the cases of Listserv and Listproc, you send the following message:

```
unsubscribe GROUP-NAME
```

You may have to include your email address if Majordomo is being used to manage a list, if you gave it when you joined the group, or if you're leaving from a different address. Send either the message above or the following:

```
unsubscribe LIST-NAME YOUR-CURRENT-EMAIL-ADDRESS
```

For example, the administrative address for the group Net-Essentials-L is **LISTPROC@listproc.mwc.edu**, so to leave you would send the following message to that address:

```
unsubscribe net-essentials-l
```

Remember: Send email to the administrative address to unsubscribe from or leave an email group.

Getting Services and Archives from a Discussion Group

All the commands for services are sent by email to the administrative address so that the software managing the list can detect the commands. Sending a command to the group generally does nothing except prompt several members of the group to reply with reminders that the commands were sent to the wrong address.

If you want more information about working with these or other types of groups, take a look at "Discussion Lists: Mailing List Manager Commands," **http://learn.ouhk.edu.hk/~u123/unit2/ mirror2/mailser.html**, by James Milles.

Access to discussion groups and their archives is becoming available through forms interfaces that are part of Web pages.

> ☑ Some discussion groups let you join, leave, and use the services of

ON CD

The CD that accompanies this book includes a table that lists many of the common services available through discussion groups.

To view it click on the hyperlink "Services Available Through Discussion Groups." in the collection of items for Chapter 7.

the group through a forms-based Web page. One example is "SF-Lovers Digest," **http:// sflovers.rutgers.edu/Digest**.

> ☑ Archives of discussion groups are usually categorized only by date, so it is difficult to search the archives for messages relating to a specific subject. Some progress is being made in this area, however. The University of Buffalo, for example, provides a forms-based interface for searching the archives of the groups hosted there. Use the URL **http://listserv.acsu.buffalo.edu/archives** to try this service.

Finding the Discussion Groups You'd Like to Join

There are thousands of email discussion groups with more added each day. Because of this large number, it is virtually impossible to keep current with the available groups. It's probably more important (and certainly more practical) for you to know how to find the names of groups that focus on a topic you'd like to find out about.

☑ F Y I **Information About Discussion Groups on the Web**

> ☑ "Email Discussion Groups/ Lists and Resources," http://www.webcom.com/ impulse/list.html

> ☑ "Internet Mailing Lists Guides and Resources," http://www.ifla.org/I/ training/listserv/lists.htm

Finding a Group Dealing with a Specific Topic

There are a number of different ways to find out about discussion groups. You're likely to hear about some groups from the folks you correspond with on the Internet. You'll also see groups mentioned if you read Usenet news, and you'll see some groups mentioned in various other publications that you read. In addition, you can use one of the services available on the Web and listed in Table 7.3.

When you use these services, you simply type in a keyword or key phrase and the software searches a database of group names, descriptions, and associated addresses. You'll get the information you need (group name, address for joining the group, address of the group, address of the group owner or moderator, etc.) for the appropriate groups.

Name	Brief Description	URL
CataList, the official catalog of LISTSERV lists	Ability to search or browse the database of more than 45,000 public groups that use LISTSERV.	http://www.lsoft.com/lists/listref.html
Publicly Accessible Mailing Lists	This Web site, maintained by Stephanie da Silva, is an authoritative resource for information about email discussion groups. You can search or browse the database.	http://paml.org
Tile.Net/List	Contains a list of discussion groups. Browse the alphabetic list.	http://tile.net/lists

Table 7.3   Web Sites for Finding Discussion Groups

The activity on the CD shows how to use the Web site "Publicly Accessible Mailing Lists" (PAML) to search for discussion groups based on a topic. For each group found, you can retrieve information about the group and ways of subscribing. PAML has discussion groups or mailing lists arranged into a subject directory. The other search services mentioned in this chapter can be used in a similar manner.

ON CD

The CD that accompanies this book includes an activity that deals with finding a discussion group.

To view it, click on the hyperlink "Finding a Discussion Group" in the collection of items for Chapter 7.

Now that we've explained how to use and find discussion groups, it's time to move on to the important issues related to etiquette and behavior in these types of Internet discussions.

Proper Etiquette and Behavior Within a Group

Discussion groups and newsgroups are great ways to communicate with people. Participants might live in other countries or across the street from you. Members have discussions, post information, and ask questions. Table 7.4 lists some tips and guidelines for proper etiquette and behavior. We'll refer to these again later in this chapter.

Tip/Guideline	Explanation
Spend some time getting to know the group.	When you first join a discussion group, take a little time to observe what kinds of things are discussed and to get a feel for the tone of the discussion. Read the articles in a newsgroup before posting. You also might find that the questions you have are currently being answered.
Posting or sending a message to the group is a public act.	Everything you write to the group may be distributed to all group members or posted worldwide through Usenet. If you're working with a group that isn't moderated (most aren't), your messages will go directly to the group. Don't embarrass yourself. A friend, relative, or supervisor also might be a member of the group.
Think before you respond to a message.	If someone writes something that upsets you, take a few minutes or hours to formulate an appropriate, considered response that deals with the issue. Think about the source of the message, and don't criticize others too hastily or without good reason.
Write easy-to-read messages.	The material you write to the group should be grammatically correct, concise, and thoughtful. If the information you have to share could go on for several screens, it's a good idea to summarize it and invite others to ask you for more information if they are interested.
Group members are people like you and need to be treated with respect and courtesy.	Respond to messages as if you were talking face to face. A member may be from a different culture, may not be familiar with your language, and may have different views and values from your own. It's better to think before you write than to be sorry afterward.
When responding, include only the pertinent portions of the original message.	Let's say that a group member starts a discussion and writes something about 40 lines long. You want to respond, but only only to one portion of it. In your follow-up message, include just the portion that's relevant to your response.
When you ask questions to the group, post a summary of the responses.	With a summary, everyone in the group benefits from the responses to your question. Naturally, this applies only if you get several responses and if the answers to the question are of general interest.
Think about whether a response to a message should go to the group or to an individual.	Messages to the group should be of general interest. They may be requests on your part for advice or for help in solving a problem. When other group members make a request, you'll know their email address, and you can send a response to that person if it's appropriate.
Post test messages to groups designed for testing.	Post messages that test whether you're following proper procedures and if your computer system is properly configured to discussion groups and newsgroups designed for that purpose. To test your hand at email discussion groups, use Net-Essentials-L, described earlier in this chapter.

Table 7.4   Tips and Guidelines for Working with a Discussion Group or Newsgroup

Another excellent source for rules of etiquette for discussion groups is the section "LISTSERVS/MAILING LISTS/ DISCUSSION GROUPS" of Arlene Rinaldi's "The Net: User Guidelines and Netiquette," **http://www.fau.edu/netiquette/net/dis.html**.

Overview and Essential Information About Usenet News

Usenet news, sometimes called just "news," is a popular means of communicating on the Internet. The news is a collection of **articles** arranged into categories called **newsgroups**. Anyone with access to a **news server** can post an article to a newsgroup and, thus, to Usenet. The articles are very much like email messages, and they have many of the same headers. The big difference is that the articles are addressed to a newsgroup and anyone with access to a **newsreader** can read any of the articles.

You use Usenet news for the same reasons you use a discussion group—to exchange or read information dealing with specific topics. These are some ways that Usenet news differs from discussion groups:

☑ With Usenet, you have access to many groups. Some sites carry thousands of groups; others carry fewer or different ones depending on the policies and procedures of that site.

☑ F Y I   **What Is Usenet?**
Some Classic Papers

☑ "What is Usenet?,"
http://www.faqs.org/faqs
/usenet/what-is/part1

☑ "What is Usenet?
A second opinion,"
http://www.faqs.org/faqs
/usenet/what-is/part2

☑ Messages to a group aren't exchanged between individuals using email; instead, messages are passed from one computer system to another.

☑ There's no formal process for subscribing to or joining newsgroups.

☑ Anyone can read and post to any newsgroup carried by his or her news server.

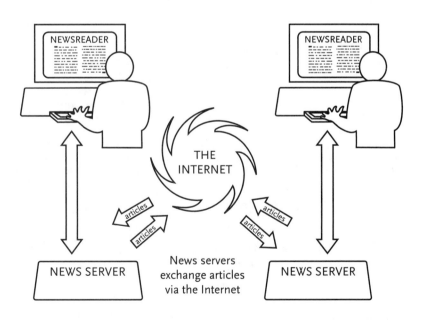

Figure 7.4   The Relationship Between Users, Newsreaders, and News Servers

Web-based services for reading and posting news are also popular. One such service is "Google Groups," **http://groups.google.com**. It gives a very easy-to-use interface to Usenet and has some excellent features you can use to search recent and archived articles for information. The archives date back to the 1980s for some newsgroups.

Once you get comfortable using Usenet news, you'll see that it is a valuable resource for finding answers to questions, getting information on a variety of topics, and keeping up with what's happening in the world and on the Internet.

Some of the essential information about Usenet news is listed in Table 7.5 below.

> There are over 30,000 newsgroups and several major, top-level categories. We won't list the categories here. A complete list, "Master List of Newsgroup Hierarchies," **http://www.magma.ca/ ~leisen/mlnh/**, is maintained by Lewis S. Eisen.

Feature/Concept	Explanation
Usenet news is a collection of articles arranged into newsgroups.	Usenet was originated so people at one computer site could exchange information or communicate with a group of users at another site. The number of articles (messages) and computer sites involved with Usenet has grown so that now people throughout the world are adding thousands of new articles daily. Having the articles arranged in categories makes it possible for a user to focus on an area or topic of interest.
An individual uses a program called a newsreader to select newsgroups and then to read and post messages.	In order to read or post articles, you need to either use a program called a newsreader, which runs as a client on your computer, or a Web-based service specifically for reading and posting articles. People at each site can read, ignore, save or print articles, respond to an article's author through e-mail, or **post** their own articles. "Post" means to compose either an original article or a response to someone else's article and then pass it on to Usenet. Microsoft Outlook Express, distributed with Internet Explorer, includes a newsreader. Netscape Communicator also includes a newsreader. (You can access it by selecting **Newsgroups** from the pull-down menu **Communicator** in the menu bar.) There are several other free newsreaders. One that's highly recommended is Free Agent, available through the Free Agent home page, **http://forteinc.com/ agent/freagent.htm**.
A news server makes the news—newsgroups and articles—available. News servers exchange articles and newsgroups.	To access Usenet news, you have to connect to a news server. Many ISPs make Usenet news available. Ask your ISP or network support group for the Internet domain name of the news server you can use. The newsreader program contacts the server so that you can access newsgroups and articles. News servers exchange newsgroups and articles. That way, when you post an article, it's made available to other servers participating in Usenet.
Each newsgroup has a name that gives the main topic for the articles in the group. The groups are arranged or named according to a hierarchy.	When you look at the name of a newsgroup, you'll see that it usually consists of several words or names separated by periods. The first part of the newsgroup name is the name of the top level of the hierarchy. Moving to the right, the names become more specific. Consider the newsgroup name **rec.music.makers.guitar.acoustic**. ☑ **rec** is the name of a top-level category that includes groups dealing with artistic activities, hobbies, or recreational activities.

☑ **music** indicates the group deals with topics related to music.

☑ **makers** tells you that this group is about performing or playing music rather than another activity such as reviewing music or collecting recordings.

☑ **guitar** identifies the group as one that deals with performing guitar music. What type of guitar? That's next.

☑ **acoustic** identifies this group as one that deals with discussions or other matters related to playing or performing acoustic guitar.

Here are a few other groups in the **rec.music** hierarchy to give you a feeling for this naming scheme:

> **rec.music.makers.piano**
>
> **rec.music.makers.percussion**
>
> **rec.music.marketplace**
>
> **rec.music.reviews**

All articles belong to one or more newsgroups.	Many newsgroups have charters that state the purpose of the newsgroup and the topics discussed within the group. An article is either a follow-up to another article or a post on a different topic. The term for posting an article to more than one newsgroup is *cross-posting*.
Articles on the same topic are sometimes arranged into threads.	There may be several articles on the same topic in a single newsgroup. If each of the articles was posted as a follow-up to some original article, then the collection of these articles is called a *thread*. If you are given the option, you'll probably want to arrange articles into threads. It really helps to organize collections of articles in this way. You can follow a thread by reading the articles in the thread one after another.
Posting to Usenet is a public act.	When you post an article or reply to one in Usenet, you're creating an article that will be available to the thousands of computer systems and millions of people who make up the infrastructure of Usenet. The information you give in the identity preferences for your newsreader or Web-based Usenet service—your email address, name, and organization—are part of the article. So think twice about what you write and check your message for spelling and grammar.
You may find some articles or discussions in some groups offensive.	There is no central control over what's posted to Usenet. What offends you may not offend others, and a topic that bothers you might be something important to others. Some of the information on Usenet concerns illegal topics, such as pirated software. Some newsgroups contain pornographic or "X-rated" material. Whether a newsgroup is available on a news server depends on the policies of the organization that provides the news server. But you always have the choice of which articles to read and which newsgroups to look through. Sometimes you can tell the nature of a group by its title. The articles in the newsgroup titled **alt.sadistic.dentists** may or may not be offensive, but you can tell from the title whether reading the articles will be worth your time. Individual users take the responsibility for what types of information they review.
There is no single person, group, or computer system in charge. There is virtually no censorship on Usenet.	All the computers and people who are part of Usenet support it and manage it. It's similar to a bulletin board system (bbs), except that most bulletin boards are managed by one person and are run on one computer. Anyone with a connection to a news server can post an article, so free speech is encouraged and tolerated even when the postings are offensive. Usenet is a community with its own generally agreed upon code of etiquette. Several articles that deal with Usenet etiquette are listed in the section "Usenet News Etiquette."

	Newsgroup availability is controlled at the local level because each news server is configured to accept or reject certain newsgroups. If you think certain newsgroups should be available to you or some should not be made available to others using the same news server, then write or call the person or group that administers or sets policy for the news server.
Using Usenet can be so appealing that you spend too much time doing it.	Remember that you have a life outside of Usenet and you should pay attention to it. Get your other work done, take a walk, and spend some time with other human beings (assuming they're not all on Usenet).

Table 7.5   Essential Information About Usenet

Now we're ready to look at the details of working with Usenet.

Details of Working With Usenet News

We'll go over some of the steps for working with Usenet news. We're going to use the newsreader that is included with Outlook Express to demonstrate the concepts involved here. Other newsreaders are similar. If you don't have access to a newsreader or a system that acts as a news server, you can read and post messages through a Web-based service such as Google Groups, **http://groups.google.com**. You will need to register—give your name and some demographic information about yourself—before you can use the service for posting articles.

Once you get your newsreader configured and set up, you'll be able to choose which newsgroups you want to read as well as one or more articles in a newsgroup. The newsreader lets you select a group from all the newsgroups available on the news server. Selecting a newsgroup is called *subscribing* in Usenet terminology. You can subscribe to newsgroups at any time. Subscribing simply adds a particular newsgroup to the list of newsgroups that you see when you start your newsreader; you won't need to send anyone your name and email address as when you subscribe to an email discussion group. After selecting a newsgroup, you're ready to read, reply to, print, save, or file articles in the newsgroup. You also can post an article to the newsgroup.

You'll find that working with articles is a lot like working with email. The major differences are that the articles or messages are arranged into groups, and instead of sending a message to an address, you post an article to a group.

Now for the Details

The first step is to set the address of the news server. We know that news servers exchange articles, and you use a newsreader to access articles and newsgroups. This means that when the newsreader is configured, or set up, you need to supply the Internet domain name or IP address of a news server so you can read or post news. The section "Getting Set for Email and Usenet" on the CD that accompanies this book covers the details of setting the address and filling in the other information to set up the newsreader.

Once the newsreader is set, you are ready to subscribe to some newsgroups. We'll go over subscribing to newsgroups and take a look at reading some articles in the activity below.

ACTIVITY 7

SUBSCRIBING TO NEWSGROUPS AND READING ARTICLES

Overview

We'll be using Outlook Express for this activity. If you're using another newsreader, you'll find the concepts are similar but the details may be different. We're assuming the Internet domain name or IP address of the Usenet news server has already been entered and the newsreader is properly configured. Check the online help for your newsreader when you have questions.

> Remember that Usenet is always changing and that your results will differ from those shown here. Don't let this confuse you. The activities demonstrate fundamental skills. These skills don't change, even though what you see will be different.

The first time you use your newsreader, you may have to subscribe to, or select, some newsgroups. We'll go through the steps to follow in this activity. We're going to subscribe to the groups **news.newusers.questions** and **news.answers**, which are all good places to start. **news.newusers.questions** is dedicated to questions from new Usenet users. There is no such thing as a "dumb question" here, but it's not a place for conversational or frivolous postings or postings to test whether you're able to post articles to Usenet. Before posting to the newsgroup, check to see if someone else has asked a similar question. The group **news.answers** is where periodic Usenet postings and frequently asked questions (FAQs) are put.

Follow these steps:

1. Start the newsreader.
2. Choose and subscribe to newsgroups from the list of available newsgroups.
3. Select a newsgroup from the list of subscribed newsgroups.
4. Read articles in the newsgroup.

Details

1. Start the newsreader.

☑ Do It! If there is an Outlook Express icon on your desktop, 📧 Outlook Express , double-click it to start the program, then click on **Read News**. Otherwise, click on **Mail** in the toolbar of Internet Explorer and select **Read News**.

We'll assume you're not subscribed to any newsgroups. When the newsreader starts, it will display a message similar to the one in Figure 7.5.

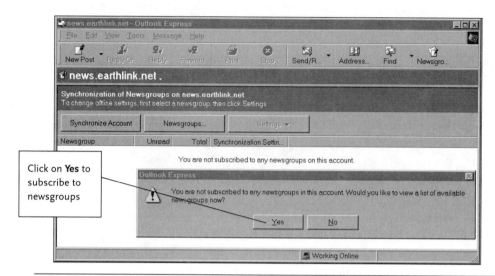

Click on **Yes** to subscribe to newsgroups

Figure 7.5   The "Not Subscribed to Any Newsgroups"
                    Message from Outlook Express

2. Choose and subscribe to newsgroups from the list of available newsgroups.

Now we're ready to select or subscribe to some newsgroups.

☑ Do It!   Click on **Yes** in the dialog box.

If the newsreader is set so that some newsgroups have already been subscribed to, click on **Newsgroups** in the toolbar to subscribe to additional newsgroups. You can do this any time you want to subscribe to a newsgroup.

Another window will appear, allowing you to subscribe to newsgroups. It is shown in Figure 7.6.

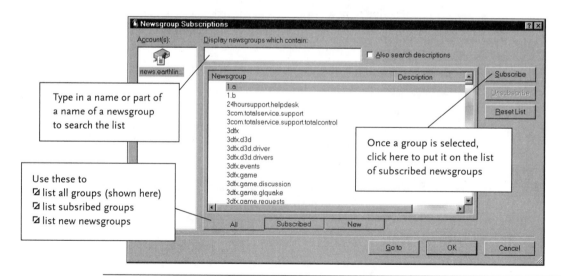

Type in a name or part of a name of a newsgroup to search the list

Once a group is selected, click here to put it on the list of subscribed newsgroups

Use these to
☑ list all groups (shown here)
☑ list subsribed groups
☑ list new newsgroups

Figure 7.6   A List of Available Newsgroups

You'll select newsgroups from the list in the window. You also can search for newsgroups by title. Click on **Reset List** to send a request to the news server to update the list of newsgroups. The list of newsgroups that you're working with now is on *your* computer, and it could be different than the list of newsgroups on the server. It could take several minutes for the list of newsgroups to appear after you click on **Reset List**. The amount of time it takes depends on the size of the list and the speed of your Internet connection. The list, which may have several thousand entries, has to be downloaded from the news server.

We'll be subscribing to **news.answers** and **news.newusers.questions**. The most direct way to do that here is to type the name of each and then select the group. There are other ways though: We could browse through the entire list, or we could type **news** in the search box and browse the resulting list.

☑ Do It! Type **news.answers** in the search form as shown in Figure 7.7.

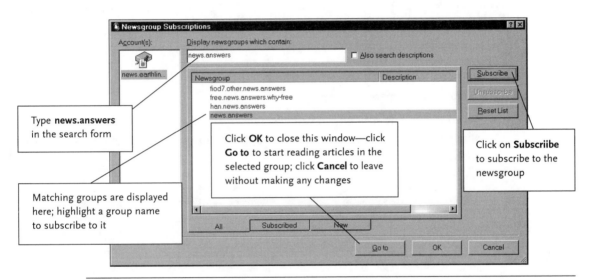

Figure 7.7   Newsgroup Subscriptions; Subscribing to news.answers

Once the name of a newsgroup is highlighted, you can subscribe to the group by clicking on **Subscribe**, as shown in Figure 7.7.

☑ Do It! Highlight **news.answers** and click on **Subscribe**.

You also can subscribe to a newsgroup by double-clicking on its name. It's not clear in Figure 7.7, but there's also a button that you can use to *unsubscribe* from a group. Clicking on **Unsubscribe** removes the name of the group from the list of subscribed groups.

You follow similar steps to subscribe to **news.newusers.questions**.

☑ Do It! Type **news.newusers.questions** in the search form, as shown in Figure 7.7.

☑ Do It! Highlight **news.newusers.questions** and click on **Subscribe**.

We'll now read some articles in the newsgroup **news.answers**.

☑ Do It! Click on **OK** to end subscribing.

Clicking on **OK** closes the window shown in Figure 7.7 and opens another, like the one shown in Figure 7.8, that lists the names of the newsgroups that have been subscribed to.

3. Select a newsgroup from the list of subscribed newsgroups.

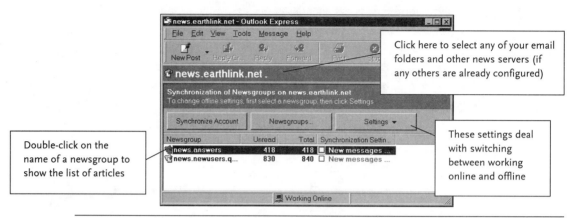

Double-click on the name of a newsgroup to show the list of articles

Click here to select any of your email folders and other news servers (if any others are already configured)

These settings deal with switching between working online and offline

Figure 7.8   A List of Subscribed Newsgroups

☑ Do It! Double-click on **news.answers**.

When you double-click on the name of a newsgroup, a window similar to the email window opens with a list of the articles in the group and a display of the current article, as shown in Figure 7.9.

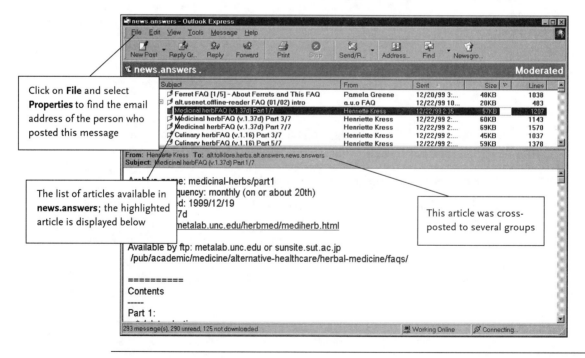

Click on **File** and select **Properties** to find the email address of the person who posted this message

The list of articles available in **news.answers**; the highlighted article is displayed below

This article was cross-posted to several groups

Figure 7.9   Reading an Article in a Newsgroup

Note: When you select a newsgroup, the newsreader first checks with the server to see if there are any new articles in the newsgroup. If so, they are listed, along with the older ones. (The articles stay on the server until you read them.)

4. Read articles in the newsgroup.

You can browse through the subject lines of each article.

You also can search for articles based on the subject or author. Articles are generally not downloaded or brought to your computer until you read them. That's why you generally won't be able to search through the body of the articles on the server.

END OF ACTIVITY 7 ◀

In the activity above, we showed how to start the newsreader, subscribe to newsgroups, and read articles in a newsgroup. You follow the same steps to subscribe to any newsgroup and to read articles in a subscribed newsgroup. To remove a newsgroup from the subscription list, display the subscription list, highlight the name of the group, and click on **Unsubscribe**.

You saw in Figure 7.9 of the activity that the window used to display the articles in a newsgroup is similar to the window used to display email messages. Indeed, working with Usenet articles is similar to working with email. Now we'll look at some of the ways to work with newsgroup articles.

Another way to see the articles in a newsgroup is to type the URL for the newsgroup in the location field of the browser window. A newsgroup URL has the form news:*newsgroup-name*. For example, the URL for the group **rec.music.makers.guitar.acoustic** is **news:rec.music.makers.guitar.acoustic**.

Type that in the location field of the browser and press Enter. If your news server carries that group, you'll be able to read articles in the group and the group will be automatically added to your list of subscribed newsgroups.

Saving, Mailing, or Printing an Article

A Usenet article can be saved to a file, mailed to someone else, or printed in much the same way you can work with an email message.

Let's suppose you're reading an article, such as the one shown in Figure 7.9.

If you want to . . .	then ...
Save the article in a file	Click on **File** in the menu bar and select **Save As**. A Save As dialog box pops up. Select or create a folder to hold the article.
File the article in a folder	Click on **Edit** in the menu bar and select **Copy to Folder**. Select a pre-existing folder or create a new one to hold the message.
Mail the article to another Internet address	Click on the item labeled **Forward** in the toolbar. **Fwd: *Title of the article*** and the article being forwarded is included.
Print the article	Click on the item **Print** in the toolbar, then click **OK** or **Cancel**.

Table 7.6   Saving, Mailing, or Printing an Article

Replying to an Article

You have the choice of posting a ***follow-up*** article (which is passed to all other Usenet sites), sending an email message directly to the author, or doing a combination of the two—posting a follow-up article and sending it to the author by email.

There are two items on the toolbar for you to use:

☑ Click on **Reply Group** to post a follow-up.

☑ Click on **Reply** to post a message only to the author.

In each case, a message composition window pops up. If the reply is a follow-up, then the message is addressed to the newsgroup. If the reply is to the author only, then it's automatically addressed to the author. In either case, the subject is **Re:** followed by the subject of the original article. The text of the original article is also included. Remember to only keep pertinent parts of the original article when posting a reply or follow-up.

Follow-up or Email?

Suppose an article is posted in **rec.music.bluenote.blues** discussing the impact of Muddy Waters' music on English rock bands, and you think something important was left out. You might want to post a follow-up responding to the original article. Your follow-up article would be sent to any site that carries **rec.music.bluenote.blues**. You ought to post a follow-up for the same reasons you would send a reply via email to an author, except your reply should be interesting to enough people to be distributed to all of Usenet.

Posting an Article

Posting an article means composing an original message or article and having it distributed throughout all of Usenet.

Before You Post

Read "A Primer on How to Work with the Usenet Community." You'll find it posted in **news .announce.newusers** and available through the URL **http://www .faqs.org/faqs/"usenet/primer/ part1**.

Be sure to select the right newsgroup for the article. Once you select a newsgroup, check the FAQ for the newsgroup to see if your question is answered there.

To post an article:

☑ Click on the item **New Post** in the toolbar.

☑ A window will pop up—the same one you use to post a follow-up article or write an email message. The name of the newsgroup will be filled automatically into the frame labeled "Newsgroups." Type the subject of your article in the frame labeled "Subject." Choose a subject that isn't too long and that clearly states the purpose of your article. Read several articles in the group to see the form that others use.

☑ Compose your article. Type it into the large frame of the window. If you have a signature file, its contents will be put automatically into the message. You can send attachments with the article by clicking on the button labeled **Attachments**. Don't include large text or binary files (usually images) unless that sort of information is normally posted to the newsgroup. Click on **Spelling** to have your spelling checked.

☑ Click on the icon labeled **Send** to post your article. If you don't want to post it—you've made too many typing mistakes or you change your mind—click on **File** in the menu bar and select **Close** or press Ctrl+**W** from the keyboard. You'll have one more chance to post the article, but if you don't want to send it, click the button labeled **No**.

☑ Use the newsgroup **alt.test** for posting an article that's meant to test your connection to Usenet. Figure 7.10 shows a test posting to **alt.test**.

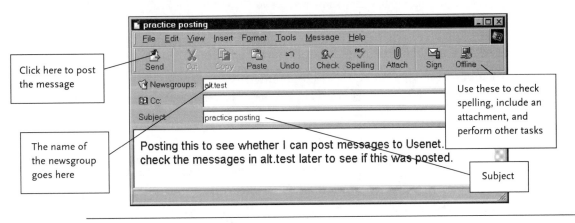

Figure 7.10   A Posting to alt.test

Using FAQs, Finding Newsgroups, and Searching Archives

FAQs

FAQ stands for *frequently asked questions*, a collection of common questions with answers. (Some people also use the term to refer to a single question.) Many of these are written and maintained by volunteers. Most newsgroups have an informative and useful FAQ. You can find it posted either in the newsgroup the FAQ was created for or in **news.answers**. Several newsgroups hold these FAQs; you'll see them referred to as the *.answers newsgroups. Some of these are **alt.answers**, **comp.answers**, and **sci.answers**. Here is a short list of FAQs to give you an idea of the variety of topics:

☑ Comp.Object FAQ

☑ comp.graphics.animation FAQ

☑ rec.games.netrek FAQ List

☑ FAQ: Old Time Radio (OTR)

☑ rec.sport.hockey FAQ

☑ FAQ: Sci.Polymers

☑ FAQ: rec.music.dylan

☑ F Y I   **More Information About Usenet**

☑ "news.newusers.questions Links Page," http://geocities.com/ResearchTriangle/8211/nnqlinks.html

☑ "Usenet: Reading and Writing the News," http://webliminal.com/Lrn-web05.html

☑ "Usenet References," http://www.faqs.org/usenet

Be sure to consult the FAQ for information before you post a question to a newsgroup. It's annoying to other people reading the newsgroup to see questions that they know are in the FAQ. It may be embarrassing for you if you post a question to a newsgroup and you get several replies (or follow-ups) letting you (and everyone else reading the newsgroup) know that you should read the FAQ before asking other questions.

The FAQ for a specific group is posted regularly to the group as well as to one of the *.answers groups, such as **news.answers**. If you can't find the FAQ you're looking for there, try looking at "Internet FAQ Archives," **http://www.faqs.org/faqs**.

Recommended Newsgroups for Information About Usenet

There are several newsgroups that a beginning or infrequent user should browse. These newsgroups include information about Usenet, lists of FAQs for Usenet and several newsgroups, and articles that will help you use Usenet.

news.announce.newgroups	This newsgroup features articles dealing with forming and announcing new newsgroups. It's also a place to get lists of all newsgroups.
news.announce.newusers	This group offers explanatory and important articles for new or infrequent Usenet users.
news.answers	This is where periodic Usenet postings are put. The periodic postings are primarily FAQs. This is often the first place you should look when you have a question.
news.newusers.questions	This newsgroup is dedicated to questions from new Usenet users. There is no such thing as a "dumb question" here. You should browse this group to see if others have asked the same question that you want to ask. Once you get some expertise in using Usenet, you can check this group from time to time to see if you can help someone else out.

Finding Newsgroups

There are thousands of newsgroups. How can you decide which ones to read or even find out which ones exist?

Several lists of newsgroups are available through Usenet. Keep your eye on the newsgroup **news.answers**, **news.lists**, or **news.groups** so you can read or save these listings when they appear (usually monthly).

Some sites on the WWW provide facilities for searching for newsgroups. In our example sites, simply use the URL to retrieve a Web page, then enter a keyword or phrase, click on the button labeled **Search**, and work with the results.

Site Name	URL	Description
Google Groups	**http://groups.google.com**	Here, you can browse Usenet groups arranged by hierarchy or search for articles.
Harley Hahn's Master List of Usenet Newsgroups	**http://www.harley.com/usenet**	Browse the list of groups or search by keyword
Tile.Net/News	**http://tile.net/news**	Use keyword searching or browsing to find newsgroups.

Searching Archives of Usenet Articles

There is a lot of useful information posted to Usenet. A search of the archives of posted articles is a good place to start when you want information about recent events, a particular product or brand, a company, or leads for jobs. Very little of this information is edited or reviewed, so you have to take time to verify information and not take it at face value.

The primary search service dedicated to Usenet archives is Google Groups, **http://groups.google.com**.

Usenet News Etiquette

Table 7.4 lists tips and guidelines for working with Usenet newsgroups and email discussion groups. Go back to take a look at them again. Think about them within the context of what you now know about Usenet.

Over the years, several documents have been developed about proper Usenet etiquette. These are regularly posted in **news.announce.newusers**, **news.answers**, or **news.newusers.questions**. Here is a list of some that you might want to take a look at:

- ☑ "A Primer on How to Work with the Usenet Community," **http://www.faqs.org/faqs/usenet/primer/part1**
- ☑ "How to Make the Best Use of Usenet News," **http://netscape.com/eng/mozilla/1.1/news/news2.html**
- ☑ "Emily Postnews Answers Your Questions on Netiquette," **http://www.faqs.org/faqs/usenet/emily-postnews/part1/**
- ☑ "Rules for Posting to Usenet," **http://www.faqs.org/faqs/usenet/posting-rules/part1/**
- ☑ "Hints on Writing Style for Usenet," **http://www.faqs.org/faqs/usenet/writing-style/part1/**
- ☑ "FAQ on Making and Using a .signature File," **http://www.faqs.org/faqs/usenet/signature-faq/**
- ☑ "How to Find the Right Place to Post (FAQ)," **http://www.faqs.org/faqs/finding-groups/general/**

Summary

Email discussion groups are examples of asynchronous group communication on the Internet. Group members communicate via email, with messages broadcast to all group members.

Several thousand discussion groups are available and active on the Internet. The email groups may be called mailing lists, discussion groups, Listserv lists, or interest groups. Regardless of the name, each consists of a group of members on the Internet. This way, communities or collections of people can discuss items related to a common topic, find information about the topic, make announcements to the group, and ask questions and receive help from other group members. The large number of groups or lists guarantees a wide range of topics. The groups are particularly useful to people who want to discuss issues with a large or diverse group. The groups extend any resources beyond a local site.

When you communicate with an email discussion group, you send messages to the list by using the group address. Commands and requests for service are usually sent to the administrative address. For example, the group SF-LIT, which deals with a variety of topics related to science fiction literature, has **SF-LIT@loc.gov** as the group address and **listserv@loc.gov** as the administrative address. You use this second address to join the group, leave or unsubscribe from the group, request archived files from the group, and get a list of the members of the group. Be sure you use the correct address when you communicate with the group or list. A discussion group also can be Web-based so that you use a Web browser to join, read, and contribute to the group.

Discussion groups and Usenet newsgroups can be thought of as communities of people sharing common interests. There are generally accepted rules of behavior or etiquette for list members. These include providing appropriate, thoughtful, and concise messages to a group, providing a summary of the responses received in answer to a question, and communicating with other group members in a civil and respectful manner.

Usenet news is a collection of messages called articles. Each article is designated as belonging to one or more newsgroups. These articles are passed from one computer system to another. The newsgroups are arranged into categories in a hierarchical manner. Users at a site can usually select any of the groups that are available and can often reply to or post an article. Some estimates put the number of participants at more than 40 million people worldwide.

Software called a newsreader allows you to work with the articles and newsgroups in Usenet news. Several different newsreaders are available. The one you use will depend on your preferences and what's available on the system with which you access Usenet.

Usenet is a valuable resource for information on a wide array of topics. It can be enjoyable to read and participate in the discussions. Services are available on the World Wide Web to search for newsgroups related to a specific topic and to search for articles that contain keywords or phrases.

Selected Terms Discussed in This Chapter

administrative address	listserv
article	lurking
cross-posting	mailing list
email discussion group	news server
fan-in	newsgroup
fan-out	newsreader
follow-up	post
frequently asked questions (FAQ)	subscribe
group address	thread
interest group	unsubscribe

Materials on CD for This Chapter

Here is a list of items for this chapter on the CD that accompanies the text:

☑ "Services Available Through Discussion Groups," A table that lists many of the common services available through discussion groups

☑ "Finding a Discussion Group," An activity that includes the steps for finding a discussion group on a specific topic using the Web site "Publicly Available Mailing Lists," **http://paml.org**

☑ All URLs mentioned in this chapter in hypertext format

☑ Selected terms discussed in this chapter with hyperlinks to the glossary

☑ Copies of the review questions in quiz format

Review Questions

True or False?

1. A discussion group is an example of asynchronous communication.
2. A group or list is managed by an individual who personally sends messages welcoming newcomers to the group.
3. Lurking behavior is discouraged in discussion groups.
4. The administrative address is used when you subscribe or unsubscribe from a group.
5. You can respond to a Usenet group by posting a follow-up article or sending an email message to the author of a particular posting.

Short Answer—Completion

1. A collection of common questions with answers is called _____.
2. There are two addresses associated with a discussion group, the administrative address and the _____.
3. Any message that you want to go to all the members of a group should be sent to the _____.
4. The news is a collection of _____ arranged into categories called newsgroups.
5. There is no formal process for subscribing to or joining _____.

Exercises and Projects

1. Search for email discussion groups. Use PAML, **http://paml.org,** to come up with a list of three discussion groups along with the administrative address and list address for each.
   Do the following:
   a. Subscribe to the three discussion groups you found. Did any require a reply or other authorization?
   b. Compare the welcome messages you get from the groups. Which was most helpful? Why?
   c. Unsubscribe from the group.
2. Go to the Web site "List-Etiquette.com," **http://List-Etiquette.com/,** and look over the rules of etiquette for discussion list members. (It's also a good site to visit if you're thinking about moderating or forming an email discussion group.)
   a. State the rules that deal with spam, copyright, and HTML.
   b. Do you think the rules are reasonable? Explain your answer.
3. Take a look at the list of discussion boards at "The New York Times: Readers' Opinions," **http://forums.nytimes.com/comment.** What are some of the topics listed? Find a posting with several replies, a threaded discussion. State the main topic, the number of replies, and a summary of the discussion.

4. Go to "news.newusers.questions Links Page," **http://web.presby.edu/~nnqadmin/nnq/ nnqlinks.html**.

    a. The page states that news.newusers.questions is a moderated newsgroup. What does that mean?

    b. Go to the section titled "What You Need to Know." What does it say about the topics "Making Money Fast Schemes" and "Advertising and Selling"?

    c. Go to the section "How Newsgroups Work." You can probably get to it by scrolling down the page. You'll see the topic "Disappearing Articles." What's it about?

5. Go to the Web site "Internet FAQ Archives," **http://www.faqs.org/faqs**.

    a. Find a FAQ that deals with health care for dogs. What is its title? When was it last updated?

    b. Is there a FAQ that deals with health care for cats? What is its title? When was it last updated?

    c. Give the title, date of the last update, author, and URL of three FAQs that deal with a topic you're studying, related to your business, or related to a hobby or recreational interest of yours.

FTP and Downloading
Web Resources

▶ the internet was primarily created so that researchers could exchange ideas and share the results of their work. It stands to reason, then, that one of the basic Internet services would be to enable people to copy files from one computer to another on the Internet. FTP, which stands for File Transfer Protocol, is that basic Internet service. It dates back almost to the beginnings of the Internet, the early 1970s, and it's used to share information in any type of file. Most of the files, accessible by FTP, are publicly available through what is called anonymous FTP, because no special login identification other than "anonymous" is needed to retrieve the files. A computer system that allows others to connect to it through anonymous FTP is called an anonymous FTP site or an FTP archive. The collection of files available at an anonymous FTP site is also called an FTP archive.

Goals/Objectives:

- ☑ Learn how to download a file by using anonymous FTP
- ☑ Know how to locate and download software
- ☑ Know how to uncompress compressed programs and files
- ☑ Learn how to use an FTP client program

Topics:

- ☑ FTP Overview
- ☑ Downloading a File by Anonymous FTP
- ☑ Locating FTP Archives and Other Sites for Finding Software
- ☑ Downloading and Working with Files from Software Archives
- ☑ Using an FTP Client Program

FTP Overview

What is now the World Wide Web wouldn't have been possible without the notions associated with FTP and its use. FTP can be used to transfer any type of file. It's commonly used to distribute software throughout the Internet. Most of these software programs are available as *shareware*, which means that you retrieve *(download)* the program from an archive, use it, and purchase it if you find the program useful. Software programs known as *freeware* are those that don't require a fee to download. FTP is an efficient way to transfer files when you know the exact name and location of the file—this information is included in the URL for the file. Using FTP, you also can transfer a file from your computer to another. This is called *uploading* a file. When you upload, you usually have to give a login name and password to the other computer system; it's not the same as anonymous FTP. This turns out to be a good way to work on one computer and transfer your work to another. Some people use this technique to update or create Web pages. They do their work on one computer and then transfer the files to a computer that acts as a Web server.

These days, much of the access to files by FTP is through a Web browser, which means you need to be familiar with the URL format for FTP. Here is the general form of a URL for anonymous FTP:

ftp://name-of-ftp-site/directory-name/file-name

Suppose a friend tells you, "I found this picture of Mars with great detail and colors. You can get it by anonymous FTP at the FTP site for the Jet Propulsion Laboratory, **ftp.jpl.nasa.gov**. You'll want to get the file **marglobe.gif**. It's in the directory **pub/images/browse**. There are also some animations at the same site in **pub/images/anim**." You'd like to view the image, and she's told you everything you need to retrieve it. The URL for that file is **ftp://ftp.jpl.nasa.gov/pub/images/browse/marglobe.gif**.

Matching this to the general form, we have the following:

You also can use a URL to refer to a directory. For example, if you use the URL **ftp://ftp.jpl.nasa.gov/pub/images/browse**, the Web browser displays a list of all the files or subdirectories in the directory **/pub/images/browse**, as displayed in Figure 8.1. Each file or subdirectory is represented as a hyperlink, and you can view it by clicking on its name.

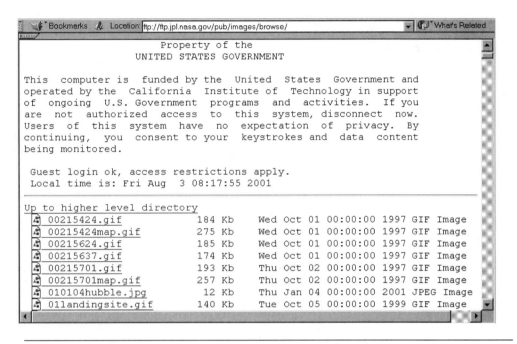

Figure 8.1   An FTP Archive Displaying Directory Files

Downloading a File by Anonymous FTP

There are two ways to retrieve a file; that is, to copy it from a remote site to the computer you're using. The browser makes it possible for you to download files using *anonymous FTP* without having to type **anonymous** as a user ID or give a password. You use standard browser techniques to do this.

Method 1: View the File First, and Then Save It Using the File Menu

If you type a file's URL or if you click on a hyperlink, the file will be transferred to the Web browser. If the browser is configured to display or play a file of that type, you'll see (and hear, if possible) the file's contents in the Web browser window. In this case, select **Save As** from the **File** pull-down menu in the menu bar. This opens a Save As dialog box on the screen. Set the directory or folder name, and then click on the button labeled **Save**.

The file also can be displayed in a window created by another program called a *helper application*. If there is no helper application installed to display the file, a message box pops up saying "No Viewer Configured for File Type." See the tip on the followin page to handle a file type that doesn't match any type that your browser can work with.

Method 2: Save the Hyperlink in a File by Using the Right Mouse Button

If a hyperlink to a file is present in the Web browser's window, you can save the hyperlink. To retrieve the file without viewing it, put the mouse pointer on the hyperlink and press the right mouse button. When a menu pops up, choose **Save Link As** (in Netscape) or **Save Target As** (in Internet Explorer). This opens a Save As dialog box on the screen. Set the directory or folder name, and then click on the **Save** button.

Locating FTP Archives and Other Sites for Finding Software

FTP archives are a collection of directories arranged according to some scheme. A common arrangement is for the top level to be arranged by the type of computer system (such as Mac, PC, or Linux) and for the levels below that to be ordered according to the type of software (such as games, utilities, or Internet software). You start at the home or root directory and, by clicking on hyperlinks that represent folders or directories, you move to or browse through the archives. Once you've located the file you want, you can download it using one of the methods described above. Because millions of files are available through FTP, it would be very difficult to find the name of a file and its archive without some automated search tool.

The FTP archives listed on the right arrange files in categories according to their function—such as sound files, desktop utilities, games, HTML editors, and so forth—and description. However, the ability to search a collection by file names and descriptions is more useful. Several of these are available on the Web. We'll look at some in the next activity and in the exercises. Many of the files accessible through these sites are programs or collections of programs and

☑ T I P ! **What to Do When "No Viewer Configured for File Type" Pops Up**

The message "No Viewer Configured for File Type" means that you've come across a file type that your browser doesn't currently know how to handle. Select the option that lets you **save to disk**. A Save As dialog box pops up, asking you to specify the folder in which you want to store the file. If you want to see or hear the file, then be sure you have any hardware and software you need to uncompress, display, or play the file after it has been transmitted. There are lots of variations and possibilities for the necessary equipment and programs you might need, so we can't cover all of them here. But if you do have everything you need, you may want to configure the browser so that it knows what to do with files of that type in the future. In your browser's help section, you can find instructions about informing the browser about a particular helper application. Click on **Preferences** on the **Edit** pull-down menu in the menu bar, select the **Applications** panel, and click on the **Help** button if you're using Netscape Navigator.

☑ F Y I **Here's a List of General-purpose FTP Archives on the Web**

☑ "UIArchive, University of Illinois at Urbana-Champaign," http://uiarchive.cso.uiuc.edu

☑ "Wuarchive, Washington University in St. Louis," http://ftp.wustl.edu

☑ "Garbo, University of Vassa, Finland," http://garbo.uwasa.fi

other files that are distributed as shareware. The files are in either executable form (their names end with **.exe**) or compressed form (their names end with **.zip** or **.gz**).

Here are a few sources on the Web that list FTP and software or shareware archives:

Source That Lists Software or Shareware Archives	URL
Librarians' Index to the Internet	**http://lii.org**, then select **Computers**, then **Software**
Nerd's Heaven: The Software Directory Directory	**http://boole.stanford.edu/nerdsheaven.html**
Yahoo!: Computers and Internet: Software: Shareware	**http://www.yahoo.com/ computers_and_internet/software/shareware**

Downloading and Working with Files from Software Archives

Several services on the Web act as archives and distributors of software in the form of shareware or freeware. Each service supplies links to the programs; when you click on the link, the software is transferred to your computer, essentially by FTP. In other words, you select the software you'd like, and you then use a Web browser to download it to your computer.

Shareware Often Comes in Packages

Most of the files in the archives are packages, or collections of related files. These are bundled together because to install, run, and use a single program usually requires several files, such as program libraries, instructions for installing and registering the program, and online help files. When you retrieve these, you get all the files you need combined in one file, the package.

The files or packages are processed by a compression program, which reduces the total number of bytes necessary to represent the information in the package. Reducing the size of a file means it takes less time to download the file. Because of this compression, you must do two things to the package after you receive it: uncompress it and extract the individual files from the package.

Compressed files or packages have names that usually end in **.zip**. Two popular compression programs are PKZIP and WinZip (which are both shareware). You will definitely want a copy of either of these utilities. We will discuss these compression programs and how to download them in Appendix A.

How can you extract the files necessary for those compression programs or similar packages? These and many other packages are in what is called a self-extracting archive. The package's file name ends in **.exe**. When you click on the name, it starts extracting its own components; for example, the software for Winamp, a popular MP3 player discussed later in this chapter, is in that format.

This compressed format isn't used only with programs. Any single file or collection of files can be compressed and transmitted in a compressed format. In the course of writing this book, we used this technology. Because each chapter has so many images, the files were quite large. We put each chapter and the images into a single package and then compressed it using either PKZIP or WinZip. We used FTP or email to send the compressed packages to the publisher.

Downloading and Installing Software

Here are the steps involved in downloading and installing shareware or freeware programs and associated files:

- ☑ Find the program you want to retrieve in a software archive.
- ☑ Create a folder or directory to hold the program from the archive on your computer.
- ☑ Click on the hyperlink in the software archive to the program. As soon as you indicate where it should go using a **Save As** dialog box, it will be transferred to your computer.
- ☑ If the file name ends in **.exe**, then it's likely a self-extracting archive. Locate it using Windows Explorer and double-click on it. It will either install itself, giving you instructions to follow, or it will extract its parts into the current directory.
- ☑ If the file name ends in **.zip**, then you have to use a program such as PKZIP or WinZip to extract the components. In this case, you usually select the folder or directory in which they will go. To obtain a copy of PKZIP or WinZip, see Appendix A.
- ☑ In any case, look for a file with a name similar to **Readme** or **Instructions** to see what steps you must follow to install the program or to work with the files in the package. In many cases, the extracted files will need to go through some other processing by a program named **Setup** before they are ready to use.
- ☑ Be sure to check the program and associated files for computer viruses. Many of the archives check for viruses before making files available to the public, but you should also check them yourself.

Acquiring Antivirus Software

You also will want a program that checks files for computer viruses. Several are available, and you can get shareware versions to evaluate and determine which you like best. One, F-PROT, makes its software free to individuals; commercial customers or organizations must pay for using it. Here are three sites that offer shareware versions of their antivirus and virus protection software:

Antivirus Shareware	URL
F-PROT, Data Fellows	http://www.frisk.is/f-prot/download
Norton AntiVirus, Symantec	http://symantec.com/avcenter
VirusScan, McAfee	http://mcaffee.com/anti-virus/default.asp

If you don't have an antivirus program on your computer, visit one of these sites, download the most recent version, and install it. Any of the antivirus programs from the sites listed above come as compressed packages. After you download one of these, you'll need to use the software to uncompress and extract the files into a folder. Once you have done that, look for a file with a name such as **Readme** to get instructions on how to install the software. In many cases, you can install the programs on your system by clicking on an application or program in the folder named **Setup**. You follow the same steps for installing these programs as for almost any other software that you download.

Using Software Archives and FTP Search Services

In an earlier section of this chapter, we gave the URLs for some lists of software archives or sites where you can find software to download through FTP.

What You'll Find in the Archives

Software archives maintain their own collections of files, and FTP archives have hyperlinks to the files, which are usually stored at the Web site of the person or organization that markets the software. Both archive types include a search form so you can search the collection for files, and several also have reviews, descriptions, and links to the software arranged into categories so you can browse the items accessible through the archive.

The files are usually arranged in categories according to the type of software, such as games, Internet, utilities, and personal use. Sometimes, they also are arranged according to the type of operating system they're designed for, such as MS-DOS, Windows 95/98/2000/ME/NT, Mac OS, or Linux.

Software Archives	URL
CNET Download.com	http://download.cnet.com
CNET Shareware.com	http://shareware.cnet.com
IT Pro Downloads	http://itprodownloads.com
Stroud's Consummate Winsock Apps List	http://cws.internet.com
TUCOWS	http://tucows.com
ZDNet Downloads	http://www.zdnet.com/downloads

Before You Download

We're going to demonstrate downloading and installing some software in the activity below. Before you download software, you need to answer a few questions for yourself.

Is the program appropriate for my computer system?

Most software archives include a description of the system requirements for each type of software available for download. Make sure that you have enough memory (RAM) to run the program (some require 32 megabytes to run properly) and that you have the correct operating system. Software that's developed for a Windows 95/98/2000 or Windows ME/NT system won't work properly if it's installed on a system running Windows 3.1 or on a Macintosh system.

Do I have enough storage space on my disk to hold the software?

Again, look at the system requirements to see that you have enough disk space to hold the new program along with your other software.

Do I meet the licensing requirements?

Most software is available as shareware to anyone, but some software is available only to educational or nonprofit institutions. The software will likely come with a licensing agreement; you'll need to read this and decide whether to consent to it.

Do I have permission to install the software?

If you're working on your home computer, then there's probably no problem. However, if you're working on a computer that's owned by your school or company—and probably being shared by others—check local policies to see whether you may install new software on the computer.

Do I have the software I need to install the software I downloaded?

Check to see if you have the proper software, such as PKZIP or WinZip, to extract the parts of the package. Often, this will be stated in the description of the software. Also look at the name of the package. If it ends with **.zip**, then you'll need a program such as the one we've mentioned to install it. For information on obtaining PKZIP or WinZip, see Appendix A.

Will the software have a detrimental impact on other software on my computer?

This isn't always easy to answer until the software is installed, in which case it may be too late. Read as much as you can about the software before installing it to see if it will negatively affect existing programs or system configuration. Be sure you can check it for viruses before installing it.

Will I be able to "uninstall" the program if things don't go well?

Most software comes with a program that makes it easy to remove the primary program and all associated files if and when you need to do this.

Now we'll go through some of the details involved in downloading and installing software from an archive.

LOCATING AND DOWNLOADING AN MP3 PLAYER AND MP3 FILES

Overview

In Chapter 3, we discussed the legal aspects of downloading and copying information from the Internet, using MP3 as an example of a file type that is frequently pirated and downloaded illegally. Not all MP3 files are illegally placed on the Web. Many artists regularly make their music available on the Web for public use. This is a convenient way for relatively new musicians to get noticed and listened to. We understand the allure of being able to play music on your computer and want to show you how to download a player that will allow you to play MP3 files. We will find an MP3 player in a software archive and download it from there. We will then locate a piece of music from an MP3 library that lists legal MP3s. We will show you how to download the file to your computer and play the music on your MP3 player. Here are the steps we'll follow:

> Remember that the Web is always changing and that your results may differ from those shown here. Don't let this confuse you. The activities demonstrate fundamental skills. These skills don't change, even though what you see when you do this activity may look different.

1. Go to the home page for ZDNet Downloads.
2. Browse the directory for MP3 players.
3. Select an MP3 player to download and check its system requirements.
4. Download the MP3 player.
5. Search an MP3 library for an MP3 file to download.

6. Download an MP3 file.
7. Open the MP3 player.
8. Play the music using the MP3 player.

Details

We'll assume that the Web browser is started and displayed on the screen. We are using Internet Explorer for this activity, but Netscape will work much the same.

1. Go to the home page for ZDNet Downloads.

☑ Do It!   Click on the address bar, type **http://www.zdnet.com/downloads**, and press **Enter**.

The ZDNet Downloads directory is a large, well-organized, and well-maintained software archive. The home page appears in Figure 8.2.

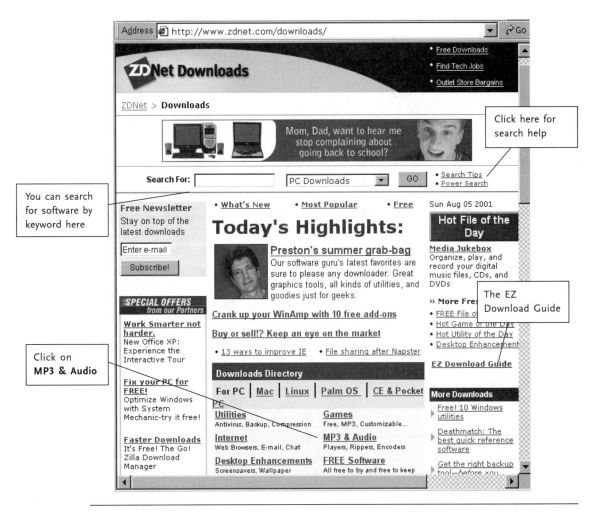

Figure 8.2   The Home Page for ZDNet Downloads

This home page shows that we can search or browse the archive either by type of software or by type of computer system. Several types of software and individual programs are listed.

Also note that there's a hyperlink called the **EZ Download Guide.** We know from using other search services that it's a good idea to click on **Search Tips** or any type of search guide available on the service's home page and do some reading before we continue.

☑ Do It!   Click on the hyperlink **EZ Download Guide.**

We'll follow the steps listed there after we select the software to download. In the next step, we'll browse the directory for MP3 players, but it's worth spending a little time looking at some of the other categories as well.

2. Browse the directory for MP3 players.

Note in Figure 8.2 that there is a category called **MP3 & Audio.** This appears to be the category where we'll find MP3 players. Note that we also could search for MP3 players by typing **mp3 players** into the search form.

☑ Do It!   Click on **MP3 & Audio.**

☑ Do It!   In the window that appears, find a hyperlink called **Players**, and click on it.

☑ Do It!   List the downloads in order of most popular by clicking on the link **Most Popular.**

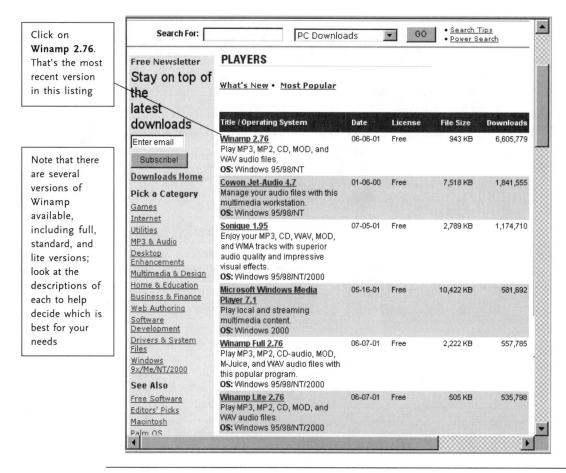

Figure 8.3   A List of the MP3 Players Available at ZDNet

3. Select an MP3 player to download and check its system requirements.

As you can see from this list, there are several MP3 players to choose from. Winamp catches our eye because we have heard about this player from friends and have read about it in other sources. Let's see what Winamp is all about.

☑ Do It! Click on **Winamp 2.76**, as shown in Figure 8.3.

Figure 8.4 shows the information that ZDNet provides about Winamp. Take some time to read the system requirements, downloads to date, compressed file size, and other facts. We see that Winamp is designed to run on a computer that uses a Windows operating system and that this version in compressed form takes up about 921 Kilobytes. Once it is expanded, we can expect it to take up about twice as much space, so we'll need to decide if we have enough disk space to install it. If we feel the software will be useful to us, and it will run on our computer, we can start downloading it.

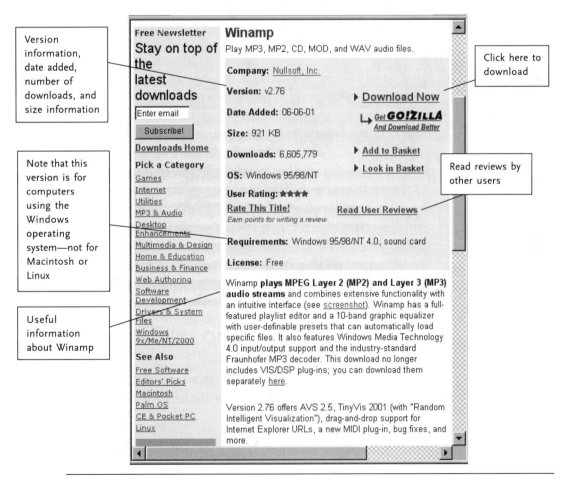

Figure 8.4 Information About Winamp

4. Download the MP3 player.

We're going to follow the steps in the ZDNet Download Guide.

☑ Do It! You'll want to put the package—or any resources that you download from the Internet—into a folder with a name that's easy to remember so that you can find it later if you need to. There may be a folder on your computer named **My Downloads**. If not, then you can create a folder. For this activity, let's suppose that we'll need to create a folder to hold this package and other things that we download. We'll name that folder "**downloads**."

☑ Do It! We're using Windows 98, so the first thing we'll do is activate Windows Explorer by clicking on the **Start** button, selecting **Programs**, and choosing **Windows Explorer.**

☑ Do It! We'll use Windows Explorer to display the contents of Drive C:. Click on **File** in the menu bar, select **New**, and then click on **Folder**.

The window you'll see appears in Figure 8.5. If you are using other software to manage your files, read the instructions in the download guide.

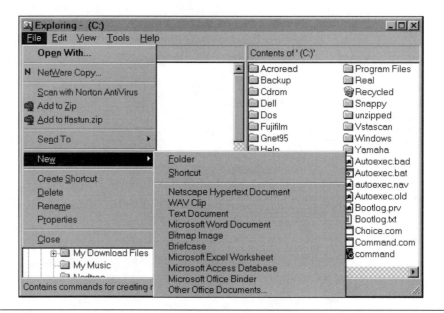

Figure 8.5   Creating a New Folder Using Windows Explorer

A new folder is created. We'll name it **downloads.**

☑ Do It! Type **downloads** for the folder's name and press **Enter**.

Now we're ready for the second step in the download process. We can use the browser to transfer the file from ZDNet Downloads to our system. Be sure that the Web page shown in Figure 8.4 is still available.

☑ Do It! Return to the browser window, and click on the hyperlink **Download Now**.

The browser will attempt to transfer the file to your computer using FTP. You'll likely get a dialog box message such as "unknown file type" or some other warning. In any case, you'll want to click on the button that lets you save the file to disk. Figure 8.6 shows the dialog box that appeared in the browser we are using (Internet Explorer).

Figure 8.6   The File Download Dialog Box

You'll want to save the file to your disk. Click on a button that lets you do this. A **Save As** dialog box will appear.

☑ Do It!   Use the controls in the Save As dialog box to select the folder **downloads**, as shown in Figure 8.7. Then click on **Save**.

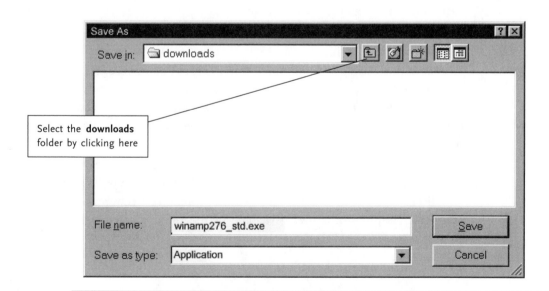

Figure 8.7   The Save As Dialog Box with **downloads** as the Selected Folder

A window titled "Saving Location" pops up on the screen to show the estimated time it will take to download the file and the progress of the download. Depending on the speed of your modem, how busy the server is at ZDNet, and current Internet traffic, it could take a few minutes or longer (up to an hour in extreme cases) to download the file. Figure 8.8 shows the "Download complete" box. It shows that the program has finished loading onto your computer.

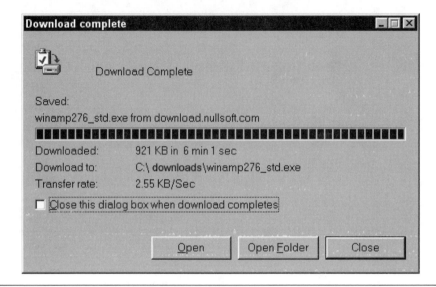

Figure 8.8   The Download Complete Dialog Box

☑ Do It!   Click on **Open** to start installing Winamp.

☑ Do It!   Now we're ready to install the MP3 player. The name of the package ends with **.exe**, which means that this is a self-installing package.

The contents indicate that the file is an executable file, as shown in Figure 8.8. Clicking on **Open** here will begin its installation.

Note: If you're using Netscape rather than Internet Explorer, the process is slightly different. The package will be downloaded to the folder **downloads**. When the download is complete, you'll have to open the folder and then double-click on the name of the package for Winamp. Following the example in this activity, you would double-click on **winamp276_std.exe**.

A program will start to lead us through the installation process. We will take all the usual options as the installation or setup program proceeds. The first thing you'll be asked to do is read a license agreement, as shown in Figure 8.9. Winamp is freeware, so there's no charge for using it. The license sets any legal liability for the company that distributes and maintains the software and asserts ownership of the program.

☑ Do It!   To install the software, click on **Next**.

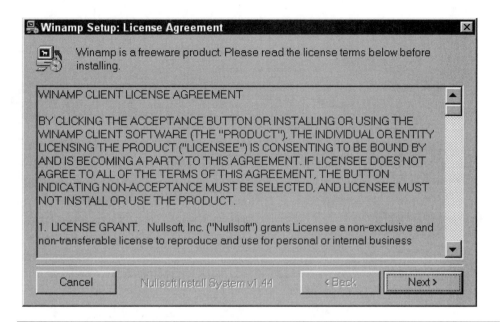

Figure 8.9   The License Agreement for Winamp

You will click on the **Next** button as you go through the setup process. You will be shown various Winamp settings that you may accept or not. One of the settings is "Add icon to desktop." All of the settings are recommended, so we'll keep all of them. When the setup program finishes, Winamp will be installed in the folder **C:\Program Files\winamp**, and Winamp will be added as an icon to your desktop. At the end of the process, a **Run Winamp** button will be provided, which you will be instructed to select.

☑ Do It!   Click on **Run Winamp**.

The Winamp player will appear on your desktop. You can close the player by clicking the ▨ in the upper-right corner.

One more thing: Now that we've installed Winamp, we don't need the files in the folder **C:\downloads** anymore. It's safe to delete them at this point.

Now let's locate some music to play on the player!

5. Search an MP3 library for an MP3 to download.

First, we need to find an MP3 library to search. One good place to go for a listing of MP3 libraries is the Librarians' Index to the Internet, **http://lii.org**. We can find a collection of MP3 libraries by entering **mp3** in the search form. One of the libraries listed is MP3.com, and it's a highly recommended site.

☑ Do It!   In the address bar, type the URL for MP3.com, **http://mp3.com**, and press ⎣Enter⎤.

Figure 8.10 shows the home page. Note that MP3.com is arranged much like other regular directories that we are familiar with. You can search the database or browse the subject categories. We are interested in downloading a piece of music by a rock band named **Skywave**.

☑ Do It!   Type **Skywave** in the search form and click on **Search**.

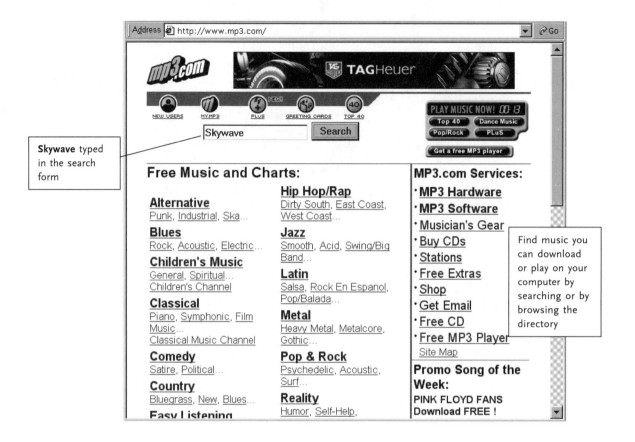

Figure 8.10   MP3.com, a Music Library

The result of this search brings up two items. When we did this search, the first result was a hyperlink to the band we were looking for. Remember that because the Internet is constantly changing, the search results can be different every time you do a search. Clicking on the link that our search found brought up the MP3.com page for the band Skywave. Figure 8.11 shows a portion of the results of this search. There are many tunes to choose from. The one titled "It's in Your Eyes" interests us the most.

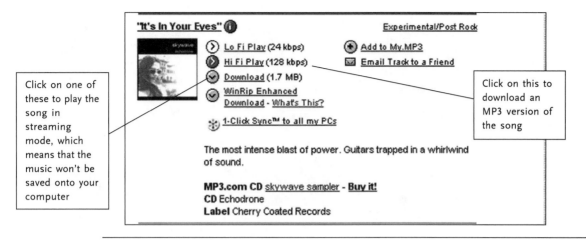

Click on one of these to play the song in streaming mode, which means that the music won't be saved onto your computer

Click on this to download an MP3 version of the song

Figure 8.11   Partial Results of a Search for Skywave in MP3.com

6. Download an MP3.

Figure 8.11 shows the information about a particular song by Skywave. Note that if you clicked on one of the **Play** options, you could hear the music in a few seconds. To download the music to your computer, you'll need to click on the **Download** hyperlink. A simple click will begin the download process.

☑ Do It!   Click on **Download**, as shown in Figure 8.11.

You may be asked to provide your email address or zip code information. You must do this in order for the download to proceed.

☑ Do It!   After you have filled in the required information, click on **Get Free Music!**

Just as when we downloaded the MP3 player, your browser will give you a choice of whether you want to open the file in the current location or if you want to save it to a disk—you should save it to a disk. You also will want to be sure that you've checked the box next to "Always ask before opening this type of file." That way, the downloaded file will be checked by the antivirus software on your computer. If you haven't downloaded and installed antivirus software yet, do it now!

☑ Do It!   Make sure the radio button next to **Save this file to disk** is selected and the check box next to **Always ask before opening this type of file** is checked. Then click on **OK**, as shown in Figure 8.12.

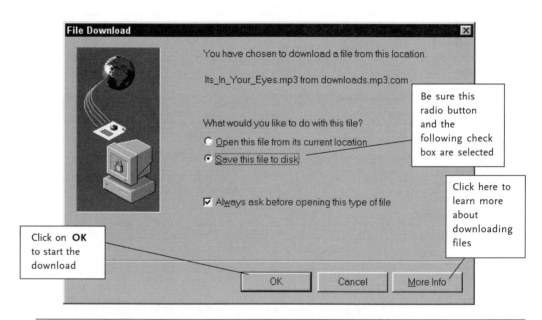

Figure 8.12   The Beginning of the MP3 Download

A **Save As** dialog box will pop up. **downloads** should appear in the **Save in** field, and the MP3 file name will appear in the **File name** field. This will allow the MP3 file to be saved in the folder named **downloads**.

☑ Do It!   Use the controls in the Save As dialog box to select the folder **downloads**, as shown in Figure 8.7. Then click **Save**, as shown in Figure 8.13.

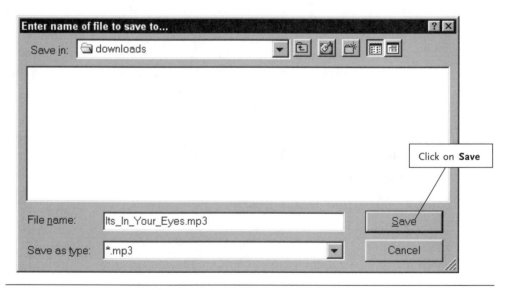

Figure 8.13   The MP3 File Being Saved in the **downloads** Folder

Then the file will download to your computer. A "Download Progress" window, similar to the one shown in Figure 8.8, will open showing the file. Depending on the speed of your connection and current Internet traffic, it could take anywhere from one minute up to 30 or more minutes.

7. Open the MP3 player.

You should see a Winamp icon on your desktop.

☑ Do It! If you have a Winamp icon on your desktop, simply click on it. If you don't have the icon, go to **Start**, (in the task bar), choose **Programs**, and find **Winamp**.

Figure 8.14 shows the top portion of the Winamp player.

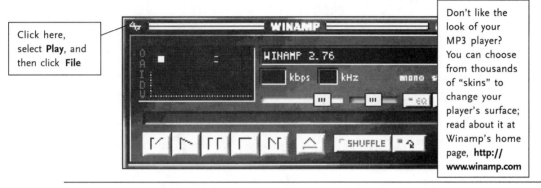

Click here, select **Play**, and then click **File**

Don't like the look of your MP3 player? You can choose from thousands of "skins" to change your player's surface; read about it at Winamp's home page, **http://www.winamp.com**

Figure 8.14   Top Portion of the Winamp Player

8. Play the music using the MP3 player.

☑ Do It! Click on the icon in the upper-left corner of the Winamp player, select **Play**, and then click on **File**.

An **Open file(s)** box will pop up.

☑ Do It! Highlight the name of the file, **Its_In_Your_Eyes.mp3**, and then click on **Open.**

The tune will open in the Winamp player.

☑ Do It! To play the music, you'll need to use the controls on the face of the player. Click on the right-facing arrow to play. The MP3 player is designed to resemble a tape or CD player, so it should be familiar to you.

☑ F Y I   **Other Sites That Offer MP3s**

☑ "EMusic.com,"
http://emusic.com

☑ "Listen.com,"
http://listen.com

☑ "Lycos Music,"
http://music.lycos.com

☑ "MP3Planet,"
http://www.mp3planet.com

END OF ACTIVITY 8 ◀

In the activity above, we downloaded and installed a program from a software archive. In this case, the software we downloaded was an MP3 player. We also downloaded a file from an MP3 music directory to our computer. The steps we followed were fairly typical, although the details can change, depending on the browser used, the program downloaded, and the software archive or library selected.

Using an FTP Client Program

In the examples and activities discussed so far in this chapter, we have used FTP through a Web browser. That may be all you need to retrieve information from the Web or Internet using FTP. Sometimes, though, you may need to use an FTP program that's separate from the browser. To use an FTP program in this way, you'll still need an Internet connection through your computer. The program you run will download files from a server or upload files from your computer to a server. In Chapter 10, we will discuss transferring source files to a Web server. The FTP program you use acts as a client.

When you work with an FTP client to contact another computer (called the *server* or *host*), you'll need to have certain pieces of information. The following list explains what you must know.

You'll need the Internet domain name or address of the server, or host.

The client uses the **domain name** to contact the server. Earlier in the chapter, in the section "FTP Overview," we pointed out the domain name portion of a URL that implies the use of FTP.

☑ F Y I **Several very good guides to using WS_FTP are available on the Web. Here's a short list:**

    ☑ "How to FTP — the Basics," http://www.zdnet.com/ devhead/stories/articles/ 0,4413,1600802,00.html

    ☑ "How to Use WS_FTP," http://library.albany.edu/ internet/ws_ftp.html

    ☑ "Installing and Configuring WS_FTP," http://usats.com/ learn/ftp.shtml

    ☑ "WS_FTP and How to Use It," http://d-na.com/ tryftp.htm

If you're going to download software, you'll need a user name and a password on the host.

If you're using anonymous FTP, the user name is *anonymous* and the password is your email address. If you're going to download some files from your user account on the server system, you'll use your assigned user name and password.

If you're going to upload files to another computer, you'll need a user name and password on the host.

The user name and password enable you to upload files to a directory or folder that isn't necessarily available to the public.

Of course, you'll also need an FTP client for your computer. Several are available as shareware, but one in particular is highly recommended. It's WS_FTP, and it's free for personal use. To get a copy appropriate for your system, go to CNET Download.com, **http://download.cnet.com/downloads**, and search for WS_FTP.

We'll briefly go over how to use WS_FTP, but look at some of these guides for more help when you're ready. First, download and install the appropriate version of the software from CNET. Use the same techniques discussed in the activity above.

After installation, start the program by selecting it from the Start menu, clicking on an icon on your desktop, or clicking on an icon in a folder. Which one of these you choose depends on how it was installed. When it starts, a session profile pops onto the screen.

Figure 8.15 shows a session profile for connecting to a system with the host name (same as the domain name) **library.mwc.edu**. The user ID or login name for this user is **khartman**. A password isn't typed in here; it will be typed in when the host system is contacted. If a password were saved with this profile, then anyone using the computer could access the files belonging to user **khartman** on **library.mwc.edu**. If this were to be an anonymous FTP session, then the box labeled **Anonymous** would be checked. You can select other servers with different profiles by clicking on the button to the right of the profile name.

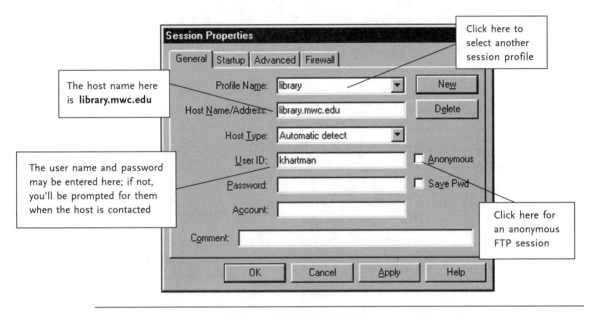

Figure 8.15   A Sample Session Profile for WS_FTP

To contact the host, click on the button labeled **OK**. Acting as a client, WS_FTP attempts to contact the host system. Another window pops up that shows whether the host has been contacted. The user then has control over the transfer of files.

Figure 8.16 shows the window that appears when WS_FTP starts an FTP session with **library.mwc.edu**. The left column lists the files in the current folder of your computer, the client. The right column lists the files in the directory on the host computer with which you've connected.

You can choose a file to transfer by selecting it from the appropriate column. You'll see that there are scroll bars to let you scroll through the list of files and directories on both the client and host computers. In each column, the subdirectories of the current directory are listed in the upper panel and the files are listed in the lower panel.

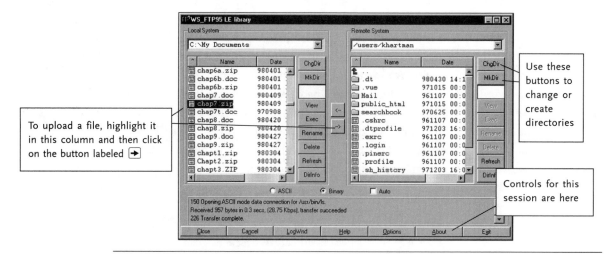

Figure 8.16   A Session Window for WS_FTP

Suppose we want to upload the file named **chap7.zip** from the client computer—that's the computer we're using—to the host. We highlight **chap7.zip** as shown in Figure 8.16 and click on the button labeled ➡. In doing so, we move the file from the client (listed on the left) to the host (listed on the right).

After we click on ➡, another dialog box called Transfer Status pops up showing information about the transfer of the file from one computer to another over the Internet. The items shown include the total number of bytes to transfer, the number transferred so far, the rate of transfer, how much time has been spent so far, and the estimated remaining time. That window will stay on the screen until the transfer is complete. You can stop the transfer by clicking on the **Cancel** button.

ON CD

The CD that accompanies this book includes a table that explains the basic FTP commands and some examples of using text-based FTP.

To view it, click on the hyperlink "Text Based FTP" in the collection of items for Chapter 8.

To download a file, select the directory on the local system that will hold the file, highlight the name of the file in the list on the right, and click on ⬅.

WS_FTP is one example of an FTP client. It presents a graphical user interface for transferring files between a client and server. Other client programs have a strictly text-based interface. With those, you use the command **get**, as in **get etiquet.zip**, to download a file. You use the command **put**, as in **put chap1.zip**, to upload a file.

Summary

FTP stands for File Transfer Protocol. With FTP, you can share or copy files from one Internet site to another. Anonymous FTP is the term used for when you copy a file from one computer to another without giving a login name or a password. Collections of files available by anonymous FTP are called anonymous FTP archives.

Literally trillions of bytes of information, programs, and resources are available by anonymous FTP. Several search services and software libraries provide facilities that allow you to search a database that holds descriptions and reviews of software available through anonymous FTP. Some of the software archives also have entries arranged by the type of program (for example, antivirus programs) or by the operating system (for example, Windows 98 or Macintosh).

Transferring a file from another computer to the computer you're using is called downloading. That's what you do when you retrieve a program from an FTP archive or software library. Many of the programs depend on a number of auxiliary files, such as online help files, to run and be used effectively. These files are put together into a package, and the contents are compressed to allow for faster transfer and easier storage.

After you retrieve one of these packages of software, you need to process it to extract the components. If the package name ends with **.exe**, then it's a self-extracting archive. Click on the name of the package, and it will unpack itself. If the name ends with **.zip**, you'll need to use a program, such as PKZIP or WinZip.

Once the files are extracted, you will run a program (application) to install the program. To be safe, you also should scan the software for computer viruses before you install it. Look for a file with a name such as **Readme**, and read it before you install the program. It might help you decide whether the program is appropriate for you and your computer system. Sometimes the **Readme** file is available only after installing the program. Finally, look for a program—often named **Setup** or **Install**—that you'll run to install the program.

An FTP client program is one that you run on your computer to exchange files with another computer, also using FTP, that acts as the host, or server. This program is not usually part of a Web browser. To access another computer through FTP, you need to give the client program the Internet domain name for the host computer. That's the part of the URL that immediately follows **ftp://**. For example, in the URL **ftp://ftp.jpl.nasa.gov/pub/images/browse/marglobe.gif**, the domain name is **ftp.jpl.nasa.gov**. Once connected, you can upload files from your computer to the host or download files from the host to your computer. You can do either one by using a graphical interface provided by the client or by using the commands **put** and **get**.

Selected Terms Discussed in This Chapter

anonymous FTP	FTP archive
domain name	shareware
download	upload
freeware	

Materials on CD for This Chapter

Here is a list of items for this chapter on the CD that accompanies the text:
- ☑ "Text-Based FTP," A table that explains the basic FTP commands and some examples of using text-based FTP
- ☑ All URLs mentioned in this chapter in hypertext format
- ☑ Selected terms discussed in this chapter with hyperlinks to the glossary
- ☑ Copies of the review questions in quiz format

Review Questions

True or False?

1. FTP stands for File Transfer Protocol.
2. Freeware is software that doesn't require a fee to download and use.
3. Uploading and using anonymous FTP is the same thing.
4. If a file name ends in **.zip**, then you will need to have hardware such as a zip drive attached to your computer to open it.
5. FTP was developed in the early 1990s.

Short Answer—Completion

1. A computer system that allows others to connect to it through anonymous FTP is called an anonymous FTP site or an _____.
2. Software programs available for downloading from the Internet that can be used for a period of time and then must be purchased are called _____.
3. Compressed files or packages have names that usually end in _____.
4. Self-extracting archive file names usually end in _____.
5. The term used for copying a file from one computer to another without giving a login name or a password is _____.

Exercises and Projects

1. Use your Web browser to take a look at the contents of the directory **/pub/usenet-by-group/rec.fitness** at the anonymous FTP site **rtfm.mit.edu**. (Hint: Use the URL **ftp://rtfm.mit.edu/pub/usenet-by-group/rec.fitness/**.)
   a. What is in that directory?
   b. What is the domain name of the site being contacted?
   c. What protocol is used to transfer the file? Explain.
   d. What's in the directory **/pub/usenet-by-group/** at **rtfm.mit.edu**?
2. Retrieve a copy of the file with the URL **ftp://nic.merit.edu/introducing.the.internet/answers.to.new.user.questions**. Using that file, write a one- or two-sentence answer to each of the following questions.
   a. What is the difference between the *Internet* and an *internet*?
   b. What is an advantage of the *domain name system* (DNS)?
   c. What is the definition of *TCP/IP*?
3. Using the images available through the URL **ftp://ftp.jpl.nasa.gov/pub/images/browse**, collect the URLs for images of all the planets in the solar system. Put them in one bookmark folder.
4. Go to the software archive "IT Pro Downloads," **http://itprodownloads.com/**, and search for a program that deals with math games. Choose one program to download and explain why you made that choice. Download and install the program. Did it work as you anticipated it would? If you're not happy with it, remove it from your computer system.
5. Go to CNET.com, **http://home.cnet.com**, and search for information using FTP as the keyword. Find and list the FTP clients that CNET recommends. What are some of the special features that make these FTP clients so attractive?

Writing
Web Pages

▶ you have seen lots of different Web pages as you've browsed and searched the World Wide Web and the Internet, and you may have been curious about how they're made. You'll soon learn that it's a straightforward process to design and put together a basic Web page.

Web pages are text or ASCII files in which HTML (hypertext markup language) is used to specify the format of the Web page, images to be displayed, hyperlinks, and other elements.

Because Web pages are text files, we don't necessarily need any special software tools or editors to create them. You'll find it's easier to create more complicated Web pages and sites using software designed for that purpose, such as Macromedia's *Dreamweaver* or Microsoft's *Front Page*, but you can get along with any word processor or editor that can create text files. If you're using Microsoft Windows, then Notepad, available through the Applications menu, is sufficient.

The browser receives the source for a Web page from a server, interprets the HTML, and displays the page. If the HTML says to display a word or phrase in the file in bold font, for example, the browser does it. If the HTML tags say to display an image, the browser takes care of that as well. If the tag indicates that what follows is a hyperlink to some other page, the browser displays the text as a hyperlink and associates it with the specified URL. Hyperlinks on a page can be to other pages or to other types of files, such as multimedia files and some types of interactive programs. Regardless of where the source for a Web page is—on your computer or on a remote Web server—it has the same format and the browser interprets it in the same way.

Goals/Objectives:

- ☑ Understand the concepts involved in writing a Web page
- ☑ Understand the relationship between a source file and a Web page
- ☑ Know basic HTML for producing a Web page
- ☑ Be capable of writing a Web page that contains one or more hyperlinks, images, or lists

Topics:

- ☑ Description of a Web Page
- ☑ Viewing the Source Version of a Web Page
- ☑ Introduction to HTML
- ☑ Style Guides: How to Do It Right, How to Do It for Impact, and How to Make It Portable
- ☑ Evaluating the Quality of a Web Page or Web Site
- ☑ Beyond HTML

Description of a Web Page

A **Web page** is a text file that contains HTML codes or tags. A **text file** is a file that contains plain printable characters. The text file is also called the **source file** or just the *source* for the Web page.

The name of the source file has to end with the extension **.htm** or **.html**. Some examples are **resources.htm**, **mvtool12.htm**, **index.html**, and **weather.html**. If the name doesn't have that form, HTML tags might not be interpreted by a Web browser. Check with the people who provide the Web services for your organization to find out the correct format for a file name. Ask whether it makes a difference if you use the extension **.htm** or **.html**, ask if your home page must be named **index.htm** or **index.html**, ask whether it matters if you use upper or lowercase letters in the name of a file, and ask whether it is advisable to include spaces in the names of files.

You can learn something about using HTML from looking at the source for a Web page, as shown in Figure 9.1, and how the page is displayed by a browser, Figure 9.2. Several items have been labeled so you can see the relationship between the HTML tags and what's displayed by the browser. Here are a few things to notice:

- ☑ The HTML tags are contained in angle brackets < >; for example, <title> and <img SRC = "intcover.gif">.
- ☑ Most HTML tags come in pairs because the browser uses them to determine how to display a particular piece of text based on the tags surrounding it. The first tag tells the browser to start a particular display mode and the second tag tells the browser to stop. The ending tag will always include a slash (/). For example,<i> tells the browser to begin and </i> tells it to stop displaying the text between in italic font.
- ☑ To write comments or notes that won't show up in the window with the document, surround the comments with <!— and —>.
- ☑ Looking at the page displayed by the browser (Figure 9.3), you can see that hard returns and spaces are generally ignored by the browser. You can use the HTML tag <p> to indicate the start of a new paragraph.

☑ <a href= "*URL*"> ... *text* ... </a> is an HTML tag for a hyperlink. Any URL may be used between the quotation marks.

☑ <img SRC = "*file name*"> is an HTML tag for an image. Put the name of the file or a hyperlink to a file containing the image between the quotation marks.

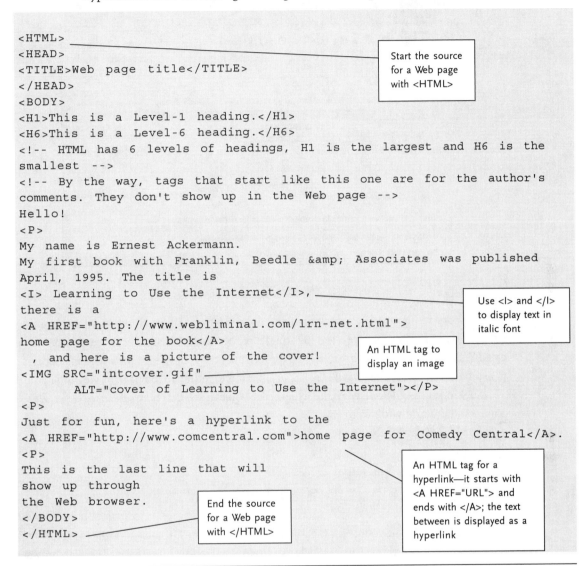

```
<HTML>
<HEAD>
<TITLE>Web page title</TITLE>
</HEAD>
<BODY>
<H1>This is a Level-1 heading.</H1>
<H6>This is a Level-6 heading.</H6>
<!-- HTML has 6 levels of headings, H1 is the largest and H6 is the
smallest -->
<!-- By the way, tags that start like this one are for the author's
comments. They don't show up in the Web page -->
Hello!
<P>
My name is Ernest Ackermann.
My first book with Franklin, Beedle &amp; Associates was published
April, 1995. The title is
<I> Learning to Use the Internet</I>,
there is a
<A HREF="http://www.webliminal.com/lrn-net.html">
home page for the book</A>
 , and here is a picture of the cover!
<IMG SRC="intcover.gif"
        ALT="cover of Learning to Use the Internet"></P>
<P>
Just for fun, here's a hyperlink to the
<A HREF="http://www.comcentral.com">home page for Comedy Central</A>.
<P>
This is the last line that will
show up through
the Web browser.
</BODY>
</HTML>
```

Start the source for a Web page with <HTML>

Use <I> and </I> to display text in italic font

An HTML tag to display an image

An HTML tag for a hyperlink—it starts with <A HREF="URL"> and ends with </A>; the text between is displayed as a hyperlink

End the source for a Web page with </HTML>

Figure 9.1   The Source for the Web Page in Figure 9.2

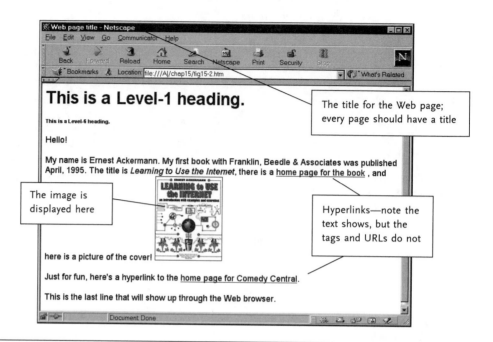

Figure 9.2   The Web Page, with the Source Shown in Figure 9.1, as Displayed by a Web Browser

The page in Figure 9.3 was written using the simple text editor Notepad, although any editor that can create and save a text file could have been used. It's easier to create more complicated Web pages using software designed for that purpose, but special software isn't necessary to get started. You can see the way HTML is used to put together a Web page by viewing its source.

Looking at the URLs used in the hyperlinks, you can see that they reference other Web pages on the World Wide Web.

The HTML tag for the image

```
<img SRC="intcover.gif"
    ALT="cover of Learning to Use the Internet">
```

uses SRC to specify the source for the image. In this case, the URL used for the image **intcover.gif** is rather plain. There's no domain name or leading directories. The Web browser interprets this to mean that the file is in the same directory and on the same server as the source for the Web page. This means that if we copy the source file to a folder on a Web server, we have to copy the image file to the same folder in order to use this simple form of a URL.

Figures 9.1 and 9.2 give you a basic idea of what a Web page contains, what HTML tags look like, and how HTML tags can be used. Regardless of how advanced or complex a Web page can be, remember that it contains the text you see on a page, HTML tags, and other items called *elements.* The elements can be images, hyperlinks to audio files, hyperlinks to other parts of the document, hyperlinks to other portions of the Web, interactive programs, scripts, and inline plug-ins.

Curious about what the source file looks like for a favorite Web page? The next section shows how you can use Netscape or Internet Explorer to view the source file for any page.

Viewing the Source Version of a Web Page

You can view the source file of any Web page. This lets you see the HTML used on the page. Here's how:

 Click on View from the menu bar and then choose Page Source.
Netscape

 Click on View from the menu bar and then choose Source.
Internet Explorer

Try it out. Take a look at the view you get of the source file for the Web page shown in Figure 9.2. It will be similar to what we've shown in Figure 9.1.

Viewing the document source with Netscape shows the HTML tags and URLs in a different font and color, making them easy to pick out.

Viewing the source is a good way to see how a Web page is constructed and to learn from the work of others. It's not intended to be used for copying someone else's work. A Web page belongs to the author just like any other work, such as a book or tape that someone has created and developed. If you see something you like, view the source, study how it was done, and then adapt the techniques you see to your own work.

Introduction to HTML

Web pages are written using **HTML (hypertext markup language)**. HTML consists of a collection of instructions, called **tags**, that the Web browser interprets to display a Web page. The commands or instructions are written in HTML, but the effects of the tags aren't seen until a Web browser or some program interprets the HTML. For example, the tags <b> and </b> placed around text indicate that the enclosed text is to be displayed in bold format. So if

```
Be sure to follow the <b>Yellow Brick Road</b> to get to Oz.
```

were part of a Web page, it would be displayed as

Be sure to follow the **Yellow Brick Road** to get to Oz.

The commands and the way browsers interpret HTML have more to do with the organization of a document than with its format. A number of commands can control the way text is displayed, but HTML emphasizes the hypermedia aspects of the World Wide Web. Extra spaces, tabs, and line lengths, for example, are generally ignored by the browser; the text is made to fit within the browser's window.

HTML includes the commands or tags to create hyperlinks from one part of a Web page to another part of the same page as well as to create hyperlinks to other Web pages or resources on the Internet. In other words, these hyperlinks are embedded into or become part of the Web page. **URLs (Uniform Resource Locators)** are used to create the hyperlinks. The same process of embedding hyperlinks in a document is used to embed images. The text, images, and hyperlinks are called the elements of a Web page.

In this section, we'll concentrate on the HTML tags that do basic formatting, create lists, include hyperlinks to other Web pages and resources, and include images in Web pages. We will talk about using background colors, background images, and tables in the material on the CD.

Numerous resources deal with creating, designing, and implementing Web pages. Two places that offer lots of help are CNET's "Web Building" site, **http://builder.cnet.com**, and "Developer's Corner," **http://www.webreference.com/dev**. A good background in the basics—what we'll cover in this chapter—is what you need to know to get started. After you understand the basics and have some confidence, you'll be ready to go forward on your own.

The General Form of HTML Tags

All HTML tags begin with the character < (left angle bracket) and end with the character > (right angle bracket). Most of the tags come in pairs surrounding or enclosing text. The second tag is identical to the first except that there's a slash (/) after the opening <. The tags tell a browser to treat the text between the tags in a certain way. You can see this in Figures 9.1 and 9.2. Some tags may occur singly and still cause an action. We've written the tags in lowercase, but the browser ignores the case of the letters in a tag. Remember, though, that in a URL, it's very important to use the proper case for names of files.

The Structure of a Web Page—Head and Body

The source file should start with the tag **<html>** and end with **</html>**. Between those tags, the source file has two distinct parts: the head or heading, which gives some information about the Web page, and the body, which contains the elements or content of the Web page. The title of the Web page, for example, goes in the heading section. Use the tags **<head>** and **</head>** to denote the heading of the Web page, and use **<body>** and **</body>** to mark off the body of the page. The items in the heading section aren't displayed as part of the Web page. Figure 9.1 shows the proper use of these tags. Figure 9.3 gives a brief outline.

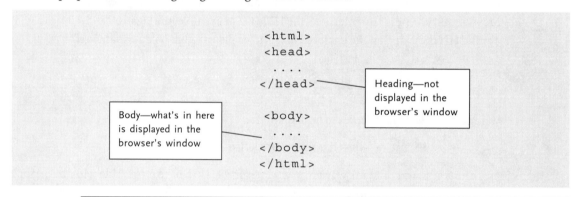

Figure 9.3   An Outline of the Head and Body Sections of a Web Page

Title

Every Web page needs a title. The title doesn't appear as part of the Web page, but it is visible at the very top of the browser window, as shown in Figure 9.2. The title is put between the tags **<title>** and **</title>**, in the heading section of a Web page, as shown in Figure 9.1. The title is important—it's the name that appears in a bookmark/favorites list, it's used for writing a citation, it's the name that appears when someone uses a search engine to find the page, and what's in the title can play a significant role in how a search engine ranks the Web page.

Author's Comments

The author of a Web page can include comments that are part of the source for the page but aren't displayed when the browser displays the page. Comments are useful as notes about how the page was constructed or what might need to be changed in the future. Comments serve as reminders not only to the person writing the page but also to anyone who might have to modify the page. Comments need to be surrounded by **<!--** and **-->**, as shown in Figure 9.1.

Headings

Web pages can be given a structure. You can start with a top-level heading and then have several levels of subheadings. One method used for constructing a Web page is to restate the title at the top of the body section as a level-1 heading using the tags **<h1>** and **</h1>**, then give a level-2 heading using **<h2>** and **</h2>**, then a third-level heading, and so on. There are six levels of headings using the tags **<h1>**, **<h2>**, **<h3>**, and on through **<h6>**. The different levels of headings control the size of the characters displayed. In Figure 9.1, we used **<h1>** and **<h6>**, and you can see the difference in Figure 9.2. Take a look at the source of the Web page with the URL **http://webliminal.com/lrn-net4.html** to see the use of several heading levels.

Paragraphs, Line Breaks, and Horizontal Lines

Blank spaces on a line and blank lines in a source document don't show up when an HTML document is displayed by a Web browser, they're ignored. The source document in Figure 9.1 contains blank spaces and lines that don't appear in the Web page in Figure 9.2. The browser adjusts and formats the lines so that they fit nicely within the window. There is a disadvantage to this, however: You need to use an HTML tag to specifically mark the beginning of a paragraph or the end of a line.

- ☑ Use **<p>** to mark the beginning of a paragraph. When the browser interprets this tag, a blank line is displayed, and the text following the **<p>** starts on a new line. Another way to think about this is that **<p>** is used to separate paragraphs.
- ☑ Use **
** to separate lines. The text following the tag **
** is placed at the beginning of the next line in the browser's window.
- ☑ **<hr>** puts a horizontal line on the Web page. The length of the line is automatically adjusted so that it's always the width of the window.

Figures 9.4 and 9.5 show the document source and the browser view of a page that uses **
, **<p>, and **<hr>**. These tags can be placed anywhere on a line or between lines.

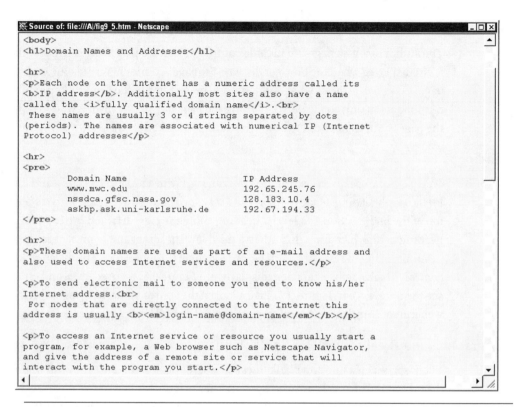

```
Source of: file:///A|/fig9_5.htm - Netscape

<body>
<h1>Domain Names and Addresses</h1>

<hr>
<p>Each node on the Internet has a numeric address called its
<b>IP address</b>. Additionally most sites also have a name
called the <i>fully qualified domain name</i>.<br>
 These names are usually 3 or 4 strings separated by dots
(periods). The names are associated with numerical IP (Internet
Protocol) addresses</p>

<hr>
<pre>
        Domain Name                     IP Address
        www.mwc.edu                     192.65.245.76
        nssdca.gfsc.nasa.gov            128.183.10.4
        askhp.ask.uni-karlsruhe.de      192.67.194.33
</pre>

<hr>
<p>These domain names are used as part of an e-mail address and
also used to access Internet services and resources.</p>

<p>To send electronic mail to someone you need to know his/her
Internet address.<br>
 For nodes that are directly connected to the Internet this
address is usually <b><em>login-name@domain-name</em></b></p>

<p>To access an Internet service or resource you usually start a
program, for example, a Web browser such as Netscape Navigator,
and give the address of a remote site or service that will
interact with the program you start.</p>
```

Figure 9.4   The Source for a Web Page Using **<B>**, **<P>**, and **<HR>**

Character Formatting—Italic, Bold, and Emphasized

HTML tags can be used to display parts of the text in bold or italic font. To display text in bold font, surround it with the tags **<b>** and **</b>**. To display text in italic font use the tags **<i>** and **</i>**. Both of these are used in the source document shown in Figure 9.4. The tags **<em>** and **</em>** are also used to display text in italic font. The portion of the source in Figure 9.4 that reads **<b><em>login-name@domain-name</em></b>** displays the enclosed text in bold and italic font.

Why use **<em>** and not **<i>** for italic font? Some browsers don't display text in italic font, and the HTML 4.01 specification, **http://www.w3.org/TR/html4**, gives a preference to these tags. **<em>** means *emphasize* to a browser, and many browsers will display the text in italics. If a browser can't display text in italic font, it will use some other font to emphasize the text. There are other tags that behave this way; **<strong>** and **<b>** can usually be used in place of each other.

Preformatted Text

Putting **<pre>** and **</pre>** around text indicates that it's preformatted and the browser shouldn't change the formatting for display. Text within the tags is displayed in fixed-width font, usually Courier, and looks different from other text displayed by the browser. Figure 9.4 shows the use of the tags **<pre>** and **</pre>**, and Figure 9.5 shows how the browser displays the text.

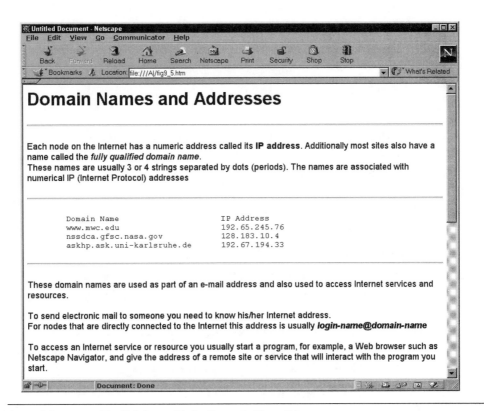

The Web page displays:

Domain Names and Addresses

Each node on the Internet has a numeric address called its **IP address**. Additionally most sites also have a name called the *fully qualified domain name*.

These names are usually 3 or 4 strings separated by dots (periods). The names are associated with numerical IP (Internet Protocol) addresses

```
Domain Name                    IP Address
www.mwc.edu                    192.65.245.76
nssdca.gfsc.nasa.gov           128.183.10.4
askhp.ask.uni-karlsruhe.de     192.67.194.33
```

These domain names are used as part of an e-mail address and also used to access Internet services and resources.

To send electronic mail to someone you need to know his/her Internet address.
For nodes that are directly connected to the Internet this address is usually *login-name@domain-name*

To access an Internet service or resource you usually start a program, for example, a Web browser such as Netscape Navigator, and give the address of a remote site or service that will interact with the program you start.

Figure 9.5   The Web Page with the Source in Figure 9.4

◢ F Y I   **Special Characters**

The special characters that can be represented with HTML are part of the standards for sets of codes defined by the International Organization for Standardization (ISO).

☑ "HTML 4.0 Character Entity References," http:// www.hclrss.demon.co .uk/demos/ansi.html

☑ "ISO8859-1/HTML Stuff," http://ppewww.ph.gla.ac .uk/~flavell/iso8859

Quoted Text, Indented Blocks

If you want to display quoted text or indent a block of text in a Web browser, use the HTML tags **<blockquote>** and **</blockquote>**. Take a look at the source of the Web page with the URL **http:// webliminal.com/Ltu/BlockquoteExample.html** for an example of the use of these tags.

Special Characters

Here's a question for you. If a Web browser interprets the character < as the beginning of an HTML tag, then how can we display < on a Web page? HTML has ways of representing that and other special characters. The format is an ampersand followed by some letters and a semicolon. Here are some examples:

<   to represent   <

>   to represent   >

&   to represent   &

"   to represent   "

     to represent   a space

Lists

HTML has tags for several different types of lists. In addition, the lists can be nested so that one type of list is inside another. The types of lists supported by HTML are as follows:

- ☑ Ordered (numbered) lists
- ☑ Unordered lists
- ☑ Descriptive lists

Hey! We just used an unordered list to show the types of lists you can represent with HTML.

Ordered or Numbered Lists

Ordered lists, also called numbered lists, are lists in which each item is numbered. You don't need to do the numbering; the Web browser does this automatically. If you change the list and add items, the browser takes care of renumbering them correctly.

The rules for using HTML to construct ordered lists are as follows:

- ☑ An ordered list starts with the tag **<ol>** and ends with the tag **</ol>**.
- ☑ Each item in the list starts with **<li>**.

Unordered Lists (Bulleted Lists)

Each item in an unordered list is marked with a dot called a bullet. The term *unordered* means the items aren't numbered, but they do appear in the order given in the source document. These lists also go by the names *unnumbered lists* or *bulleted lists.*

The rules for using HTML to construct unordered lists are as follows:

- ☑ An unordered list starts with the tag **<ul>** and ends with the tag **</ul>**.
- ☑ Each item in the list starts with **<li>**.

Descriptive Lists (Indenting)

Each item in a descriptive list has a title and then an indented description of the title. The items aren't marked with numbers or dots (bullets) as are ordered or unordered lists.

The rules for using HTML to construct descriptive lists are as follows:

- ☑ Tags—The descriptive list starts and ends with the tags **<dl>** and **</dl>**, respectively.
- ☑ Title—The descriptive title for each item starts with the tag **<dt>**.
- ☑ Description—The indented description for a title is marked with **<dd>**.

Examples of Lists

Figure 9.6 shows the source code for the Web page shown in Figure 9.7.

```
An example of an <b>ordered list</b>.
<br>
What is the Internet?
We'll look at it from these points of view.
<ol>
<li>From a social point of view.
<li>From a practical point of view emphasizing resources.
<li>From a technical point of view.
</ol>

An example of an <b>unordered or bulleted list</b>. <br>
What is the Internet? We'll look at it from these points of view.
<ul>
<li>From a social point of view.
<li>From a practical point of view emphasizing resources.
<li>From a technical point of view.
</ul>

An example of a <b>descriptive list</b>. <br>
What is the Internet? We'll look at it from these points of view.
<dl>
<dt>From a social point of view.
<dd>Consider the Internet in terms of individuals and groups of
users. We'll focus on using the Internet for communication and the
virtual communities that have arisen in recent times.
<dt>From a practical point of view emphasizing resources.
<dd>Consider the Internet as a vast storehouse of information. We'll
also stress the fact that the information isn't only "on the shelf,"
but that there are lots of people to answer questions and give
support.
<dt>From a technical point of view.
<dd>Here's where we give an introduction to some of the technical
details and issues. We'll look at the Internet as a network of
networks, explain how the networks can communicate, and cover some
details about connecting to the Internet.
</dl>
```

Figure 9.6   An Example Using HTML for Different Types of Lists

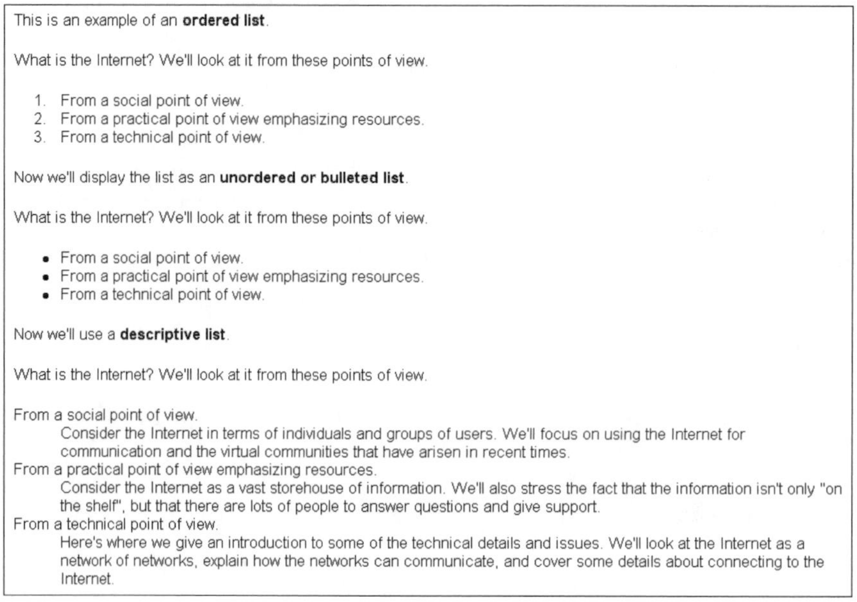

This is an example of an **ordered list**.

What is the Internet? We'll look at it from these points of view.

1. From a social point of view.
2. From a practical point of view emphasizing resources.
3. From a technical point of view.

Now we'll display the list as an **unordered or bulleted list**.

What is the Internet? We'll look at it from these points of view.

- From a social point of view.
- From a practical point of view emphasizing resources.
- From a technical point of view.

Now we'll use a **descriptive list**.

What is the Internet? We'll look at it from these points of view.

From a social point of view.
Consider the Internet in terms of individuals and groups of users. We'll focus on using the Internet for communication and the virtual communities that have arisen in recent times.
From a practical point of view emphasizing resources.
Consider the Internet as a vast storehouse of information. We'll also stress the fact that the information isn't only "on the shelf", but that there are lots of people to answer questions and give support.
From a technical point of view.
Here's where we give an introduction to some of the technical details and issues. We'll look at the Internet as a network of networks, explain how the networks can communicate, and cover some details about connecting to the Internet.

Figure 9.7   The Web Page Showing the Effects of Using Different Types of HTML Lists

Nested Lists

Any of the types of lists can be nested; that is, one put inside another. You'll notice that the symbol used to mark items in unordered lists changes shape when these lists are nested. Take a look at the Web page with the URL **http://webliminal.com/Ltu/NestedListExample.html** to see the effect of nesting lists. Don't forget to look at the source, too. The important thing to remember when you're writing nested lists is that the types can't overlap—they have to be contained within each other, in other words, nested.

Hyperlinks

HTML was designed to allow for the construction of hypertext, hypermedia documents, or Web pages. One of the advantages of HTML is that, with it, we can create *hyperlinks* from a resource on the World Wide Web to another Web page or from one part of a Web page to another part of the same page. We'll cover both of these types of hyperlinks in this section.

Hyperlinks to Other Resources on the Web

To use HTML to represent a hyperlink to a resource on the WWW, you use two tags, with text or an image between them. The first tag starts with **<a href="** and includes the URL or link for the resource. The matching tag is **</a>**. As you've already seen, many HTML tags appear in pairs. We'll look at an example before giving the rules for these types of tags.

Here's an example of the HTML tags used for creating a hyperlink:

```
The home page for <a href="http://www1.mwc.edu/~ernie/index.html">
Ernest Ackermann</a> has a link to materials for workshops and
tutorials.
```

A Web browser would display that HTML as follows:

The home page for <u>Ernest Ackermann</u> has a link to materials for workshops and tutorials.

When someone clicks on <u>Ernest Ackermann</u> in the browser's window, the browser opens the location and retrieves the resource given by the URL.

The HTML rules for creating hyperlinks are generalizations of the example above.

- ☑ The first tag has the form **<a href="** *URL***">**. A URL for an actual Web page is substituted for *URL* between the pair of quotation marks (**"**).
- ☑ The closing tag is **</a>**.
- ☑ The tags aren't visible on the Web page.
- ☑ The text between the two tags appears on the Web page as underlined or highlighted text.
- ☑ If there's an image between the two tags, its border is highlighted.
- ☑ Clicking on the text or image opens the location or takes the user to the Web resource given by the URL.

Figures 9.8 and 9.9 show the use of HTML tags for hyperlinks from a Web page to other resources on the Web. Figure 9.8 shows the HTML source, and Figure 9.9 shows the Web page. There are hyperlinks to sites at more than one location—a Web page can contain hyperlinks to many different locations and resources. Near the bottom of the page, an image is used within the tags for a hyperlink; otherwise, the hyperlinks all appear as text. We'll discuss displaying images in the next section. You'll notice that Figure 9.8 shows some HTML tags that we've discussed. Try to discern what the page will look like before looking at Figure 9.9.

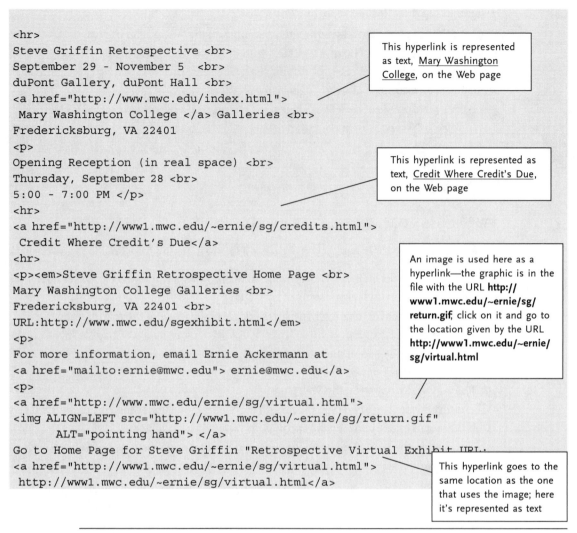

```
<hr>
Steve Griffin Retrospective <br>
September 29 - November 5  <br>
duPont Gallery, duPont Hall <br>
<a href="http://www.mwc.edu/index.html">
 Mary Washington College </a> Galleries <br>
Fredericksburg, VA 22401
<p>
Opening Reception (in real space) <br>
Thursday, September 28 <br>
5:00 - 7:00 PM </p>
<hr>
<a href="http://www1.mwc.edu/~ernie/sg/credits.html">
 Credit Where Credit's Due</a>
<hr>
<p><em>Steve Griffin Retrospective Home Page <br>
Mary Washington College Galleries <br>
Fredericksburg, VA 22401 <br>
URL:http://www.mwc.edu/sgexhibit.html</em>
<p>
For more information, email Ernie Ackermann at
<a href="mailto:ernie@mwc.edu"> ernie@mwc.edu</a>
<p>
<a href="http://www.mwc.edu/ernie/sg/virtual.html">
<img ALIGN=LEFT src="http://www1.mwc.edu/~ernie/sg/return.gif"
     ALT="pointing hand"> </a>
Go to Home Page for Steve Griffin "Retrospective Virtual Exhibit URL:
<a href="http://www1.mwc.edu/~ernie/sg/virtual.html">
 http://www1.mwc.edu/~ernie/sg/virtual.html</a>
```

This hyperlink is represented as text, Mary Washington College, on the Web page

This hyperlink is represented as text, Credit Where Credit's Due, on the Web page

An image is used here as a hyperlink—the graphic is in the file with the URL **http://www1.mwc.edu/~ernie/sg/return.gif**; click on it and go to the location given by the URL **http://www1.mwc.edu/~ernie/sg/virtual.html**

This hyperlink goes to the same location as the one that uses the image; here it's represented as text

Figure 9.8   The Source for the Hyperlinks Example

Hyperlinks to Other Parts of a Web Page

HTML also can be used to create hyperlinks between several parts of the same document. This is useful when dealing with a long document. Hyperlinks for a table of contents or a list of sections can take the reader to specific parts of the document. Hyperlinks within a document also are appropriate when constructing a glossary—a list of terms and definitions—to allow the reader to consider some items in context.

Making a link from one part of the document to another section involves link tags and an anchor tag. The anchor marks a spot within the document, and the link tags are ties to that specific anchor. Figure 9.10 shows an example of the source for these types of hyperlinks, and Figure 9.11 shows how they would be displayed by a Web browser.

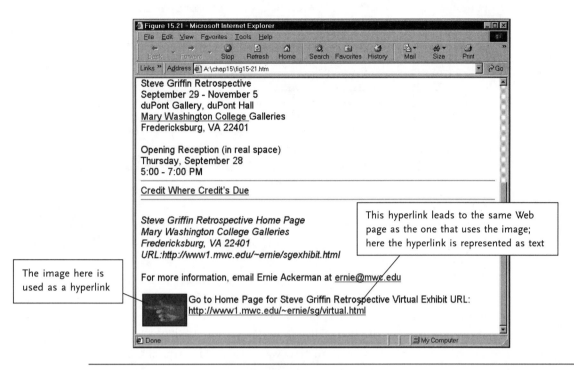

The image here is used as a hyperlink

This hyperlink leads to the same Web page as the one that uses the image; here the hyperlink is represented as text

Figure 9.9   The Web Page Produced by the Source in Figure 9.8

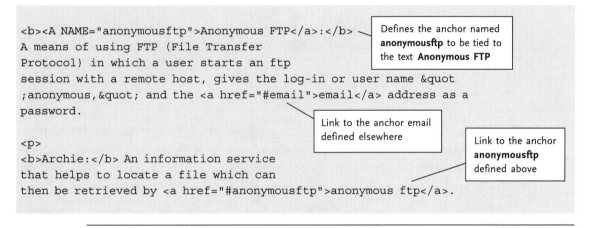

Figure 9.10   The Source for Hyperlinks Within a Document

Anonymous FTP: A means of using FTP (File Transfer Protocol) in
which a user starts an ftp session with a remote host, gives the
log-in or user name "anonymous," and the <u>email</u> address as a password.

Archie: An information service that helps to locate a file which can
then be retrieved by <u>anonymous ftp</u>.

Figure 9.11   The Web Browser Display of the Source in Figure 9.10

Clicking on a hyperlink in Figure 9.11 takes the user to a portion of the document marked by anchor tags. Looking at the example in Figure 9.10, you see:

- ☑ Anchor tags have the form **<A NAME="*word*">*portion-of-document*</a>** where *word* is some term that's used in the link tags. When the link is selected, the page is displayed starting here.

- ☑ Hyperlinks to portions of a document have the form **<a href="#*word*">*text or image*</a>**. Clicking on the hyperlink takes the user to the portion of the document where the anchor word's definition appears.

The **#** character identifies the link as going to a portion of a document. The hyperlinks we've shown here are within one document or Web page. You can use the same idea to set up hyperlinks to portions of other documents, provided that the document has anchors defined in it. The material in Figure 9.11 was taken from the Web page with the following URL: **http://users.mwc.edu/~ernie/glossary.html**. If we wanted to make a hyperlink from another Web page to the portion of the glossary that gives the definition of anonymous FTP, we'd use the URL **http://users.mwc.edu/~ernie/glossary.html#anonymousftp** in a link, as shown below.

```
Before 1990, you needed to learn how to use
<a href="http://users.mwc.edu/~ernie/glossary.html#anonymousftp">
anonymous ftp</a> to access most of the material on the Internet.
```

Images

A Web browser is capable of displaying images as part of a Web page. The basic HTML tag to use for an image has the form **<img src="*URL*">**, where *URL* is the URL of a file that contains a digital representation of the image. Browsers can display images that are in GIF or JPEG format. The browser determines the format only by the name of the file. If the image is in GIF format, store it in a file that has a name ending with **.gif**. For an image in JPEG format, store it in a file with a name ending in **.jpg**.

We've used HTML tags for images that appear in Web pages for some of the previous figures:

- ☑ Figure 9.1: **<img src="intcover.gif" ALT="cover of Learning to Use the Internet">**
- ☑ Figure 9.8: **<img ALIGN=LEFT src="http://www1.mwc.edu/~ernie/sg/return.gif" ALT="pointing hand">**

The second URL uses a complete qualified domain name. The first uses a relative name for the URL. A relative URL is easier to type in, but remember that using a relative URL implies that the image is in the same directory or folder as the Web page source, which restricts the location of pages and images. In some cases, it may be too restricting.

ALT is used to specify what is called ***alternate text***. This type of text is displayed when someone selects or moves the mouse over an image. The text is used to provide some information about the image—it's important to include alternate text in this way to further describe a Web site and to make a Web site accessible to people who are visually impaired.

You can also give directions to the browser as to where the accompanying text will be displayed in relation to the image. Text can be displayed aligned at the top, middle, or bottom of an image. It's usually displayed to the left of the image. Use ALIGN="BOTTOM", ALIGN="MIDDLE", or ALIGN="TOP" within the IMG tag; for example, **<img ALIGN="TOP" src="http:// www.mwc.edu/ernie/InternetToday/ intcover.gif" ALT="cover of Internet Today!">**. With this type of alignment only one line is displayed in the specified position and the remaining text (if there is any) is displayed under the image. It's also possible to align text with the entire image, starting at the top, using ALIGN="LEFT" or ALIGN="RIGHT". This puts the image to the left or to the right of the text. Take a look at the Web page with the URL **http:// webliminal.com/Ltu/ ImageAlignExample.html** for some examples of using the ALIGN attribute with the IMG tag.

Make Sure Others Can Find Your Images and Hyperlinks

Avoid using a URL or file name that references a local file in terms of its location on your computer without giving the Internet address of the computer. An example of this would be the HTML tag **<img SRC="file:///C|nicestuff/ greatpic.gif">**.

That tag instructs the browser to display a file that's on the computer that's being used to run the Web browser, which means if users viewing the page aren't using that same computer, then they won't be able to see it! Hyperlinks to resources that start with **file://** and don't give the Internet domain name will have the same problem. If you want the image or the hyperlink to be accessible from other computers on the Internet, you need to use a URL that includes the domain name of the system that's running the Web server. If the image were to be displayed as part of a Web page with the URL http://www.circlea.com/ nicestuf/coolpage.html, for example, you would put the image in the same directory or folder as the Web page and make its tag **<img SRC="greatpic.gif">**.

The examples above show how to align text with images. We've used the attribute ALIGN to align an image with relatively small amounts of text. The attribute is part of the HTML tag, and it gives an attribute to the image that's displayed. There are other attributes that you can use. The list below describes some of them.

ALT="*text*"	The text is displayed when the mouse pointer is moved over an image. This is useful to describe the image. For example, moving the mouse pointer over the image of Ernest Ackermann on his home page, **http:// webliminal.com/ernie**, displays **"picture of ernie"** because the IMG tag contains ALT="picture of ernie".
ALIGN="*alignment*"	This attribute aligns the image with the border of the Web page. ALIGN="LEFT" puts it on the left of a page, and ALIGN="RIGHT" puts it on the right.

HSPACE="*width*"	This attribute specifies the number of pixels between the left and right sides of the image and other elements of the Web page. For example, using HSPACE="5" places five pixels between the left and right sides of the image and other items on a Web page.
VSPACE="*width*"	This attribute specifies the number of pixels between the top and bottom of the image and other elements of the Web page. For example, using VSPACE="8" places eight pixels between the top and bottom of the image and other items on a Web page.
BORDER="*width*"	This specifies the border around an image. Using BORDER="0" gives no border. To get a thick border, use BORDER="5".
HEIGHT="*size*" and WIDTH="*size*"	Use these to specify the height and width of an image in pixels. If you position the mouse pointer over an image, right-click, and select **View Image**, the image is displayed in its own window with the size specified. Setting these attributes makes a page load faster because the browser knows how many pixels to allocate for the image. For example, HEIGHT="181" WIDTH="163" specifies that an image will be 181 pixels high and 163 pixels wide.

Table 9.1   IMG Tag Attributes

Background Colors and Images

Using HTML, you can set the background for a Web page so that it is a solid color or an image. You do this by setting an attribute in the **<body>** HTML tag. For example, to have a white background on a Web page use **<body bgcolor="WHITE">**. To set the background of a Web page to an image, such as one that's in the file **mwc.gif**, use **<body background="mwc.gif">**. Only one of these, **bgcolor** or **background**, may be set in the **<body>** tag because the background can be either a color or an image, but not both. Setting a color or an image as the background on a Web page displays all the other text or images on top of the background.

The rules for the file name that's used with background are the same as for any image used in HTML. The file name can be a fully qualified URL with the domain name and the path, or it can be relative to the location of the file that holds the source for the Web page. Take a look at the Web page with the URL **http://webliminal.com/Ltu/BackGroundExample.html** to see an example.

Colors may be designated by name—such as white, blue, or palegoldenrod—or they can be designated by a six-digit hexadecimal (base sixteen) numeral. Most folks are more comfortable with the names for colors. A guide to the names of the colors and a display of what the colors look like is available at "HTML Color Names," **http://www.w3schools.com/html/html_colornames.asp**. (That's how we know the name palegoldenrod can be used for a color!)

☑ F Y I   **Web Page Colors**

Here are two places to look for advice and more information about using color in Web pages:

- ☑ "Annabella's HTML Help — Colors," http://geocities.com/Heartland/Plains/6446/color.html

- ☑ "The Browser-Safe Color Palette," http://lynda.com/hex.html

The six-digit number indicates the amount of red, green, and blue in the color. The colors are formed in a similar way to how light is mixed. By that, we mean that giving the highest value to all three colors (designated by #FFFFFF) results in white, and giving the least value to each (designated by #000000) results in black. The first two characters after the # represent the amount of red, the next two the amount of green, and the last two the amount of blue. Using hexadecimal digits allows for 16 * 16 possibilities for each of the three colors and thus over 16 million possible colors. Before you get too carried away with color possibilities, remember that for best results you ought to stick with the 216 browser-safe colors as mentioned in the resources listed in the FYI on the previous page.

Now that we've looked at some of the basics of HTML, we'll present an example of how to construct a Web page.

WRITING WEB PAGES

Overview

Now that we know something about HTML, HTML tags, and URLs, we'll put together a Web page. This Web page could be called a **_personal home page_** because it will give information about an individual. Thousands of folks have personal home pages. It's a way of letting others on the Internet know about you. An example of an excellent personal home page is "Jan's Home Page," **http://jan.redmood .com**, created by Jan Hanford.

ON CD: Tables in HTML

The CD that accompanies this book includes information about using tables or rectangular grids to position information on a Web page.

Click on the hyperlink "Tables in HTML" in the collection of materials for Chapter 9.

ON CD: HTML Tags

The CD that accompanies this book includes a list of the HTML tags we've discussed in the text and on the CD.

Click on the hyperlink "HTML Tags" in the collection of materials for Chapter 9.

☑ F Y I   **Personal Web Pages**

Here are two interesting articles on the reasons people create personal Web pages:

☑ "The World Wide Web as Social Hypertext," http:// pliant.org/personal/ Tom_Erickson/ SocialHypertext.html

☑ "Personal Home Pages and the Construction of Identities on the Web," http://www.aber.ac.uk/ media/Documents/short/ webident.html

In this activity, we'll create two Web pages. One will give some work-related information and the other will give information about hobbies and interests. We'll put an image on each, and the pages will be linked. This activity shows some of the beginning stages of designing a personal Web site.

At the end of each page, we'll include an email address to use if readers have any questions about the Web page, and the date the Web page was last modified or changed.

You create the Web page by typing the HTML tags and text into a file on your computer using an editor or word-processing program. No matter what software you use to create the page, your work will be saved in a text or *ASCII* file. The image file with a picture of Ernest Ackermann was created by using a scanner to scan a photograph.

We're going to write the pages in stages; first we'll write the HTML statements, then save them to a file, and finally use the Web browser to view what we've done. We'll use the editor Notepad, which is part of the basic accessories for a Microsoft Windows system. You can use whatever tool for creating or maintaining Web pages you'd like.

These are the steps we'll follow for this activity:

1. Start Notepad.
2. Type the HTML and text for the first Web page.
3. Save the work into a file named **activity9p1.html**.
4. Use the Web browser to view the page.
5. Add the image near the top of the page and other information at the end of the page.
6. Create another Web page in the same manner. Save it as **activity9p2.html**. Include a hyperlink on both pages so that a visitor can go from one to the other.

ON CD

The images and the source files for the Web pages in this activity are all in the collection of items for Chapter 9.

To access them, click on the hyperlink titled "Activity—Writing Web Pages."

Details

1. Start Notepad.

You start Notepad by selecting or clicking on its icon in the Accessories section of Microsoft Windows.

☑ Do It! Click on the **Start** button, move the pointer to **Programs**, then move the pointer to **Accessories**, and click on **Notepad**.

Once Notepad starts, you'll see a window similar to the one in Figure 9.12, except there won't be any text in the window.

2. Type the HTML and text for the first Web page.

☑ Do It! Start by typing the HTML and tags necessary for the items on the first page.

Figure 9.12 shows the HTML tags and text to type in.

The heading section including the title

A level-2 heading; <H2> makes **Hi!** stand out

The end of the document

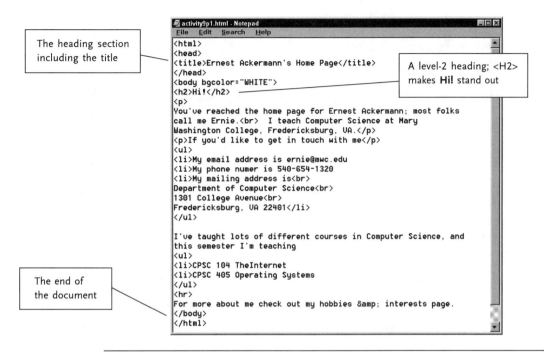

```
activity9p1.html - Notepad
File   Edit   Search   Help
<html>
<head>
<title>Ernest Ackermann's Home Page</title>
</head>
<body bgcolor="WHITE">
<h2>Hi!</h2>
<p>
You've reached the home page for Ernest Ackermann; most folks
call me Ernie.<br>  I teach Computer Science at Mary
Washington College, Fredericksburg, VA.</p>
<p>If you'd like to get in touch with me</p>
<ul>
<li>My email address is ernie@mwc.edu
<li>My phone numer is 540-654-1320
<li>My mailing address is<br>
Department of Computer Science<br>
1301 College Avenue<br>
Fredericksburg, VA 22401</li>
</ul>

I've taught lots of different courses in Computer Science, and
this semester I'm teaching
<ul>
<li>CPSC 104 TheInternet
<li>CPSC 405 Operating Systems
</ul>
<hr>
For more about me check out my hobbies &amp; interests page.
</body>
</html>
```

Figure 9.12   The Initial Text and HTML Tags for the Web Page

3. **Save the work into a file named activity9p1.html.**

To use a Web browser to look at what's been done so far, you need to save the work to a file. You should save your work periodically anyway, say every 15 minutes or so, so that if your computer crashes or the power goes out, you won't lose anything.

☑ Do It!   To save a file while using Notepad, click on **File** in the menu bar, choose **Save As**, and then give the file a name.

You'll want to be sure of two things:
1.   The name of the file ends with **.htm** or .html, such as **activity9p1.html**.
2.   You know the name of the directory or folder that holds the file so you can find it later.
       If you have the opportunity, be sure to select an appropriate folder to hold the file. You might want to create a folder named **WebPages** to hold your work. Just to be specific for this example, the work will be saved in a file named **activity9p1.html** in a folder (directory) named **WebPages** on Drive C:.

☑ Do It!   First, create the folder or directory named **WebPages** using My Computer or Windows Explorer. After you select **Save As,** a dialog box will appear on the screen. Type **C:\WebPages\activity9p1.html** in the portion of the dialog box labeled **File name**.

4. **Use the Web browser to view the page.**

First, be sure the Web browser is started. You don't necessarily have to connect to the Internet to view the file holding the Web page because it's a local file. We'll use Internet Explorer to view the file. Everything would look about the same and the steps would be very similar if we were using Navigator.

☑ Do It! Click on **File** in the menu bar, and then select **Open**.

This opens a dialog box labeled **Open**.

☑ Do It! Click on the button labeled **Browse**.

A dialog box will appear on the screen.

☑ Do It! Use the controls to get to the folder named **WebPages** on Drive C:.

☑ Do It! Double-click on **activity9p1.html** to view the Web page in the browser.

☑ Do It! Only one more step to get the file displayed in the browser. Click on **OK** in the Open dialog box.

These steps cause the browser to display the Web page written above. It's shown in Figure 9.13.

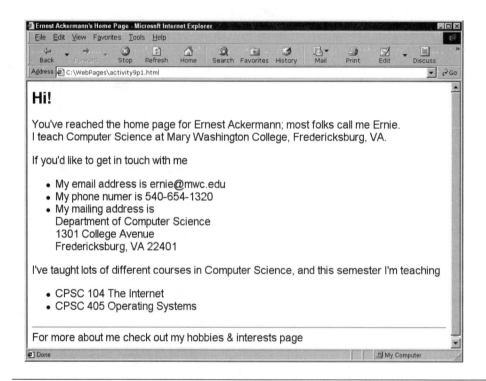

Figure 9.13   The Web Browser View of **activity9p1.html**

How do you like it? It's not bad, but we're going to change it by adding some hyperlinks. Since Mary Washington College has a home page, we'll add a hyperlink to it through the college's name. We'll also add a hyperlink so that folks can send email by clicking on the email address on the screen. In addition, we'll make hyperlinks to the Web pages for the courses listed and to the Web page that's going to list hobbies and interests. That Web page might not exist yet, but we can still make the hyperlink. We just have to be sure about the name of the file. Here's how we would do that:

1. Use the editor or word-processing program to edit or change the file holding the Web page.
2. Save the changes.
3. View the Web page with the browser again.

   If both the editor and the browser are still on the screen, you have to click on the appropriate windows to use them. Otherwise, you need to start them.

   As you make changes to **activity9p1.html**, it's a good idea to keep viewing it with the browser. Make changes, save the changes, and then click on the icon labeled **Refresh** from the browser's toolbar. It's really useful to be able to make changes and see what they look like almost immediately, particularly when trying new things.

   Figure 9.14 shows the portion of **activity9p1.html** with the hyperlinks added. We've pointed out the tags to add. Note that we've used a relative URL—just the name of the file **activity9p2.html**—for the hyperlink to the next Web page we're going to write.

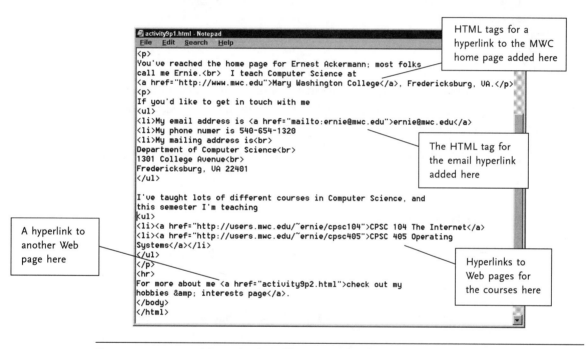

Figure 9.14   **activity9p1.html** Modified with Added Hyperlinks

☑ Do It!   Click on **File** and select **Save** to save the modified source in the file **activity9p1.html**.

How do you like it now? Make any changes you'd like. We're going to add an image near the top and put some information at the bottom of the page.

5. **Add the image near the top of the page and other information at the end of the page.**

   We're going to add a picture at the top of the page and some information at the end. The picture is in a file in GIF format, and we'll use an **IMG SRC** tag to display it. The information at the end includes an email address to use if readers have questions about the Web page, and the date the Web page was last modified or changed. We'll call this the "footer information."

To add the image, we'll include the HTML tag for the image between the lines

```
<p>
You've reached the home page for Ernest Ackermann; most folks call
me Ernie.
<br>
```

in the source.

☑ Do It! Add the line **<img ALIGN="RIGHT" src="erniebw.gif" alt="picture of Ernie">**.

With this addition, the source now contains.

```
<p>
<img ALIGN=RIGHT src="erniebw.gif" alt="picture of Ernie">
You've reached the home page for Ernest Ackermann; most folks call me
 Ernie.
<br>
```

Using **src="erniebw.gif"** implies that the image is in the same directory as the Web page. We've made sure that's the case, so the Web page now looks like the one shown in Figure 9.15.

☑ Do It! Add the following information near the end of the file just before the tag **</body>**:

<hr>

Contact Ernest Ackermann,

<a href="mailto:ernie@mwc.edu">ernie@mwc.edu</a>,

for any questions/rants/raves about this Web page.

**
Last modified March 4, 2002.** (You'll want to put the current date in here.)

☑ Do It! Select **Save** to save the modified source in the file **activity9p1.html**.

The Web page now looks like the one in Figure 9.15.

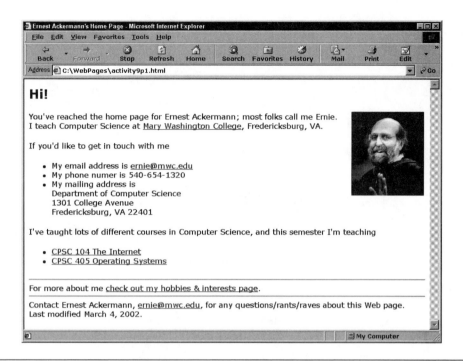

Figure 9.15   **activity9p1.html** with an Image and Footer Information Added

Now on to writing another Web page to list hobbies and interests.

6. Create another Web page in the same manner. Save it as activity9p2.html. **Include a hyperlink on both pages so that viewers can go from one to the other.**

We're going to write a Web page that lists hobbies and interests. Before we get to that, we have to spend some time deciding on and finding the content. We want to list some hyperlinks to Web sites related to our chosen topics. Let's assume the hobbies and interests are gardening and photography, and we've collected some hyperlinks to the sites we want to list. We also need to decide on the design of the page. There are many possibilities. We'll look at one example in this section and another in the next. Figure 9.16 shows a sketch of one design.

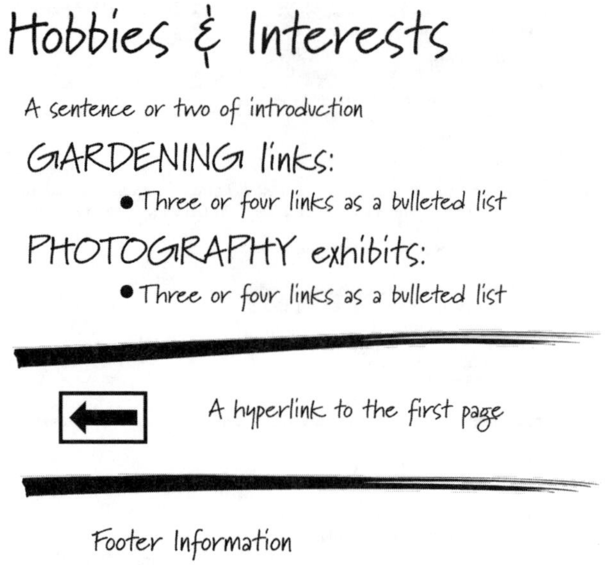

Figure 9.16   A Hobbies & Interests Web Page Design That Uses Lists

We'll use an image of an arrow that we've retrieved from the MediaBuilder Icon Library, **http://www.mediabuilder.com/ds_icons_blocks_page_aa.html**, which is a good resource for free images.

Now we need to write the HTML for this page. The page will include a main heading, some text, and two lists of hyperlinks. We also need to insert an image, a hyperlink to get us back to **activity9p1.html**, and the footer information. Previous sections explain the HTML necessary for all these items.

Figure 9.17 shows some of the HTML for the page. To see all of the HTML, use Notepad to view the file **activity9p2.html** on the CD that's included with this book.

The main heading

A bulleted list for gardening links

Hyperlinks for photography

HTML for the arrow image

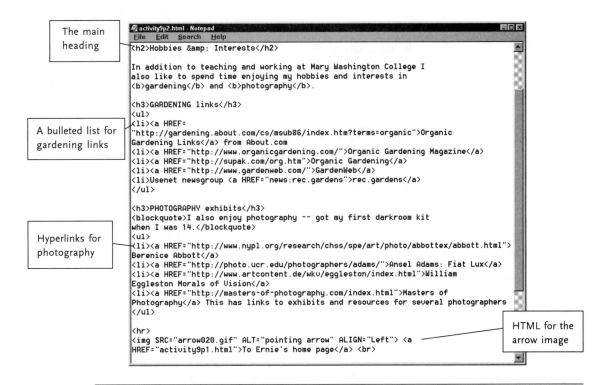

```
activity9p2.html - Notepad
File   Edit   Search   Help
<h2>Hobbies &amp; Interests</h2>

In addition to teaching and working at Mary Washington College I
also like to spend time enjoying my hobbies and interests in
<b>gardening</b> and <b>photography</b>.

<h3>GARDENING links</h3>
<ul>
<li><a HREF=
"http://gardening.about.com/cs/msub86/index.htm?terms=organic">Organic
Gardening Links</a> from About.com
<li><a HREF="http://www.organicgardening.com/">Organic Gardening Magazine</a>
<li><a HREF="http://supak.com/org.htm">Organic Gardening</a>
<li><a HREF="http://www.gardenweb.com/">GardenWeb</a>
<li>Usenet newsgroup <a HREF="news:rec.gardens">rec.gardens</a>
</ul>

<h3>PHOTOGRAPHY exhibits</h3>
<blockquote>I also enjoy photography -- got my first darkroom kit
when I was 14.</blockquote>
<ul>
<li><a HREF="http://www.nypl.org/research/chss/spe/art/photo/abbottex/abbott.html">
Berenice Abbott</a>
<li><a HREF="http://photo.ucr.edu/photographers/adams/">Ansel Adams: Fiat Lux</a>
<li><a HREF="http://www.artcontent.de/wku/eggleston/index.html">William
Eggleston Morals of Vision</a>
<li><a HREF="http://masters-of-photography.com/index.html">Masters of
Photography</a> This has links to exhibits and resources for several photographers
</ul>

<hr>
<img SRC="arrow020.gif" ALT="pointing arrow" ALIGN="Left"> <a
HREF="activity9p1.html">To Ernie's home page</a> <br>
```

Figure 9.17   HTML for **activity9p2.html**, Hobbies & Interests, Using Lists

☑ Do It!   Save the HTML in the file **activity9p2.html.**

☑ Do It!   View the Web page.

The Web page is shown in Figure 9.18.

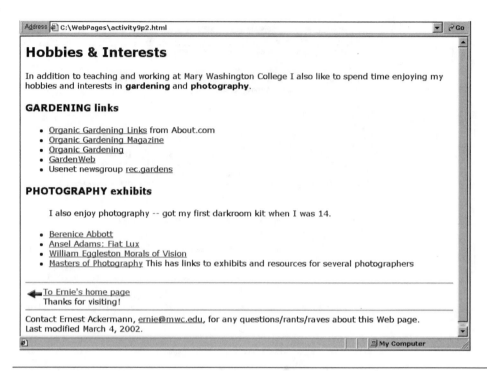

Figure 9.18   The Web Page View of the File **activity9p2.html**, Hobbies & Interests, Using Lists

It has taken some work to develop the two pages, but it's a good start on writing Web pages.

END OF ACTIVITY 9 ◀

The activity above showed just one possibility for design and linking Web pages. A Web page for a business or organization should present the organization's image, describe its services offered, and strive to get the reader interested in requesting information, services, or products.

ON CD

The CD that accompanies this book includes an example of constructing a Web page using tables.

To view it, click on the hyperlink "Writing Web Pages with Tables" in the collection of items for Chapter 9.

A page that focuses on a theme (such as guitars) or an event (such as an art exhibit) should present information, provide a means for folks to participate, and include hyperlinks to related resources or Web pages. Some pages are pure whimsy, entertainment, or playfulness. No matter what type of Web page you're constructing, think carefully about its purpose and design before writing, and search for Web pages with a similar topic or purpose to get ideas. We can learn a lot from looking at each other's work.

Tools to Help Create Web Pages

In the previous section, you learned that to create Web pages, you need an editor that lets you save your work in text or ASCII format. In fact, that's all you need to create relatively simple pages. When you have to create lots of pages or pages with lots of HTML, you'll want to use something that makes the task easier.

There are several programs that can help you create Web pages. Working with them is like working with a word processor. They have a menu bar and toolbar that let you create the page as you'd see it through a Web browser. The tags are often inserted automatically. For example, to create a hyperlink, you highlight text, click on the icon for creating a link, and type the URL for the link in a dialog box. Several of the programs are available on the Web as shareware or evaluation copies. The current version of Netscape Communicator includes Composer, an easy-to-use, visual Web page editor. Several popular word-processor and spreadsheet programs include tools to save documents in HTML format. These are useful for situations in which a number of documents have to be converted or when documents have to be produced in two formats—one for the printed page and one for the Web.

☑ F Y I **Lists of Tools for Creating Web Pages**

☑ "Resources for Creating Web Sites," http://home.netscape.com/browsers/createsites/index.html

☑ The Web Developer's Virtual Library "VL-WWW: HTML_Editors," http://wdvl.internet.com/Vlib/Authoring/HTML_Editors.html

☑ The Open Directory Category "Computers: Software: Internet: Authoring," http://dmoz.org/Computers/Software/Internet/Authoring/

Style Guides—How to Do It Right, How to Do It for Impact, and How to Make It Portable

Now that you've learned the basics of creating a Web page, you should consider issues of style: how to create a Web page that is enjoyable to look at, easy to read, and effective. Creating an effective Web page deals with issues of content, HTML, and design. The two primary components are effective language and solid two-dimensional design, or layout. You'll also need an understanding of the technical issues involved in creating and viewing Web pages—a good understanding of HTML and the characteristics and limitations of Web browsers.

One difficulty with designing a Web page is that a number of technical conditions affecting the way a page looks can't be controlled by the creator of the site. For example, the size and type of font used in the browser may be set by an individual user. In addition, the number of colors displayed and the screen resolution vary from monitor to monitor. Options can be set on a Web browser controlling the type and size of font used to display text, so text that looks "just right" in terms of size and placement may appear differently to different users.

There's no control over the type of monitor or display used to view a Web page. Some monitors will be set to display 256 colors, and others will use millions of colors. An image that looks great on a display capable of displaying lots of colors may not look very good when fewer colors are available. The screen resolution or number of pixels in the viewing window also affects the way a Web page appears. Images and text have their dimensions ultimately specified in terms of pixels regardless of what's being used to view them. The greater the number of pixels, the finer the resolution. An image on a screen with a resolution of 1024 by 768 pixels will generally look better and be sharper than an image on a screen with a resolution of 800 by 600 pixels or 640 by 480 pixels. So an image that's 300 by 400 pixels, say, will appear much smaller on a screen whose resolution is 1024 by 768 pixels than it would appear on a screen with a resolution of 640 by 480 pixels. Furthermore, the size of the browser window can be changed by the user. So as you design a page, you should think about what it will look like on different types of monitors and with different user configurations.

A middle-of-the-road approach would be to design a Web page to look good on a monitor that displays 256 colors and that has a resolution of 800 by 600 pixels. Compromises have to be made because it's impossible to predict the type of monitor your readers will be using and the way their Web browser options will be set.

Also, you can control a number of style elements to create appealing and effective Web pages.

Use HTML that most browsers can deal with.

The HTML code presented in this chapter is interpreted in the same way by most browsers, but other HTML tags, such as those for creating tables and setting background colors, aren't interpreted in the same way by all Web browsers. So the HTML you use in a Web page should be chosen to give the page the format you'd like and be viewable in that format by most Web browsers; not everyone will be using Internet Explorer. Try viewing a Web page with different browsers to learn what works best. To read more about current trends and developments regarding HTML, look at the Web page "HyperText Markup Language Home Page," **http://www.w3.org/pub/WWW/MarkUp**.

Use relatively small images and limit the number of images in a Web page.

It can take many bytes to represent an image, which means it may take a long time for someone to view a Web page with many images or one large image. We'll calculate how long it would take for an image that is 54 Kbytes in size to be displayed on a computer using a 57.6 Kbps (kilobits per second) modem. The modem can receive information at a maximum rate of about 57,600 bits per second. Since each byte consists of eight bits, the modem can receive information at 57,600/8 = 1,800 bytes per second. Since the size of the file holding the image is approximately 54,000 bytes, it takes 54,000/1,800 = 7.5 seconds to deliver the image to the browser. Notice that we're ignoring any delay due to Internet traffic. Some, but not all, folks might be willing to wait that long for the image. If several images that size are on the page, the wait becomes unreasonable. One thing to do is to represent the image on the page by a small version called a thumbnail. Another possibility is to reduce the number of colors in the image (this is also called reducing the color depth) so that the image can be represented with fewer bytes. Either version can be made into a hyperlink to the full image. This gives readers access to the image in all its glory, but doesn't necessarily delay viewing the entire Web page.

Use proper grammar and spelling.

You want your page to be effective and well-received. Grammatical or spelling errors don't give a good impression of you and can turn off a reader pretty quickly.

Use proper spacing and emphasis.

Let the spacing reflect the organization of the text and content of the Web page. If the page has several distinct sections, separate them with a shaded bar (**<hr>**) or blank spaces. Use bold or italic fonts appropriately. Section headings should be emphasized as well as important subsections or words. On the other hand, don't overdo the use of spacing, shaded bars, and emphasized text. Just because something can be done doesn't mean it has to be done.

Include an email address for comments, the name of the author/designer/producer of the Web page, the URL for the page, and the date that the Web page was last modified.

These items are usually placed at the end of the Web page. The email address is there in case someone reading the page has a question or suggestions about the Web page or its content. You can use the mailto: URL to give the email address a hyperlink; clicking on it will bring up a window to create an email message. Web pages should contain the name(s) of the person(s) responsible for developing the Web page. It gives credit and responsibility where they are due. The URL for the page is included so that someone reading it will know how to reach it on the Web in case the page is printed or reproduced in some other manner. Knowing when something was changed last is helpful for readers to keep track of the most recent version of a document, and it also gives an indication of the content's timeliness.

☑ F Y I   **Web Design Style Guides**

☑ "Art and the Zen of Web Sites," http://tlc-systems.com/webtips.shtml

☑ "Elements of Web Design," http://builder.cnet.com/webbuilding/pages/Graphics/Design/index.html

☑ "Yale Style Manual," http://info.med.yale.edu/caim/manual/index.html

---

Rather than creating long documents, create a collection of shorter ones with a table of contents.

The difficulty with long documents is that they can take a long time to transfer before they can be viewed. In addition, it's more time consuming to scroll or sift through pages of text to find the information you are looking for. It's generally better to divide a long Web page into several smaller ones and provide a contents page, making the items in the table of contents hyperlinks to the appropriate sections.

Think about what you're going to write, and think about the layout before writing the HTML.

There's no substitute for planning and design. Take the time to think about what you want to do and how you can do it.

Evaluating the Quality of a Web Page or Web Site

You've seen and worked with quite a few Web pages and Web sites by now, and you probably have a good idea of what makes some sites more effective or more valuable than others. Here, we'll consider some criteria for evaluating the quality of a Web page and a Web site.

☑ **Content:** The content of a Web page or Web site needs to be accurate, focused, and appropriate with correct grammar and spelling. It should address the topic of the page or site at the appropriate level of depth, and it should be interesting or valuable to the reader.

☑ **Design:** The design of a Web page in this context deals with the appearance and presentation of the material. The design should be attractive in a way that enhances or explains the topic—never distracting. The colors and images should be appropriate and chosen so they complement the topic and each other. The same holds true for using animations or other media.

- ☑ **Accessibility:** Accessibility refers to the availability of the Web page and its components. The page should load quickly, all the hyperlinks should be valid, and it should be compatible with the major Web browsers. Use ALT tags with images or other nontext items.

- ☑ **Navigation:** Here, we're referring to the capabilities for getting around a single page if it doesn't normally fit within a window and moving through a collection of pages that make up a Web site. A single page

---

ON CD

The CD that accompanies this book includes a checklist for evaluating a Web page.

To view it, click on the hyperlink "Web Page Evaluation Checklist" in the collection of items for Chapter 9.

---

that doesn't fit in a window should contain links to other parts of the page. Likewise, a page that's part of a Web site should have clearly identifiable links to other pages in the Web site. Furthermore, the navigation between pages should be clear and should follow a pattern that's easy to determine.

Beyond HTML

Other popular technologies can be used to create and enhance Web pages. We'll give a brief description of some of them here. For more details about these topics, take a look at what's available on the CD in the items for Chapter 9.

XHTML

People who have given careful thought to HTML (including its inventor) have realized a number of its limitations. One such limitation is the fact that it can't be extended so that a browser will recognize new tags. In addition, HTML doesn't contain any tags that refer to the mean-

---

ON CD

The CD that accompanies this book includes more details about the technologies listed in this section.

To read about them, click on the hyperlink "Beyond HTML" in the collection of items for Chapter 9.

---

ing of a document. A standard called XML, extensible markup language, has been proposed to help with these limitations. XML is a meta language, meaning that it can be used to define other languages. *XHTML* is the XML definition of HTML.

JavaScript

JavaScript is a programming language used exclusively within Web pages. The statements in the language are included as part of a source file to enable certain interactive features, such as an action in response to a mouse movement and input to a form. The JavaScript source is part of the source for a Web page, so it's sent from a Web server to a client. The client or local computer executes all of the statements. JavaScript is not based on or part of Java. Examples of the use of JavaScript include changing an image on a Web page if the mouse pointer is moved over a certain region of the page and verifying input that is typed into a form.

Java

The programming language *Java* was originally designed to be used for the development of applications in networked devices. It has been used very successfully to make small applications available through Web pages in a platform-independent format as bytecodes. The small applications are called "applets," and they are passed from a Web server to a client and then executed or run on the client. This is an effective way to send a program and include an executing program as part of a Web page. For example, an applet may be used to represent an analog clock as part of a Web page.

CGI

CGI stands for ***Common Gateway Interface***. It is a specification for transferring information between programs that execute on a Web server and the server software itself. One example of how a CGI program operates is that it might take input from the server software, process it, and write the output in the form of a Web page that is then passed to a client by the server. This is typically what happens when you fill in a form on a Web site and submit it to be processed.

Summary

Web pages are text or ASCII files in which HTML, hypertext markup language, has been added to specify the page's format, images to be displayed, hyperlinks, and possibly other elements. A Web browser interprets the HTML in the file, called the source file, and then displays the Web page accordingly. One part of writing Web pages is learning how to use HTML to design and implement appropriate and effective pages.

The source file for a Web page consists of text, URLs, and other elements along with tags or directives written according to the rules of HTML. HTML tags are enclosed between < and >. Some tags occur in pairs with the second being identical to the first, except with a slash added after the < to indicate that it's the matching tag; for example, **<i>** and **</i>** would work together to indicate text to be italicized. Other tags occur as single entities, such as **<hr>**. Tags should be written using lowercase letters, although HTML ignores the case of letters in a tag. With URLs, you have to pay strict attention to the case of the letters. An HTML document should have two parts: a heading and a body. The heading contains the title for the Web page, and the body holds the content—the text and images that will be displayed on the actual Web page. HTML tags can be used for some control over vertical spacing, such as ending lines and starting paragraphs, but otherwise most horizontal and vertical spacing within a source file is ignored. The browser takes care of fitting the page within its own window. HTML tags also can be used to specify up to six levels of headings in a document and can control whether text is displayed in bold, italic, or plain font. Lists—numbered, bulleted, or descriptive—can be specified with HTML tags. HTML is also used to create and specify hyperlinks and to place images within a Web page. The hyperlinks start with a tag of the form **<a href="*URL*">** (where you substitute an actual URL for *URL*), followed by text or a tag for an image, and then terminated with **</a>**. The following:

```
It appears that <a href="http://users.mwc.edu/~ernie/index.html">
Ernest Ackermann</a> is the culprit!
```

would appear on a Web page as

It appears that <u>Ernest Ackermann</u> is the culprit!

From this Web page, clicking on <u>Ernest Ackermann</u> would cause the browser to open the location associated with **http://users.mwc.edu/~ernie/index.html**. Images are put into Web pages using a tag of the form **<img src="*URL*">** where the URL for an image is put in the place of *URL*. The image must be either in GIF or JPEG format to be displayed by a Web browser. Text can be aligned with an image, either at the top, middle, or bottom. Images can be placed to the left or right of text. HTML has many other tags, but we've covered the basic ones in this chapter.

Because a source file is in text format, it can be created with any editor or word-processing program that allows you to save a file in text or ASCII form. No special program is needed to create a Web page, but when you have a lot of pages to create or you have to convert information from another format into a Web document, it's useful to have a program designed to create Web pages. Some are available as shareware, some as freeware, and some must be purchased before using them.

Learning HTML is one part of being able to create interesting and effective Web pages. You also need to be concerned with the content and the layout of the content.

Designing, creating, or writing a Web page is generally very satisfying. You create something and then let people around the world see it. Before making the page available to the world, you can develop it on your computer and view it with your own Web browser. If you need help or want to learn more about creating or authoring Web pages, there are a number of resources and guides available on the Web. What fun!

Selected Terms Discussed in This Chapter

alternate text	personal home page
ASCII	source file
CGI (Common Gateway Interface)	tag
HTML (hypertext markup language)	text file
hyperlinks	Uniform Resource Locator (URL)
Java	Web page
JavaScript	XHTML

Materials on CD for This Chapter

Here is a list of items for this chapter on the CD that accompanies the text:
- ☑ "Writing Web Pages With Tables," An example of using a table to display information on a Web page
- ☑ "HTML Tags," A table of the HTML tags discussed in this chapter
- ☑ "Web Page Evaluation Checklist," A checklist to use for evaluating Web pages
- ☑ "Beyond HTML," A survey of other technologies used to create Web pages including XHTML, Java, JavaScript, and CGI
- ☑ "Activity—Writing Web Pages," The source files and images used in the activity in this chapter

☑ **Exercise1.htm.** The source file necessary to complete Exercise 1 below

☑ All URLs mentioned in this chapter in hypertext format

☑ Selected terms discussed in this chapter with hyperlinks to the glossary

☑ Copies of the review questions in quiz format

Review Questions

True or False?

1. Web pages are text or ASCII files in which HTML is used to specify the format of the Web page.
2. Notepad is a simple text editor.
3. The source file always starts with the tag **<head>** and ends with **</head>**.
4. Each item in an ordered list is marked with a bullet.
5. Each item in an unordered list is marked with a number.

Short Answer—Completion

1. The Web page _____ is what is visible at the very top of the browser window and also in a bookmark or favorites list.
2. The basic HTML tag to use for an image has the form _____.
3. To set the background color for a Web page, you set a(n) _____ in the **<body>** HTML tag.
4. Colors may be designated by name, such as white, blue, etc., or by a six-digit _____ numeral.
5. CGI stands for _____.

Exercises and Projects

1. The file **exercise1.htm** in the collection of materials for Chapter 9 on the CD is the source for a Web page that you are to complete.
   a. View the Web page in your browser, and use Notepad to open the source file.
   b. Use Notepad, as described in the activity in this chapter, or another HTML editor to modify the source file so that the Web page contains an ordered (numbered) list of items that you enjoy under the heading "Things I enjoy."
   c. Modify the source file so that the Web page contains a bulleted list of hyperlinks under the heading "Hyperlinks to selected Web sites."
2. Work with the source files for the activity in this chapter on the CD to create two Web pages that give information about you rather than information about Ernest Ackermann.
   a. Copy the files from the CD to a folder or disk where you can modify the files.
   b. Use Notepad, as described in the activity in this chapter, or another HTML editor to modify the source files.
   c. Replace the picture of Ackermann with another. Try using a picture of yourself or an image that is related to your interests.

3. Think about designing a one-page Web site for a company that bakes and sells chocolate-chip cookies.
   a. What's the purpose of the page? (Be specific.)
   b. Who is the audience?
   c. What should the page contain? (Be specific)
   d. Use Notepad, as described in the activity in this chapter, or another HTML editor to create the page.

4. Using the information in "Writing Web Pages With Tables" on the CD that accompanies this text, modify the page you wrote in Exercise 1 so that it now uses tables.

5. Samantha Bailey writes about information architecture. Read her article "Navigating the Information Architecture Maze," **http://webreview.com/1997/11_14/strategists/ 11_14_97_6.shtml.**
   a. She mentions five shortcuts to use. What are they?
   b. What does she mean by a "content inventory"?
   c. Which of the shortcuts do you think would take the most time to accomplish? Explain.

6. Go to the Web page "Searching and Researching on the Internet and the World Wide Web," **http://webliminal.com/search/index.html**. Evaluate the page using the "Web Page Evaluation Checklist" in the collection of items for Chapter 9 on the CD that accompanies this text.

C H A P T E R   10

Web Publishing: Putting Information on the Web

▶ the growth of the Internet and the Web has increased the opportunities for making information available to a wide audience. This is no accident—the structure of the Internet, the protocols (HTTP, for example), and HTML are all designed so that they may be used by anyone. We can contribute to the Internet and the World Wide Web because the protocols that form the technical basis for the Internet treat all networks as equal. This is different from traditional broadcast media, where there is generally a definite separation between systems that transmit information and those that receive it. Participation and involvement have always been important parts of the culture and social aspects of the Internet.

It's common nowadays to have a Web site. Organizations, businesses, and schools have Web sites. There are Web sites for individuals, clubs, products, movies, and political parties. A large number of sites deal with scientific and other scholarly research, technical subjects, and health issues. And some sites are part of the Web just for fun!

The Web is becoming one of the preferred means of distributing information and conducting business. If you haven't done so already, is very likely that you will create a Web page or site for a personal or business reason in the near future. In any case, your use of the Web—as both a consumer and a producer—will increase in the future.

Goals/Objectives:

- ☑ Understand the concepts associated with putting information on the Web
- ☑ Know the primary issues related to designing a Web page or site
- ☑ Know the steps for acquiring a domain name
- ☑ Know the means and resources to announce and publicize a Web site

Topics:

- ☑ Overview of Concepts Related to Writing and Publishing a Web Page
- ☑ Design Considerations for a Web Page and a Web Site
- ☑ Selecting a Web-hosting Service and Acquiring a Domain Name
- ☑ Transferring Information to a Web Host
- ☑ Publicizing a Web Site

Overview of Concepts Related to Writing and Publishing a Web Page

The tremendous increase in the amount of resources on and use of the Internet in recent years is partly due to graphical Web browsers and the ease with which people can make information available as a Web page or Web site. The number of host systems went from approximately two million in 1993 to almost 60 million at the beginning of 2000. There were essentially only a handful of Web pages available in the early part of 1993, and estimates at the time of this writing now put the number of Web pages at over 1 billion, with thousands being added each day.

The protocol for exchanging information on the Web, HTTP, supports hypertext and hypermedia, which make for interesting, intuitive, and useful ways of communicating information. The language used to specify the content on Web pages (HTML) is not difficult to learn and makes it possible to construct attractive, well-designed documents (Web pages).

Here are some essential points about the technical aspects of writing and publishing Web pages. Having a good understanding of what a Web page is and how it's handled by the client and the server will help us when we construct, design, and discuss Web pages.

- ☑ Web pages are files in which **HTML** (hypertext markup language) is used to specify the format of the Web page, images to be displayed, hyperlinks, and sometimes other elements.
- ☑ A Web browser interprets the HTML in the file and displays the Web page. The HTML gives the browser information about how to represent or render the information in the file.
- ☑ To make an HTML file part of the Web and available to anyone on the Internet, the file has to be stored on a computer that acts as a Web server, which means that it's connected to the Internet and running Web server software. The file is then available to anyone on the Internet through its URL, which contains the **Internet domain name** of the computer that hosts the Web server. In many cases, the file is viewed as a Web page by using a Web browser. The Web page that lists Ernest Ackermann's office hours, for example, is in a file named **offhrs.html.** This file is in his home Web directory on a computer with the Internet domain name of **users.mwc.edu.** All of this information is reflected in the URL for the page listing the office hours, **http://users.mwc.edu/~ernie/offhrs.html**.
- ☑ The Web browser acts as a client and sends requests to the Web server for the files that are displayed as Web pages. Several events occur when a Web page is requested. Here are the four primary events:

1. You click on a hyperlink or type a URL in the location field.
2. The browser formulates a request to a Web server. The server is simply software that is running on a computer with the Internet domain name designated in the URL after the first double slash (**//**) and before the first single slash (**/**). For example, if you use the URL **http://www.webliminal.com/search/10steps.html**, then a request for a Web page is sent from your browser to the computer whose Internet domain name is **www.webliminal.com**.
3. The server processes the request. If it's possible, it sends the file that represents the Web page that you requested to the browser.
4. The browser interprets the contents of the file and displays the Web page.

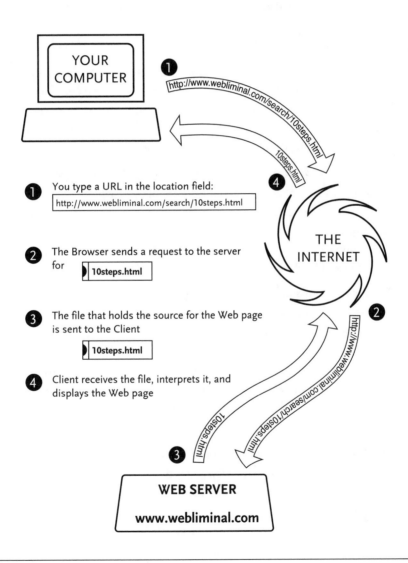

Figure 10.1   How Servers and Clients Work with Each Other

You can see, then, that to make a Web page available on the Web, you have to put the source on a computer system that is a Web server. Furthermore, the ***source file*** has to be in a folder or directory that the server can access when the page is requested. Your school, organization, or company may provide the file space and Web server. If you want or need the information hosted somewhere else, then you might want to think about acquiring your own domain name. Whether you have your own domain name or not, you'll still have to make arrangements for the domain and possibly your Web pages to be hosted on a computer system with an Internet connection.

Getting a domain name and getting files hosted at a Web server is important, but the design and content of your Web pages or site is more crucial. Before we go into the details of establishing a domain name and getting your files hosted, we're going to focus on some Web design issues. We mentioned some design issues in Chapter 9, but we'll go into more detail here.

Design Considerations for a Web Page and a Web Site

There's no substitute for planning and design. Take the time to think about what you want to do and how you can accomplish it. Virtually everyone who writes about Web page design stresses the importance of developing and including good content. Some people may be attracted by a flashy Web page, but they're not likely to come back unless the page has the content they need. We'll look at several design considerations here.

Develop a clear statement of the purpose of the Web page or Web site.

What do you want to accomplish through your Web page? Do you want to write a personal Web page, provide information about a certain topic, describe a concept or process, serve as a gateway to other information, sell a product, or advocate a cause? These aren't the only things you might want to accomplish. What's important is that you spend some time coming up with the purpose and objective of your Web page.

Identify your audience.

Identifying the audience helps you to develop the proper content and design. Do you expect the page or topic to appeal to people in a specific age group? Will the readers likely be experienced Internet or computer users? Can you make any assumptions about the type of network or computer equipment your readers will have? These are just some of the questions you'll need to consider. For example, suppose the topic is international trade agreements. If the target audience is people in the banking industry, then the Web page or Web site will probably be markedly different from a site designed for high school students.

Take a look at other sites or pages that have a similar purpose.

See what others have done for Web pages that have a purpose similar to yours. Make a note of appealing style elements and useful features. Here's a list of some Web sites arranged by their purpose.

Purpose	Title	URL
Personal home page	"Welcome to Karen Hartman's home page"	http://users.mwc.edu/~khartman/
Explain a topic or concept	"The Trail You Leave On the Web"	http://webliminal.com/trail.html
Explain a process	"Basic Search Strategy: The Ten Steps"	http://webliminal.com/search /10steps.htm
Serve as a gateway to other information	"Authoring Resources and Information"	http://www.webreference.com/ authoring
Provide information about a topic	"Directories and Virtual Libraries"	http://webliminal.com/search /search-web04.html
Sell a product	"Amazon.com"	http://www.amazon.com
Advocate a cause	"Support Our Effort to Stop Spam!"	http://www.cauce.org/join.shtml
Act as a portal	"My Excite"	http://www.excite.com

Identify the material you will use to accomplish your purpose.

Focus on the content you'll be providing on the Web page or Web site. Develop an outline for the Web page. Think about the major topics, images, or hyperlinks you'll include. Then develop each of these with enough detail so that they can be fleshed out after making final design decisions.

Establish the layout or format of the Web page. Adopt a uniform and appropriate style for a single Web page that can be used for all the pages in the site.

Think about the structure of the Web page. If the page can't be displayed in one window, you'll want to give important information a prominent position at the top of the page, and you'll probably want to provide a table of contents or links to other parts of the document or other pages in your site. See, for example, the Web page "Internet Today! Finding Information," **http://webliminal.com/internet-today/it-chap04.html**.

Include an email address for comments, the name of the author/designer/producer, the URL for the page, and the date that the Web page was last modified. These items are usually placed at the bottom of the Web page. The email address is there in case someone reading the page has a question or suggestion about the Web page or its content. Web pages should contain the name(s) of the person(s) responsible for developing the Web page. This gives credit and responsibility where they are due. The URL for the page is included so that if someone is reading it from a printout or other type of reproduction, she or he will know how to find it on the Web. Knowing when something was changed last is helpful for readers to keep track of the most recent version of a document, and it also gives an indication of the timeliness of the content of the Web page.

Consider drawing a design or diagram that shows the layout of the pages. Figure 10.2 shows two possible layout schemes. In any case, keep the design simple. It will be easier for you to create, and it will be easier for your readers to deal with.

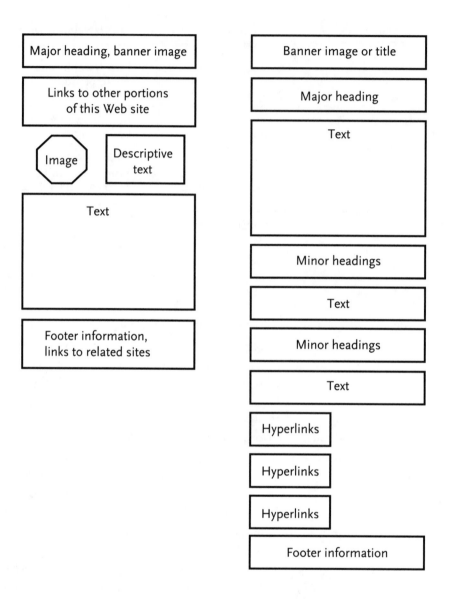

Figure 10.2   Page Layouts for Text and Images on a Web Page

Go over all the previous items, consider the points we raised about design in Chapter 9, think more about your purpose, and improve your design.

The design process goes on and on. The initial design could be implemented as a Web page that can be viewed as a file on one computer system or perhaps set up on a local network so that a team of people can review it. Use the opportunities you have to revise and improve the design. Eventually, a version will be placed on the Web, but there is still chance for revision. Some people put icons or images on their pages that state the page is "under construction." The truth is that most pages are often modified regularly and even adopt new designs over time. Plan to revise and reevaluate your work.

Web Site Design Considerations

A Web site is a collection of Web pages that have a common theme or purpose. For example, most organizations have Web sites that provide information about the organization. The Web site for a college or university will usually consist of a collection of Web sites, one for the institution with links to the Web sites for individual departments and offices.

In some cases, it's best to take a long document and divide it into several smaller documents with ways to move between them.

When people visit your Web site, you'll want them to be able to navigate through the site—get from one page to another—in an easy and logical manner. You'll also want the pages in the site to have a similar format or design so that visitors will recognize a common theme, creating a sense of place. It's also important to have a sound information architecture, which is the arrangement of information on your Web site. With this in mind, we can add these things to consider when you're putting together a Web site:

☑ Adopt a uniform format or style for the pages that make up the Web site.

☑ Make it easy for visitors to find the information that you want them to access.

☑ Provide each page with some navigational tools to help visitors go through the Web site.

Web pages that make up a Web site can be connected in several ways. It's important to plan the arrangement of pages so that it accomplishes the purpose you've set for the Web site, while meeting your visitor's needs.

Now we'll look at how to get a domain name and select a Web-hosting service.

☑ F Y I   **Information Architecture**

The arrangement and accessibility of information at your Web site is very important to visitors. Information architecture deals with the structure of information in a usable form.

☑ "Web Architect," http://webreview.com/1998/08_14/

☑ "Information Architecture Tutorial," http://hotwired.lycos.com/webmonkey/design/tutorials/tutorial1.html

ON CD

The CD that accompanies this book includes some typical arrangements of Web sites.

To view them, click on the hyperlink "Web Page Site Structures" in the collection of items for Chapter 10.

Selecting a Web-hosting Service and Acquiring a Domain Name

To make your Web pages available to everyone else on the Internet, the Web page and all supporting files have to be placed on a computer that acts as a **Web server**. That computer runs the software and has the Internet connection, allowing information on it to be retrieved through a URL that starts with **http://**. Most Internet service providers offer this service to their customers at no charge. If your organization, school, or company has a Web server, check to see what specific procedures and policies you need to follow to make your Web page available on the Web.

There are a number of "free" ***Web-hosting services***. These providers generally allow you to put files on their servers in exchange for an advertisement that they display each time someone views one of your Web pages. People tend to use these services for putting personal information on the Web such as a personal home page or resume, for listing resources about an interest or hobby, or for a local club. These services aren't appropriate for commercial or nonprofit organizations that need to establish their own Web presence and publish their own message without unrelated advertisements. Also, these free services generally won't host your information with your individual domain name. Two popular free Web-hosting services are Angelfire, **http://angelfire.lycos.com**, and Geocities, **http://geocities.yahoo.com/home.** The Open Directory has a long list of these types of services available in the category "Computers: Internet: Web Design and Development: Hosting: Free: Personal," **http://dmoz.org/Computers/Internet/Web_Design_and_Development/Hosting/Free/Personal.**

You may want to acquire a domain name and make arrangements to have the site hosted by a commercial hosting service. This would be the best approach if you were planning to set up a commercial Web site or one for an organization. Having the site hosted by a firm that specializes in providing a Web presence for companies and organizations is usually more economical than supplying and maintaining the network connections, computer systems, and associated staff.

You'll need to select and register a domain name for your site, such as **mycompany.com**. There can't be two domains on the Internet with the same name, so you may not be able to get your first choice. You need to exercise some care in choosing a name. It should reflect the purpose of your Web site—for example, the name of your business or organization—and it shouldn't be difficult for people to type in or remember. The Web site "DomainSurfer," **http://domainsurfer.com,** has a searchable database of domain names. You can use this site to see what names are already taken.

☑ F Y I   **Selecting a Web-hosting Service**

☑ "How to Choose a Web Host," http://thesitewizard.com/archive/findhost.shtml

☑ "Web Design and Development: Hosting" http://dmoz.org/Computers/Internet/Web_Design_and_Development/Hosting/

☑ F Y I   **Choosing and Registering a Domain Name**

Here are some articles about choosing and registering a domain name.

☑ "Choose and Register a Domain Name," http://hotwired.lycos.com/webmonkey/00/25/index1a.html

☑ "Tips on Choosing a Domain Name," http://thesitewizard.com/archive/domainname.shtml

Once you've chosen a domain name, you'll have to register it. The Internet Corporation for Assigned Names and Numbers (ICANN) is the nonprofit organization that oversees the registration and assignment of domain names. You can register your domain name through any of the ICANN-accredited registrars. These are companies that handle the process of domain name registration. A list is available at "ICANN | gTLD Registrar List," **http://www.icann.org/ registrars/accredited-list.html**. At the time of this writing, several dozen accredited registrars are in existence. You must pay a yearly fee for registration, and you have to register a domain name for at least two years. The costs vary among the different registrars from just under $10 to a maximum of $35 per domain name. When you register a domain name, you have to specify a host where the domain name will be located. Some registrars offer the service of "parking" a domain name. This means that the domain will be listed as residing at one of their hosts. This "parking" doesn't include the actual hosting fees, but it's a way to get started until you've decided where your site will be hosted.

You'll also need to choose a service, or company, to host your Web site. A Web-hosting company provides you with space to hold the files associated with your Web site and possibly some other services. These other services might include the use of a counter on your Web pages or software that enables visitors to fill out a form and send information to you. If you're using the site for business, you might want to find a Web-hosting company that also provides the software and tools to enable online ordering. This is usually called a *shopping cart*. Most Web-hosting services will handle the registration process for you at no charge, but you will still have to pay the yearly registration charges mentioned above. Fees for hosting a Web site range from about $10 per month to a few hundred dollars per month depending on the types of services you want to provide, the amount of disk space you'll need for your site, and other factors. Some providers base their fee on the amount of traffic measured in the amount of bytes transferred per month. You should choose a Web presence provider that has the services you need at a price you can afford. Ask about the support services offered for developing Web pages. You also should consider the provider's reputation, its past service record, and the type and speed of connection it has to the Internet.

Naming Source Files

Check with the people in charge of the Web server to see if there are any special rules you have to follow when you name your source files. You will want to know what extension(s), such as **.htm** or **.html**, you should use for file names. You'll also want to know whether the server distinguishes between upper- and lowercase letters in a file name.

The file names you choose will be part of the URL that someone might have to type. Make it as easy as possible for them. Use relatively short but meaningful names without spaces or other punctuation.

When you have a domain name registered and signed up with a Web-hosting service, you're ready to transfer the information associated with your Web site to a system that will serve as the Web host.

Transferring Information to a Web Host

When you have made arrangements and checked the policies for putting information on the Web, you are ready to move the file or files from your computer to the computer that will be the Web server. You'll need to check with your Web-hosting service to know the exact procedures to follow.

If your organization has a campuswide or companywide network, your files will probably have to be placed in a specific folder or directory that is accessible from your computer.

If you're using software that allows you to design and manage your Web site, such as *Front Page* or *Dreamweaver*, then you'll have to know the structure of your Web site on the remote server and set up a corresponding copy on the computer you use to design and write your Web pages.

In other situations, you'll use FTP (File Transfer Protocol), which we discussed in Chapter 8.

In any case, it's important for you to know the following:

- ☑ The location on your computer of the source files for your Web page(s) so that you'll be able to give the appropriate commands by clicking on icons or selecting items from a menu that will transfer the files to and from the Web server
- ☑ Where to place the files on the Web server
- ☑ What rules you have to follow for naming your source files

Publicizing a Web Site

Once you put your page on a Web server, you're a (Web) published author! There are a number of ways to publicize your Web page. You can submit the URL to several search engines and directories, announce it on certain Usenet newsgroups, or submit the URL and a description to Web sites that announce new Web pages or sites. Here are some other alternatives:

- ☑ Pay for advertising on other Web sites.
- ☑ Join a free banner exchange program. You make up an image with a hyperlink to your Web page that can be displayed on other members' Web

ON CD

The CD that accompanies this book includes an example that shows how to transfer a Web page from a computer to a Web server using FTP and Netscape Navigator. We used Netscape Navigator because it includes the utilities and features that make it relatively easy to upload a file.

To view it, click on "Transferring the Source File for a Web Page" in the collection of items for Chapter 10.

☑ F Y I **Getting Your Web Site Noticed**

- ☑ "Search Engine Submission Tips" http://searchenginewatch.com/webmasters/index.html
- ☑ "Search Engine Placement Tips, Techniques and Help in Ten Steps," http://infoscavenger.com/engine.htm
- ☑ "Promotion 101: Web Site Marketing and Promotion Info Center," http://www.promotion101.com

sites. In exchange, you agree to display banners from other sites on your page. For more information, see "LinkExchange Banner Network," **http://adnetwork.bcentral.com**.

- ☑ Join a Web ring. A Web ring is a collection of Web sites covering a specific topic, each with a link to another site that's part of the ring. Several Web rings are set up to include a Web site on any topic. WebRing maintains a directory of Web rings. Give it a look at "WebRing,," **http://dir.webring.com/rw**.

Before you start publicizing your Web site, you will want to do what you can to make it easy for people to find your Web pages by using a search tool. When a search tool searches its database, it returns a list of URLs to Web pages ranked according to some relevancy scheme.

Search tools don't give out the details of the schemes or algorithms they use to rank results. However, they seem to follow some general rules:

- ☑ Words or phrases in the title and headings carry more weight than those in the text
- ☑ The number of times a word or phrase appears increases the relevancy ranking.

As you might guess, commercial organizations have a relatively high stake in getting their sites to appear when someone searches for information on the topic of their Web site. Several sites give detailed information about getting a Web site noticed by a search engine.

You can announce your page by submitting it to several special locations on the World Wide Web: What's New Web pages, Web directories, and search engines. To take advantage of these services, you must submit forms that provide the URL for your page, your name and email address, and some descriptive information about the Web page. Depending on an organization's workload, it can take a service several days or weeks to list your Web page. There's generally no charge to have a Web page listed by these services. When you submit a request to be listed in a direc-

☑ F Y I   **Publicizing a Web Site**

Tips and Lists of Services:

- ☑ "FAQ: How to Announce Your New Web Site," http://ep.com/faq/webannounce.html
- ☑ "How to Publicize Your Web Site Over the Internet," http://samizdat.com/public.html
- ☑ "Free Web Site Promotion Guides and Tools," http://bizmove.com/website_promotion/WebsitePromotion.htm
- ☑ "Web Site Promotion Tutorial," http://apromotionguide.com

Directories:

- ☑ "Open Directory—Web Design and Development: Promotion," http://dmoz.org/Computers/Internet/WWW/Website_Promotion
- ☑ "Yahoo! Site Announcement and Promotion," http://dir.yahoo.com/Computers_and_Internet/Internet/World_Wide_Web/Site_Announcement_and_Promotion

tory, you'll also have to pick the category that you'd like to contain the listing. To choose the appropriate category, find pages on the same or a similar topic within the directory and use that category. You also can submit an announcement of your page to a mailing list and to Usenet newsgroups. Find a newsgroup that deals with the topic of your site and read articles in the group to see if other announcements of new sites are posted to the group. If others are announcing new sites, then post an article announcing your site.

In addition to individual services and sites that can help you with publicity, certain Web pages can help you submit a URL to several services at once. One of these is "Information City: Promote Your Site," **http://FreeReports.net/submit.html**. This site can be used to submit a Web page's URL to several search engines and directories. You can even use it to join a Web ring. A number of services advertised on the Web will even help you market your Web site and submit it to several search engines and directories. These services generally are not free. You can submit your URLs to sites just as well as they can.

Properly announcing your Web page can take some work, but people are going to need some help to find it among the millions on the World Wide Web.

Summary

The Internet and the Web have been designed so that individuals can be both information providers and consumers. The protocols that support the Internet give all networks equal status. Web browsers with graphical interfaces are commonly used, and the means for preparing Web pages are not difficult. This easy access has led to a large amount of information being available in the form of Web pages, and people have come to expect that nearly every organization or business has a Web presence. These factors make it important for you to understand the technical and design issues involved in creating, providing, and evaluating Web pages and Web sites.

The source for a Web page is a plain text file that contains HTML tags. A browser, acting as a client, requests the source for a Web page from a computer that acts as a Web server. When the file is retrieved, the browser displays it in its window. Therefore, to make information available on the Web, it is necessary to place the source on a Web server.

Designing a Web page involves several facets. Most important, you need to identify the purpose of the page. In addition, you should consider the technical aspects of displaying a Web page, your audience, how other Web pages with a similar purpose are set up, your content, and how to create an appropriate design. The Web page should be tested with more than one computer system and browser.

A Web site is a collection of Web pages with a common theme or purpose. When designing a Web site, you need to come up with a scheme for presenting and arranging the information. The presentation should make it clear that the information on each page of the site is related, and the arrangement often should mirror the logical structure of the information.

Putting information on the Web means taking your source files and placing them on a Web server. Some Internet service providers, Web-based services, and organizations provide space for Web pages. If these don't suit your needs, you can pay a monthly fee to a Web-hosting service, which is a company that provides space for and tools to create and maintain a Web site. FTP is often used to transfer a source file to a Web server.

Once a Web page or site is on a Web server, you'll want to make it possible for other people to find it easily. There are several services that will submit the URL to various search engines and directories. It's also possible to advertise your site on the Web either through paid advertisements or so-called link exchanges. Be sure to read tips available on the Web about ways to announce your Web site and to get it noticed.

Selected Terms Discussed in This Chapter

HTML	Web server
Internet domain name	Web-hosting
source file	service

Materials on CD for This Chapter

Here is a list of items for this chapter on the CD that accompanies the text:

- ☑ "Web Page Site Structures," Some typical arrangements of Web sites
- ☑ "Transferring the Source File for a Web Page," An example that shows how to transfer a Web page from a computer to a Web server using FTP and Netscape Navigator. We use Netscape Navigator because it includes the utilities and features that make it relatively easy to upload a file.
- ☑ All URLs mentioned in this chapter in hypertext format
- ☑ Selected terms discussed in this chapter with hyperlinks to the glossary
- ☑ Copies of the review questions in quiz format

Review Questions

True or False?

1. In order to make a Web page available on the Web, you have to put the source of the page on a Web server.
2. It isn't important to include the date a Web page was last modified on the Web page.
3. The browser acts as a client when it requests the source for a Web page from a computer that acts as a Web server.
4. The most important and time-consuming activity in putting information on the Web is finding a Web-hosting service.
5. A Web site is a collection of Web pages with a common theme or purpose.

Short Answer—Completion

1. Free _____ are providers that generally allow you to put files on their servers at no charge in exchange for an advertisement that they display each time someone views one of your Web pages.
2. There cannot be two _____ on the Internet with the same name.
3. A Web _____ interprets the HTML in a file and displays the Web page.
4. Virtually everyone who writes about Web page design stresses the importance of developing good _____.
5. Four elements should be included on every Web page: the _____ of the page, the _____ that the Web page was last modified, the _____ of the author, and an _____ for comments or questions.

Exercises and Projects

1. "Information Architecture Tutorial," **http://hotwired.lycos.com/webmonkey/design/tutorials/tutorial1.html**, by Jon Shiple consists of five lessons.
   a. What are the topics of each of the lessons?
   b. Pick one of the lessons and give a summary of what it contains.

2. Visit the home page for ICANN, **http://www.icann.org**. Using the information on links from that page, answer the following:

   a. What is the purpose of ICANN?

   b. According to the FAQ available at the ICANN site, what does it mean to register a domain name?

   c. Suppose you wanted to register the domain name **redrock.com**. List three places where that could be done.

   d. Suppose I have a dispute with someone else about registering a domain name. How could that be resolved?

3. Suppose you're in charge of finding a home for a Web site for a local charitable, nonprofit organization. The Web site will need between 10 and 20 megabytes of space. The organization would like to be able to use forms to collect information from visitors and prefers that no ads be placed on the Web pages. The organization would like it very much if they didn't have to pay for the service. Fortunately, you know about FreeWebspace.net, **http://freewebspace.net**. Use the facilities at that site to develop a recommendation of at most three servers that would be appropriate for the organization. Write a one-page report explaining why you chose the servers.

4. Suppose you've been selected to serve as webmaster for Way-Cool Music! The company has released five new CDs and has 15 others that it markets. It's up to you to recommend three Web-hosting services to meet the information and e-commerce needs of the company. Some friends recommend that you use the facilities at "HostSearch," **http://hostsearch.com**. Come up with at most three servers and appropriate Web-hosting packages for the company. Write your recommendation as a two-page report.

5. It's your job to be sure that the Web site designed for the company in Exercise 4 is submitted to several search engines.

   a. Visit the Web page "Search Engine Submission Tips," **http://searchenginewatch.com/webmasters/index.html.** Read the entire article and pay special attention to the section "Search Engine Design Tips," **http://searchenginewatch.com/webmasters/tips.html**. Using the tips in that section, write some specific recommendations for the design of the Web site for the company in the exercise above.

   b. The Web site "Promotion 101: Web Site Marketing and Promotion Info Center," **http://promotion101.com**, has a link to a Web page where you can register your site with up to 20 search engines. Is this the same as registering a domain name? Explain.

   c. Why is registering your site with search engines important?

Managing and Using Information from the Internet and the World Wide Web

Once you become adept at searching for and finding relevant information on the Internet, you may next want to learn more about how to manage and use the information you find. Several helpful ways to use Internet information include saving and printing Web pages and frames, emailing Web pages to other people, capturing images and using them in other documents, and downloading data into spreadsheets. Many of the procedures and tips shown in this appendix concern browser functions, while others require an understanding of the different types of files (text, image, or data files) that are on the Internet and how to manipulate them using various kinds of software.

Taking information from the Internet and either sharing it with or distributing it to others requires a familiarity with copyright and intellectual property issues. Much of what you find on the Internet and the World Wide Web can be downloaded and distributed to others easily. Only the owners of the information can grant the right to copy or duplicate it. This is called the copyright. In almost every case, you are required to obtain written permission from the copyright holder before distributing information on the Internet. Most copyright laws include a provision that makes it possible for individuals to copy portions of a document for short-term use for research or academic purposes. This is known as fair use.

Common Types of Files on the Internet and the Web

Information About File Formats

- ☑ "Every File Format in the World," http://www.whatis.com/ff.htm

- ☑ "File Extensions, Formats, and Utilities," http://www.stack.com

Web pages can contain text, images, video, audio, and other types of information. These will be part of the Web page, or the Web page will have hyperlinks to the information. Although information can appear as text, it is sometimes stored in a compressed format (to save space) or other format. In many cases, your browser can display the information—if it's an image or a video, for example—or convert it to sound—if it's an audio file (and if your computer is equipped with a sound card and speakers or earphones). Other types of files will require you to load the appropriate software onto your computer.

Sometimes you can tell a file's type by its name. The letters following the dot (.) at the end of a file name are called the file extension portion of the file name. Files with names that end in **.txt** or **.text**, for example, usually contain only plain, printable characters.

Table A.1 covers some of the more common file formats. For more information about working with different file formats, check the help in the menu bars of your browser.

File Type	File Extension	Specific Format	Description
Text files	.txt .asc	Plain text files	Plain text files contain printable characters, like the ones you see on this page, but without special fonts or typefaces, such as italic or bold. They're also called ASCII (rhymes with "pass key") files. ASCII stands for American Standard Code for Information Interchange, and it is the standard code used to represent characters in digital format in a computer. All browsers can display these files. The files often appear as if they were typed on a typewriter or computer terminal.
	.ps	PostScript files	The PostScript file format was invented by Adobe Systems. The files contain text but usually not in a readable format. The files also contain commands that a printer or display device interprets; the commands pertain to the formatting of different fonts, font sizes, and images in the file.
	.pdf	Portable Document Format	Adobe Systems also invented PDF. These files contain instructions that allow them to be displayed with different fonts, typefaces, colors, and images. You can view these files on your computer if you have Acrobat Reader, which is free from the Adobe Acrobat Web site, **http://adobe.com/prodindex/acrobat.**
	.doc .wpd .rtf	Word-processing files	Files produced by word-processing software contain text along with commands that format the text. Most of these files are in a format that other word-processing software can deal with, usually after being converted from one form to another. They can't be displayed as plain text files, however. Files produced by Microsoft Word usually have names ending with **.doc**, and files produced by WordPerfect have names ending with **.wpd**. RTF stands for Rich Text Format, a format that can be interpreted by several different word-processing programs.
Data files	.xls .wks .wk1	Spreadsheet files	Files produced by spreadsheet programs are in a special nontext format that's interpreted and used by the software. Two major types of files are produced by Microsoft Excel and Lotus 1-2-3. Excel spreadsheet file names end with **.xls**, and Lotus 1-2-3 file names end with **.wks** or **.wk1**. If you see file extensions like this on files you want to use, you'll need a spreadsheet program to display them. The newer versions of Excel and Lotus 1-2-3 can deal with data with any of the file extensions listed.

Image files	.gif	Graphic Interchange Format	Graphic images are stored in files in a variety of formats. As a part of a Web page or on their own, most browsers can display images stored in GIF or JPEG format. Another format, TIFF, can store high-quality images. If your browser cannot display files in TIFF, you'll have to get some other software to display them. These two shareware programs can display images in various formats and can convert them from one format to another: ☑ Lview Pro, **http://www.lview.com** ☑ Paint Shop Pro, **http://www.jasc.com/ psp.html**
	.jpg .jpeg	Joint Photographic Expert Group	
	.tif .tiff	Tagged Image File Format	
Audio files	.au	Next/Sun format	These files contain information in an audio or sound format. With a sound card and speakers, you can play such files on your computer. If you're using Netscape Navigator or Microsoft Internet Explorer, the browser contains the software to deal with all these types. Next/Sun and WAV files tend to be very large and thus may take a long time to retrieve. The RealAudio uses a different technology, called streaming technology, by which sound becomes available as it is being transferred to your computer through the Internet. RealPlayer, a free player for RealAudio files, is available using the URL **http://www.real.com/ player/index.html**. MP3 is a format and a method for compressing audio files. The compression scheme results in files that are less than a tenth of the original size with virtually no loss of sound quality.
	.wav	A standard format for computers using MS Windows	
	.ra .ram	RealAudio format	
	.mp3	MP3 or MPEG-1 Audio Layer3	
Multi-media files	.mpg .mpeg	Moving Picture Expert Group	With these types of files, you can view video and hear accompanying sound. It's similar to viewing a movie or television show. There are several popular formats, including MPEG, QuickTime (created by Apple Computer, Inc.), RealVideo (created by RealNetworks, Inc.), and Shockwave (created by Macromedia, Inc.). Netscape Navigator version 3.0 or later can display files in the the MPEG format. A QuickTime player is available at no cost at **http://quicktime.apple.com/sw**. RealPlayer, a free player for RealVideo files, is available at **http://www.real.com/products/playerdl.html**. A free player for Macromedia Shockwave files is available at **http://www.macromedia.com/ shockwave/download/**.
	.mov .qt	QuickTime	
	.rm .ram	RealVideo	
	.dcr .dir .dxr	Shockwave	
Com-pressed files	.zip .gz	Most com-mon types of com-pressed format files	A file is compressed to save space on a server or to be transferred over the Internet more quickly. There are many types of compressed files, but the most common are those ending with **.zip**. If you retrieve a file in compressed format, you'll need software to uncompress the file. Two popular shareware programs work with these types of files: ☑ PKZIP, **http://www.pkware.com** ☑ WinZip, **http://www.winzip.com** See "A Note About Compressed Files" in the section that follows this table.

Table A.1   File Types and Their Extensions

A Note About Compressed Files

At some point, you are likely to have to deal with compressed files. Many sites on the Web make compressed files available to the public. You may want to retrieve, copy, or download one of these compressed files to your computer. Often these files are packages or collections of related files. The files, or packages, are processed by a compression program, which reduces the total number of bytes necessary to represent the information in the package. Reducing the size of the file means that it takes less time to download the file. Before you can use a compressed file, you must uncompress it, using PKZIP or WinZip, as listed in Table A.1.

Any single file or collection of files can be compressed and transmitted. In the course of writing this book, we used this technology to transfer chapters back and forth between the publisher, editors, and ourselves. Because each chapter has so many images, the files were quite large. To solve this size problem, we put each chapter and the images into a single package and then compressed it using either PKZIP or WinZip. We then attached the files to email messages or sent them using FTP. The people on either end uncompressed the files using PKZIP or WinZip.

To get your own copy of either utility, follow these directions:

To get a copy of PKZIP

Go to the home page for PKWARE, **http://www.pkware.com**. Spend a little time reading about PKZIP, the way it works, and file compression in general. Click on the hyperlink that takes you through the steps of downloading the software. Store the software in a new folder. Once it has finished downloading, there will be a new application (program) in the folder. Click on it and follow the instructions. It will install itself in a directory or folder. Once it's installed, go to that directory, using Windows Explorer. Read the file named **Readme**, which contains information about the files you've installed. The program's name is PKZIP; click on it when you need to use it.

To get a copy of WinZip

Go to the home page for WinZip with the URL **http://www.winzip.com**. Spend a little time reading about WinZip, how it works, and about file compression. Click on the hyperlink that takes you through the steps of downloading the software. Store the software in a new folder. Once it's finished downloading, there will be a new application (program) in the folder. Click on it, and it will lead you through the steps of installing the program in a folder on your computer. The name of the program is WinZip; click on it when you need it.

Capturing and Using Text, Images, and Data from the Web and the Internet

There are several browser options for retrieving material from the Web. The following section will provide brief step-by-step instructions on how to work with the information you find. If the procedures differ between Netscape and Internet Explorer, then the details will be shown for both.

Printing an Entire Web Page

You've found a Web page with information that you need. You can print it out if you want, but before you print the page in its entirety, you might want to find out how many pages it contains. You can do this by accessing Print Preview, which is located in the File menu, as shown in Figure A.1. Without checking on the total number of pages first, you might print out more than you actually need.

In Netscape, do the following:

Netscape

1. After determining that you want the entire Web page printed, simply click on **File** in the menu bar and select **Print**.
2. When the Print menu pops up, click on **OK**.

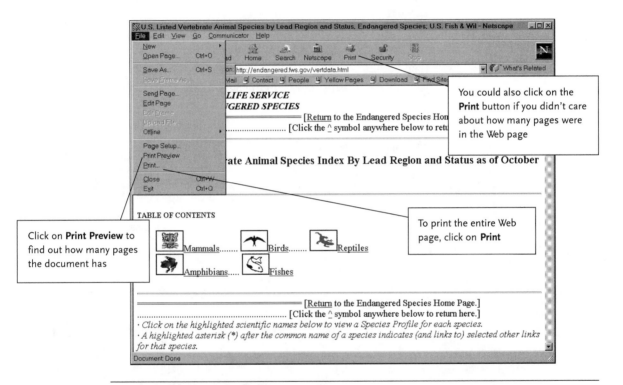

Figure A.1   How to Print an Entire Web Page

In Internet Explorer, do the following:

Internet Explorer doesn't have the Print Preview option, so it is impossible to find out how many printed pages the Web page will produce.

Internet Explorer

1. Click on **File** and select **Print**.
2. When the Print menu pops up, click on **OK**.

Saving the Text of a Web Page

You have found a valuable resource on the Web, and you'd like to read the information later, but you're not connected to a printer. You can download the page to a diskette in the A: drive or to another drive on your computer. Remember that when you download a Web page, you'll be obtaining the text only, and not any images that may be in the page. Images must be captured separately.

In Netscape, do the following:

Netscape

1. While viewing the desired Web page, click on **File**.
2. Choose **Save As** from the pull-down menu.
3. Click on the down arrow next to the **Save in** field, and choose the appropriate drive and/or folder in which to place the Web page. In Figure A.2, we chose the A: drive.
4. If you are saving to the A: drive, put a diskette in the drive before saving.
5. You can rename the file if you want by typing a name in the **File name** field.
6. Choose **Plain Text (*.txt)** from the **Save as type** pull-down menu.
7. Click on **Save**.

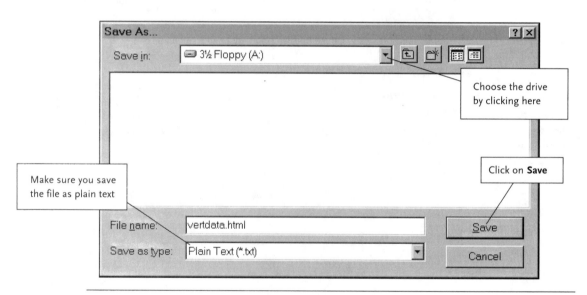

Figure A.2   Saving a Web Page to the A: Drive

In Internet Explorer, do the following:

Internet
Explorer

1. Click on **File** and select **Save As**.
2. Choose which drive you want the file to be saved in.
3. Choose **Text file (*.txt)** from the pull-down menu next to **Save as type**.
4. Click on **Save**.

Printing Part of a Web Site

You have found useful information that exists on a couple of pages of a much larger Web site. You can print just one section of a Web site if you'd like.

In Netscape, do the following:

Netscape

1. While you are viewing the Web page, click on **File**.
2. Select **Print Preview**.
3. Note the page numbers in the bottom-left corner of each page.
4. Click on **Next Page** until you come to the page(s) you want to print.
5. When you come to the page(s) you want to print, click on **Print,** as shown in Figure A.3.
6. After the Print menu appears, click on the radio button next to **Pages** and type the page number(s) that you need to print.
7. Click on **OK**.
8. When you're finished with Print Preview, click on **Close**.

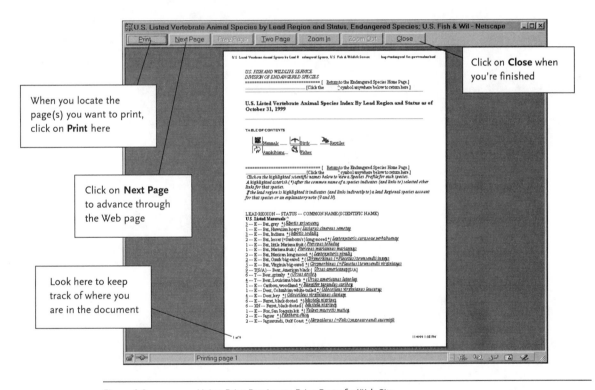

Figure A.3   Using Print Preview to Print Part of a Web Site

In Internet Explorer, do the following:

Internet
Explorer

1. Use the left mouse button to highlight the section of text that you want to print.
2. Click on **File** and then select **Print.**
3. In the Print menu, click on the radio button next to **Selection,** as shown in Figure A.4.
4. Click on **OK.**

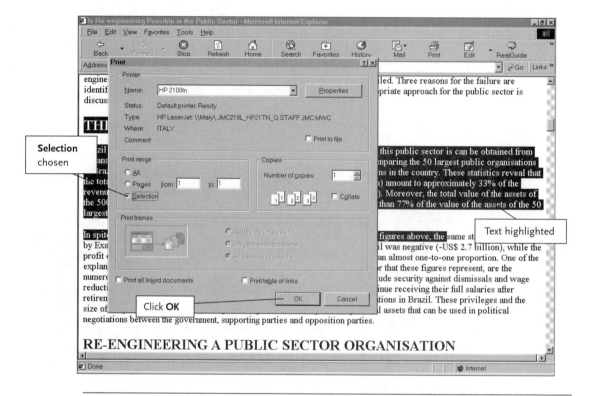

Figure A.4   Printing Part of a Web Site in Internet Explorer

Saving Part of a Web Page

Here are a few examples of when you would save part of a Web page onto your computer instead of printing it:

☑ You aren't attached to a printer, and you want to have the information that you found accessible at a later time, but you don't want the entire page saved.

☑ You want to save less than one page—for example, a paragraph or a table.

☑ You want to have the information in electronic form.

Remember, if you download the text from a Web page and plan to use the information you located in a paper or presentation, you must cite the information properly.

The following are the simple steps for saving parts of a Web page:

1. Highlight the part of the Web page you want to save by holding down the left mouse button and dragging the cursor across the text that you want. When you have reached the last line, release the mouse button.

2. Click on **Edit** in the menu bar and select **Copy.**

3. Open the word-processing program that you intend to use and create a new document.

4. Click on **Edit** in the menu bar and select **Paste**.

Note: If you are using a computer that doesn't have word-processing software installed, you can use Notepad, which is available in Windows. Notepad is located in the **Accessories** folder under **Programs**. You can copy the part of the Web page that you want into Notepad and then save the file (click on **File** and select **Save As**) to a diskette in the A: drive or to your computer.

Capturing Images

When you want to save an image and use it for your own purposes, you should try to notify the person responsible for putting the image on the Web to ask permission to use the image. Sometimes this is impossible, and if you aren't using the image for commercial purposes, it might fall within the realm of "fair use," especially if you want to use it for educational reasons. In any case, it's still a courtesy to try to obtain permission.

The following explains how to save an image:

1. Place your mouse on the image you want to save, and right-click.

2. A menu will appear, as shown in Figure A.5.

3. Choose **Save Image As** (if you're using Internet Explorer, the choice will be **Save Picture As**).

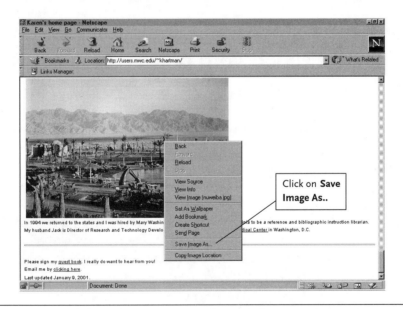

Figure A.5   Saving an Image That You Find on the World Wide Web

4. Next, you'll have to decide where to put the image. You should save it to the drive that's most convenient for you. In this example, we'll save it to a diskette in the A: drive. Click on the arrow next to the field labeled **Save in**. Choose **3½ Floppy (A:)**, as shown in Figure A.6.

5. Click on **Save**.

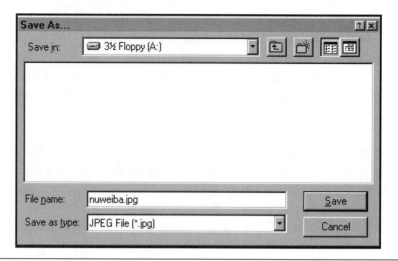

Figure A.6   Saving an Image to the A: Drive

That's all there is to capturing and saving an image. You can now insert it into other documents or programs by following the instructions in the section titled "Procedures and Steps for Managing Internet and Web" Information later in this appendix.

Capturing and Downloading Statistical Tables into a Spreadsheet or Word-processing Document

Statistical tables abound on the Internet, especially in government Web sites. Because government data is in the public domain and free to use as you want, you won't have to ask permission to use it, but you will need to cite it properly so that people know where you got the data. In this example, we'll show you how to download a statistical table that is in worksheet format (**.wk1**) into a spreadsheet program. Using a spreadsheet allows you to perform calculations with the numbers that are in the columns and rows. We'll be using Microsoft Excel, but another spreadsheet program would follow a similar procedure.

Some statistical tables are not in a worksheet format, but they may be in delimited format, which means that the data fields are separated by commas, tabs, semicolons, or some other delimiter. Excel makes it easy for you to download a file that is delimited. Many other statistical tables are in text format. If the data is in text format, you can still download it into a spreadsheet program, but you'll need to change the column sizes to accommodate the data.

Figure A.7 shows a list of statistical information you can download from the *Economic Report of the President*. The URL is **http://w3.access.gpo.gov/usbudget/fy1998/erp_wk1.html**.

1. To download an individual file from the list, hold down the **Shift** key and click with the left mouse button on the file you want. In this example, we'll click on the first one listed, as shown in Figure A.7.

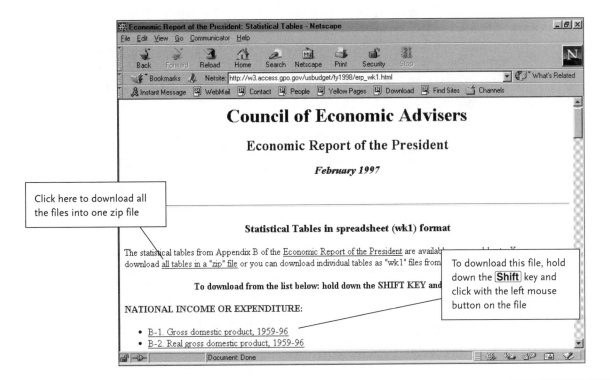

Figure A.7   Economic Report of the President Statistical Tables

2. A dialog box will pop up on the screen, as shown in Figure A.8. You'll need to decide where to save the file. You can choose a folder from the pull-down menu next to **Save in**. In this example, we will put the file directly into the **Excel** folder, which is on the C: drive in the **Msoffice** folder. Note that the file is named **b001**. Click on **Save**.

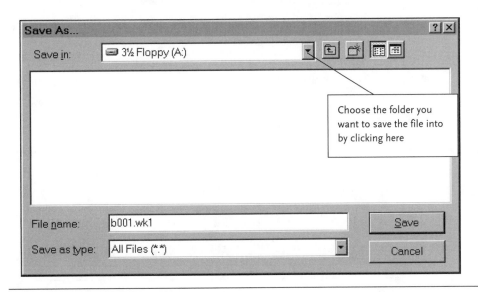

Figure A.8   Saving a Spreadsheet File

Now you need to open the Microsoft Excel spreadsheet program. Click on **Start** and then choose **Programs**. Choose **Microsoft Excel** from the menu. When Excel is open, click on **File** and choose **Open** from the menu. You'll want to look in the **Excel** folder for the file we downloaded. You'll need to choose **All Files** from the pull-down menu next to **Files of type**.

3. You should see the file named **b001.wk1** on the list of files. Click on it, as shown in Figure A.9.

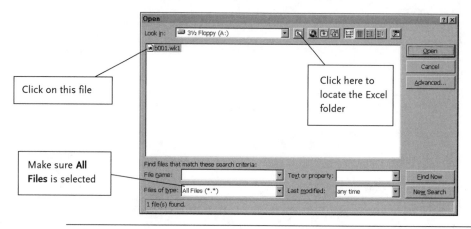

Figure A.9   Opening a File in Excel

The file is automatically placed into a spreadsheet. Because this file was already in worksheet format (**.wk1**), it downloaded directly into the Excel program, as shown in Figure A.10.

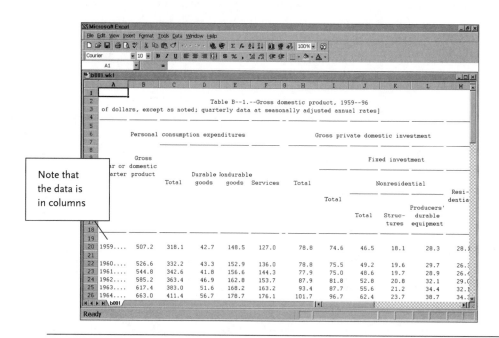

Figure A.10   The File **b001.wk1** as an Excel Spreadsheet

Sometimes you might want to capture statistical data to insert into a word-processing document. To do this, follow these steps:

1. Copy and paste the statistical table like you would copy a portion of any Web page. If the tabular configuration is distorted, you might want to try changing the font to Courier or some other nonproportional font so that the columns don't appear crooked.
2. Save the file as a text file, just as you would save a Web page.

Procedures and Steps for Managing Internet and Web Information

The following chart is a helpful reference to procedures outlined in this appendix and to some others that weren't discussed. (If steps differ between the two browsers, individual instructions are given.)

Procedure		Steps
Saving the text of a Web page (remember to cite the Web page properly if you're incorporating it into your own work)	Netscape	1. Click on **File**. 2. Choose **Save As**. 3. Choose the drive and folder in which to place the Web page. 4. Select **Plain Text (*.txt)** from the pulldown menu. 5. Click on **Save**.
	Internet Explorer	1. Click on **File**. 2. Choose **Save As**. 3. Choose the drive and folder in which to place the Web page. 4. Select **Text File (*.txt)** from the pulldown menu. 5. Click on **Save**.
Saving a portion of a Web page (remember to cite the page properly)		1. Highlight the portion of the Web page you want by holding down the left mouse button and dragging the cursor down the screen. 2. Choose **Edit**, then **Copy**. 3. Open a word-processor or Notepad, which is located under Accessories in Windows 95/98. 4. Choose **Edit**, then **Paste**. 5. The portion of the Web page you highlighted will be placed in the document.
Saving items on a Web page into a file (without viewing them first)	Netscape	1. Move the mouse pointer to the hyperlink and click the right mouse button. 2. Select **Save Link As** from the menu that appears. 3. A **Save As** dialog box will pop up where you can select the drive to save to. 4. Click on **Save**.

Procedure	Steps
	Internet Explorer 1. Move the mouse pointer to the hyperlink and click the right mouse button. 2. Select **Save Target As** from the menu that appears. 3. A **Save As** dialog box will pop up. You'll need to select the drive where you want the link to be copied to. 4. Click on **Save**. Whenever you save a file from the Internet, there's a possibility that the file will contain a computer virus or other software that may damage or erase files. A good source for information about computer viruses is "virus - PC Webopaedia," **http://www.pcwebopedia.com/virus.htm**.
Printing a Web page	1. Click on **File** in the menu bar. 2. Choose **Print**. 3. Click **OK**.
Printing parts of a Web page	**Netscape** 1. Click on **File** in the menu bar. 2. Select **Print Preview**. 3. Click on **Next Page** until you find the page you want to print. 4. Click on **Print**. 5. Select the page number(s) you want printed. 6. Click **OK**. **Internet Explorer** 1. Highlight the portion of the Web page you want to print by holding down the left mouse button and dragging the cursor down the screen. 2. Click on **File** in the menu bar. 3. Select **Print**. 4. In the box labeled **Print range**, choose the **Selection** option. 5. Click **OK**.
Emailing a Web page (emailing a Web page means sending sending the source)	**Netscape** 1. Click on **File** in the menu bar. 2. Select **Send Page**. (If the page you're trying to send is a frame, you'll select **Send Frame**.) 3. Type the email address of the person you are sending the message to in the line next to **To**. 4. To send the Web page text in the body of the email message, click **Quote**. The Web page is automatically made an attachment. 5. Click on **Send**. **Internet Explorer** 1. Click on **File** in the menu bar. 2. Select **Send**. 3. You can choose **Page by email** or **Link by email**. 4. Type the email address of the person you are sending the message to in the line next to **To**. 5. Click on **Send**.

Procedure	Steps
Printing a page that is wider than 8½ inches	1. Click on **File** in the menu bar. 2. Select **Print**. 3. Click on **Properties** in the Print menu. 4. Choose **Landscape**. 5. Click **OK**.
Printing pages with dark backgrounds Netscape	1. Click on **Edit** in the menu bar. 2. Select **Preferences** from the menu. 3. Click on **Colors** in the menu of categories. (It's a subcategory of **Appearance**.) 4. Select a background color. Since you want to be able to print, white would be a good choice. 5. Select a text color. You might want to choose black. 6. Check the box next to **Always use my colors, overriding document**. 7. Click **OK**. 8. Proceed with printing the Web page.
Internet Explorer	1. Click on **Tools** in the menu bar. 2. Select **Internet Options** from the menu. 3. Click on **Colors**. 4. Deselect **Use Windows Colors** by clicking the radio button next to it. 5. Select the background color you want; usually white is a good choice. 6. Click **OK**.
Saving a frame Netscape	1. Click on the frame you want to save. 2. Click on **File**. 3. Choose **Save Frame As**. 4. Select **Plain Text (*.txt)** from the pulldown menu next to **Save as type**. 5. Create a new file name if you want. 6. Click on **Save**.
Internet Explorer	1. Click on the frame you want to save. 2. Click on **File**. 3. Choose **Save As**. 4. Select **Text File (*.txt)** from the pulldown menu. 5. Create a new file name if you want. 6. Click on **Save**.
Printing a frame Netscape	1. Click on the frame you want to print. 2. Click on **File** in the menu bar. 3. Choose **Print Frame**. 4. Click **OK** on the print menu.
Internet Explorer	1. Click on the frame you want to print. 2. Click on **File** in the menu bar. 3. Choose **Print**. 4. Click **OK** on the Print menu.

Procedure	Steps
Using your browser to view local files	**Netscape** 1. Choose **File** from the menu bar. 2. Select **Open Page**. 3. You can type in the file name or click on **Choose File** and search until you find the one you want to view. 4. Click on **Open**. **Internet Explorer** 1. Choose **File** from the menu bar. 2. Select **Open**. 3. You can type the file name or click on **Browse** and search until you find the one you want to view. 4. Click **OK**.
Capturing images (it's a good idea to ask permission before you use an image, and remember to cite it properly)	**Netscape** 1. Right-click on the image. 2. Choose **Save As** from the pop-up menu. 3. Click on **Save** to save the image in the drive and folder listed, or use the other buttons next to the folder names to select another drive and folder. **Internet Explorer** 1. Right-click on the image. 2. Choose **Save Picture As** from the pop-up menu. 3. Click on **Save** to save the image in the drive and folder listed, or use the other buttons next to the folder names to select another drive and folder.
Inserting images into documents (Word documents, Web pages, or PowerPoint presentations)	1. Open the document in which you want to have the image inserted. 2. Make sure your cursor is located where you want the image to be located. 3. Click on **Insert** in the menu bar. 4. Choose **Picture**. 5. Choose **From File**. 6. Locate the drive and folder name that holds the image. (If the image is on a diskette, insert the diskette in the A: drive.) 7. After locating the image file, highlight it and click on **Insert**.

Procedure	Steps
Downloading statistical tables into a spreadsheet	1. If the table is already in a worksheet format, either follow the directions from the Web page or click on **File** and select **Save As**. 2. Choose a folder in which to place the file. You can choose the Excel folder if you like. 3. Open the Microsoft Excel program by clicking on **Start** and then **Programs**. Choose **Microsoft Excel** from the menu. 4. When Excel is open, click on **File** and choose **Open** from the menu. 5. Choose **All Files** from the pulldown menu next to **Files of type**. 6. Click on the file you downloaded. If the file is delimited or in fixed-width format, you'll have to indicate which format. If it is delimited, you'll need to determine which delimiter the file uses: commas, tabs, semicolons, or some other delimiter. Click on **Next** until the spreadsheet is ready to load. If the file is already in a spreadsheet format, it will automatically load into the spreadsheet.
Downloading statistical tables into word-processing documents	1. Highlight the table by holding down the left mouse button and dragging the cursor down the screen until the table is highlighted. 2. Choose **Edit**, then **Copy**. 3. Open a word-processing document or Notepad, which is located under Accessories in Windows. 4. Choose **Edit**, then **Paste**. 5. If the tabular configuration is distorted, change the font to Courier or some other nonproportional font. OR 1. If the table is an entire Web page, click on **File**, choose **Save As**, and place the file in a folder. 2. Select **Plain Text (*.txt)** from the pulldown menu and name it something new. 3. Click on **Save**. 4. Open a word-processing program or Notepad, open the saved text file, and save it using the menu provided. 5. If the tabular configuration is distorted, change the font to Courier or some other nonproportional font.

Table A.2   Procedures and Steps in Netscape and Internet Explorer

Evaluating and Citing Information from the Internet and the World Wide Web

Critical thinking skills have always been important to the process of searching for and using information from media such as books, journals, radio broadcasts, television reports, and so forth. With the advent of the Internet and the World Wide Web, these skills have become even more crucial. Traditional books and journal articles generally need to pass some kind of editorial scrutiny before being published. Web pages, however, can appear without a single person ever reading them to check for accuracy. Libraries have collection development policies that govern what material they will and will not buy; the Internet and the Web have no such policies and collect anything. This isn't to say that there isn't high-quality information on the Internet. There are thousands of high-caliber Web pages and well-regarded databases. It's up to you to decide whether a page or site is worth selecting and then determine, using well-established guidelines, whether the information is worth using in your research paper, project, or presentation.

After you determine that a resource is worthy of inclusion as support for a research paper, it is important that you cite it properly so that others who read your work can refer to it. Citing information is as important for Internet resources as it is for any traditional resource. Readers can view or read the original sources to check for accuracy, to see excerpts or ideas in the context of the original piece, or to obtain more information about the subject being covered. You also will want to cite resources to let people know where they can find the information on the Internet,

☑ F Y I   **Information About Plagiarism**

☑ "Plagiarism: What It Is and How to Recognize and Avoid It," http://www .indiana.edu/~wts/wts /plagiarism.html

☑ "Avoiding Plagiarism," http: //owl.English.purdue .edu/handouts/research /r_plagiary.html

☑ "Avoiding Plagiarism: A Writer's Perspective," http://www.Winthrop .edu/wcenter/wcenter /dontplag.htm

☑ "The Correct Use of Borrowed Information," http://www.Winthrop.edu/ English/WritingProgram/ plagiar.htm

whether you are preparing a formal research paper or sharing information about a resource in an email message to a friend. Properly acknowledging your information sources gives credit to others whose ideas or expressions you have used in your writing. Remember to avoid plagiarizing material from the Internet. It is very easy to copy and paste information from the Web, as you saw in Appendix A. However, if you copy material from a source without using quotation marks and you present the information as your own work, you are committing an unethical act that may result in grave consequences. You also should be careful when paraphrasing an author's work. Use your own words, don't just rearrange the author's words to make it appear as if it is your own writing.

In essence, to avoid plagiarism, you must cite another's work when you incorporate the following into your work:

- ☑ Any theories, ideas, opinions, and interview responses of others.
- ☑ Facts and statistics that aren't common knowledge (Common knowledge refers to facts that can be corroborated by several sources. For example, *Jimmy Carter was elected President of the United States in 1976* is common knowledge, and therefore need not be cited.)
- ☑ Copies of diagrams, charts, pictures, and illustrations.
- ☑ Another's words or ideas from a myriad of sources, including movies, TV programs, books, periodical articles, Web pages, or any other media.

Citing information that helped you formulate your own ideas is a way to make your writing and scholarship stronger and more worthy of others' admiration. It is also a way to show respect for other writers' thoughts and their intellectual property.

Reasons to Evaluate

We use the information we find on the Internet or Web for a variety of purposes. Sometimes we use it for entertainment, recreation, or casual conversation. When we use it for research, to bolster a belief, or to choose a particular course of action, we have to be sure the information is reliable and authoritative. That puts us in the position of having to verify the information and make judgments about its appropriateness.

☑ F Y I   **Web Pages That Focus on Evaluating Web Resources**

- ☑ "Evaluating Information Found on the Internet," http://milton.mse.jhu.edu /research/education /net.html

- ☑ "Evaluating the Documents You Have Found on the World Wide Web," http:// www.curtin.edu.au /curtin/library/staffpages /gwpersonal/senginestudy /zeval.htm

- ☑ "Bibliography on Evaluating Web Information," http:// www.lib.vt.edu/research/ evaluate/evalbiblio.html

- ☑ "Evaluating Quality on the Net," http:// www.hopetillman .com/findqual.html

Reliable information is one of the most important things in life. To make decisions and understand our world, we need the most truthful information that we can find.

The nature of the Internet and the World Wide Web makes it easy for almost anyone to create and disperse information. People also have the freedom to design their pages to advertise products or disseminate propaganda unnoticeable within the context of a research report. To think critically about information and its sources means being able to separate fact from opinion. We have to be able to verify information and know its source, we have to determine whether the facts are current, and we need to know why someone offered the information in the first place. In some situations, we don't have to do all the work ourselves. Some librarians and other information specialists have established virtual libraries on the Web in which the listed sources have been reviewed and evaluated. The following are the major virtual libraries:

Virtual Library	URL
Academic Info: Your Gateway to Quality Educational Resources	http://www.academicinfo.net
Argus Clearinghouse	http://www.clearinghouse.net
INFOMINE	http://infomine.ucr.edu
Internet Public Library	http://www.ipl.org
Librarians' Index to the Internet	http://lii.org
Library Spot	http://libraryspot.com
World Wide Web Virtual Library	http://vlib.org

Table B.1—Virtual libraries

Although these sites can be very useful in helping you find authoritative and reliable information, you still need to decide if the information is appropriate for your purposes. For example, say you are looking for product information before buying a CD player. Product announcements from manufacturers would give you some data, but they would probably not be the best source for impartial brand comparisons. If, however, you are researching techniques for advertising electronic consumer products, the advertisements would probably be good resource material.

Once you find some information, regardless of whether the resource is a book, journal article, Web page, or data from a CD-ROM, a librarian can help you evaluate its usefulness and quality. Librarians, particularly reference librarians, are trained professionals who have lots of experience with evaluating resources. They can tell you within seconds if information is relevant, authoritative, and appropriate for your research needs.

Guidelines for Evaluation

After typing an appropriate search expression in a search tool, scan the results. Open a document, and if it isn't readily apparent why that resource has come up in your hit list, activate the Find operation by clicking on **Edit**, choose **Find in Page** or **Find in Frame**, and type one of your keywords in the search form. Find will take you to the part of the Web page where the word or phrase appears. Sometimes the Find option won't locate the keyword or phrase in the page. This may mean that an earlier version of the page contained the keyword. Your keyword will often be used in a context that is irrelevant to your research needs. Once you've found a page that appears to be fairly applicable to your topic, you can begin to use the guidelines for evaluation. The determination of information quality is not a cut-and-dried process. You can infer quality by clues that will either support or negate your research. Sometimes you need to rely on your intuition or your own previous knowledge about a particular piece of information. With this in mind, realize that the following guidelines are just that—guidelines. They are not meant to be absolute rules for evaluating documents found on the Internet and the Web. They are questions that you should ask yourself when looking at Web pages and other Internet sources.

Who Is the Author or Institution?

☑ If the resource was written by an individual, does it offer or give links to biographical information about the author? For example, does it mention educational or other credentials, an occupation, or an institutional affiliation?

☑ What clues does the URL give you about the source's authority? A tilde (~) in the Web page's URL usually indicates that it is a personal page, rather than part of an institutional Web site. Also, make a mental note of the domain section of the URL, as follows:

.edu	educational (can be anything from serious university research to a student's or faculty member's home page, which vary in reliability)
.gov	governmental (usually contains fairly reliable data)
.com	commercial (may be trying to sell a product)
.net	network (may provide services to commercial or individual customers)
.org	organization (usually created by a nonprofit institution, may be trying to persuade the reader, may be biased)
.mil	United States military sites, agencies, and some academies

Countries other than the United States use two-letter codes as the final part of their domain names. The United States uses **us** in the domain name when designating state and local government hosts, as well as public schools (**k12** is often used).

Who Is the Audience?

☑ Is the Web page intended for the general public, or is it meant for scholars, certain professional practitioners, or children? Is the audience clearly stated?

☑ Does the Web page meet the needs of its stated audience?

Is the Content Accurate, Objective, and Supported by Other Sources?

☑ Are there political, ideological, cultural, religious, or institutional biases?

☑ Is the content intended to be a brief overview of the topic or an in-depth analysis?

☑ If the information is opinion, is this clearly stated?

☑ If there are facts and statistics included, are they properly cited?

☑ Is it clear how the data was collected, and is it presented in a logical, organized way?

☑ Is there a bibliography at the end of the document?

What Is the Purpose of the Information?

- ☑ Is the purpose of the information to inform, explain, persuade, market a product, or advocate a cause?
- ☑ Is the purpose clearly stated?
- ☑ Does the resource fulfill the stated purpose?

How Current Is the Information?

- ☑ Does the Web page have a date that indicates when it was placed on the Web?
- ☑ Is it clear when the page was last updated?
- ☑ Is some of the information obviously out of date?
- ☑ Does the page creator mention how frequently the material is updated?

Discussion and Tips

Who Is the Author or Institution?

If you are not familiar with the author or institution responsible for producing the information, you'll need to do some checking to determine if the source is reliable and authoritative. You can't consider the resource reliable if you don't know who wrote it or what institution published it. A well-designed Web page makes it easy for you to find information about the author, company, institution, or organization that published the page. Usually there is a hyperlink to this information from each major page you access. For example, consider the document "Children's Privacy," **http:// www.cdt.org/privacy/children/ index.html**. When we look at this Web page, we can see that the Center for Democracy and Telecommunications (CDT) has made it available. There are hyperlinks from the "Children's Privacy" page to the home page for CDT. You can follow the hyperlinks to find out more about the CDT, or you can go to the home page by typing the URL **http:// www.cdt.org** into the location field and pressing **Enter**. When you are unable to find your way to a home page or other information, try using a search engine, directory, or some other service to search the Web or Usenet for the information.

Shortening URLs

If a Web page doesn't contain the name of its author or institution and there are no hyperlinks to Web pages that give that information, you can manipulate the URL to try to find it. For example, if you found material at the URL **http://www .ncrel.org/sdrs/areas/ma0bibp .htm**, and you want to quickly find out the name of the publishing body, you could delete the parts of the URL back to the domain section (everything after org/) and press **Enter**. This would give you **http://www.ncrel.org**, the home page for this institution, which happens to be the North Central Regional Educational Laboratory. To find out more about this organization, you could do a search in a search engine by typing in its name as a phrase. You also could go to a proprietary or print source such as *The Encyclopedia of Associations* to get more information. Also, some sites list association Web pages and might include the organization you are looking for. To find information about individual authors, you can search Usenet and discussion group archives, perform a search for the author's name in search engines, search newspaper archives, or access association directories.

Who Is the Audience?

Web pages are sometimes written to give information to a specific group: the general public, researchers and scholars, professionals in a specific field, children, potential customers, or others. By determining the intended audience, you will be better able to decide if the information is relevant and appropriate for your purpose. Suppose you are preparing a report on sustainable forest management. An appropriate information resource, whether in print or on the Web, is one that is written for your level of expertise and for the expertise of your audience. The Web page "Forest Service Mission, Vision, and Guiding Principles," by the United States Department of Agriculture, Forest Service, **http://www.fs.fed.us/intro/mvgp.html**, might be useful for a general overview of the issues and principles involved in forest management. On the other hand, the Web page "Alternatives to Methyl Bromide: Research Needs for California," **http://www.cdpr.ca.gov/docs/dprdocs/methbrom/mb4chg.htm**, is more appropriate for a specialized audience.

Knowing who the intended audience is also can alert you to possible bias. For example, let's say you are looking for information on the anti-acne drug Accutane. You find an in-depth article called "Should Your Teenager Use Accutane?" and learn about both the negatives and positives of this drug, complete with explanations of the possible side effects. By examining the URL and accessing hyperlinks within the document, you find out that the page was published by a well-known pharmaceutical company. Immediately you should realize that the likely intended audience for this page is potential customers. This doesn't mean that you couldn't use the information. But it is important to be aware of bias and hidden persuasion in Web pages.

Is the Content Accurate, Objective, and Supported by Other Sources?

One of the first things to look for in a Web page is spelling errors. Spelling and grammatical errors not only indicate a lack of editorial control but also undermine the accuracy of the information. It is also extremely important that statistics, research findings, and other claims are documented and cited very carefully. Otherwise, the author could be distorting information or using unreliable data. In the best situations, claims or statistics on Web pages are supported by original research or by hyperlinks or footnotes to the primary sources of the information.

Sometimes, however, you will have to verify the accuracy and objectivity of published information on your own. A good way to do this is by checking to see if the information can be corroborated by other sources. Some researchers promote the triangulation process: finding at least three sources that agree with the opinion or findings that the author expounds as fact. If the sources don't agree, you'll need to do more work before you conclude your research. Remember that traditional resources such as books, journal articles, and other material available in libraries may contain more comprehensive information than what is on the Web. You can use those resources as part of the triangulation process as well.

What Is the Purpose of the Information?

When you are evaluating information that you have found on the World Wide Web, on the Internet, or in print, you need to consider its purpose. You need to ask yourself, "Is this page on the Web to persuade, inform, teach, or entertain?" Information on the Web can be produced in a variety of formats and styles, and the appearance sometimes gives a clue to its intent. Web pages aimed to market something are often designed in a clever way to catch our attention and emphasize a product. Some Web pages that were created primarily for marketing a product do not clearly distinguish between the informational content of the page and the advertising. It might appear to be an informational page, but is actually an advertisement.

How Current Is the Information?

You must note when the material you find was created and then decide if it is still useful for your purposes. If you are doing research in an area that is constantly changing, such as business, technology, political science, or medicine, the date is very important. For example, a Web page dated 1995 on the latest techniques in biotechnology should not be relied upon to give state-of-the-art information, because the field is changing so quickly. In other fields, the date may not be so important; for example, a site created in 1995 that covers the U.S. Civil War may be as relevant and useful as one published in 2002. In any case, a Web page should include the date it was created or last modified. Usually this information can be found at the top or bottom of a Web page. If it isn't displayed, you might be able to find the date that the page was last modified on the server. If you are using Netscape Navigator, click on **View** in the menu bar and select **Page Info**. That will sometimes tell you the date of the last modification to the file. While Microsoft Internet Explorer has no similar feature, there are ways to enable the browser to create this information. We will discuss this in detail later in the appendix. Email messages and Usenet news articles usually have the date the message was posted. This information is generally either part of the message or is in the header information.

Citing Internet and Web Information: URL Formats

Unlike a citation for a printed work, a citation for a Web or Internet resource must have information about how to access it. This is often indicated through the work's URL. In addition to telling you where to access a work, a URL serves to retrieve the work. For that reason, we have to be precise about all the symbols in the URL and about capitalization.

There are other differences as well. Works that appear in print, such as books, essays, articles, or songs, have a definite publication date associated with them. Documents on the Web sometimes include information about when they were first created or last revised, but not always. Add to that the fact that authors can revise work on the Web at any time. It might be more important to cite the date on which a work was viewed or retrieved.

Everything on the Web has a URL, indicating where the resource is located and how to access it. We have seen several URLs throughout this text. Here are some examples:

http://www.loc.gov	The home page for the Library of Congress
http://vlib.org/Overview.html	The WWW Virtual Library arranged by subject
http://users.mwc.edu/~khartman/educom98.html	A presentation given at Educom 98 by Karen Hartman and Ernest Ackermann
ftp://ftp.jpl.nasa.gov/pub/images/browse	The NASA Jet Propulsion Laboratory's directory of image files

You'll find it helpful to think of a URL as having the following form:

how-to-get-there://where-to-go/what-to-get

or, in more technical language:

transfer protocol://domain name/directory/subdirectory/file name.file type

For example, take the URL **http://users.mwc.edu/~khartman/educom98.html**.

> **http** is the transfer protocol; **users.mwc.edu** is the domain name (also called the host computer name); **~khartman** is the directory name; **educom98** is the file name; and **html** is its file type.

You probably already know some ways in which URLs are used. For example, all hyperlinks on Web pages are represented as URLs. Entries in bookmark and history files are stored as URLs as well. You type in a URL when you want to direct your browser to go to a specific Web page. When you cite a resource on the World Wide Web, you need to include its URL. You also will want to include the URL when you are telling someone else about a resource, such as in an email message. Here's an example:

```
If you haven't already seen this fabulous page, you must look at it. It's
called "A Business Researcher's Interests" and is hosted by @BRINT. The URL
is: http://www.brint.com. It's one of the best subject guides I've ever used.
```

By including the URL in your message, friends can use their browsers to go directly to the items you mention.

A URL tells you how to retrieve information by providing the name of a Web server and the name of a file or directory where the information is located. From the URL alone, you know which Internet protocol to use when retrieving the information and where it's located. If only a domain or server name is present, as in **http://www.loc.gov**, then a file will still be retrieved. Web servers are configured to pass along a certain file (usually named **index.html** or **index.htm**) when the URL contains only the name of the server or only the name of a directory.

It's important to be precise when you type in a URL because that is all the Web browser has to go on when attempting to access the file you are looking for. You have to be careful about spaces (generally there aren't any blank spaces in URLs), symbols (interchanging a slash and a period won't retrieve appropriate results), and capitalization.

Guidelines for Citing Internet and Web Resources

When looking for the proper way to cite resources in a report or research paper, you must first see if there is a required or accepted citation style. If you are writing a paper for a class, check with your instructor. If you are writing for a periodical or some other publication (either in print or electronic form), see if the editor or publisher has guidelines.

Proper formats for citations from printed sources are very well-established. Three commonly used formats are American Psychological Association (APA) style, Modern Language Association (MLA) style, and the Chicago Manual of Style (from the University of Chicago). Each of these institutions publishes a handbook or guide that explains how to cite information. These organizations have accepted guidelines for citing information from the Internet and the Web.

☑ F Y I   **Web Resources About Citing Information Found on the Internet and the World Wide Web**

☑ "MLA" (choose **MLA Style** for a brief overview), http://www.mla.org/

☑ "APA Style," http://www.apastyle.org/elecref.html

☑ "net.TUTOR: Citing Net Sources," http://gateway.lib.ohio-state.edu/tutor/les7/guide.html

☑ "IPL FARQ: Citing Electronic Resources," http://www.ipl.org/ref/QUE/FARQ/netciteFARQ.html

☑ "ONLINE! Citation Styles," http://www.bedfordstmartins.com/online/citex.html

Difficulties in Citing Web or Internet Resources

☑ Web and Internet resources may be updated or modified at any time.
☑ These resources may not have titles or major headings.
☑ Web pages lack page numbers.
☑ While thoughtful people have been working to expand existing standards, there are some differences of opinion about the format of citations for Web and Internet items.

Differences Between Styles

Some formats include a URL in angle brackets (< >), and others do not. Some advise including the place of publication if the Web resource is a copy of a printed work. Some say to put the date of last revision and to place in parentheses the date on which you accessed the document, whereas others do not make this recommendation. There is, however, considerable agreement on the basic information to be included in a citation of a Web resource.

When you have specific questions about citing Internet and Web sources, check some of the Web resources listed on page 261, and be sure to check with whoever is going to be evaluating or editing your work.

The Dates Are Important

You'll see that the guidelines for citations or references to Web or Internet resources all contain two dates: the date of publication or revision and the date of last access. The reason we need both dates has to do with the nature of digital media as it's made available or published on the Web. Works in print form are different from digital works; printed documents have a tangible, physical form. We all know we can pick up and feel a magazine or journal in our hands, or we can use a book or periodical as a pillow. It's pretty hard to do that with a Web page! This tangible nature of a printed work also gives an edition or revision a permanent nature. It's usually possible to assign a date of publication to a work, and if there are revisions or different editions of a work, it's possible to date and look at the revisions. If a new edition of a printed work exists, that doesn't mean that older editions or versions were destroyed.

The situation is different for Web documents and other items in digital form on the Internet, for several reasons. These documents don't have a tangible form. It's relatively easy for an author to publish a work (the work usually only needs to be in a certain directory on a computer that functions as a Web server). It's easy to modify or revise a work. Furthermore, when a work is revised, the previous version is often replaced by or overwritten with the new version. Because of this last point, the most recent version may be the only one that exists. The version you cited might not exist anymore. It is therefore necessary to include the date that you accessed or read a work listed in a citation or reference. You also might want to keep a copy of the document in a file (save it while browsing) or print a copy of it to provide as documentation if someone questions your sources.

Ways to Find Out When a Page Was Modified

To find the date that a work was last revised, see if the date is mentioned as part of the work. You often will see a line such as **Last modified: Wednesday, Jan. 15, 2002,** in a Web document.

If you don't find this information on the Web page or you want to verify this date, you can do the following:

- ☑ If you are using Netscape Navigator, click on **View** in the menu bar and select **Page Info**. This will tell you the date on which the file was last modified, as well as the document's title. If the page you are citing is a frame, first right-click on the frame, choose **View**, and then select **Frame Info**.
- ☑ If you are using Microsoft Internet Explorer version 5, there's nothing that will bring up the date last modified as Page Info does in Navigator. Selecting **Properties** from the menu you see when you click on **File** in the menu bar only tells you the current date or the date you saved a shortcut to the Web page. There is a tool named Page Freshness available at a Web site called "Bookmarklets," **http://www.bookmarklets.com**. The items at the Web site are small programs written in JavaScript. You can add any of them to your favorites list. Once they're in the favorites list, you can use them by clicking on **Favorites** in the navigation toolbar and then clicking on the bookmarklet in the favorites list. (You can add these to the bookmark list if you're using Navigator and use them in a similar manner.) Follow these steps to obtain and use the Page Freshness bookmarklet:
  1. Type the URL **http://www.bookmarklets.com/tools/frames.phtml#pgfrshfrm** in the address box, and press ⎡Enter⎤.

2. Move the mouse pointer over the hyperlink **Page Freshness**, read its description, and click the right mouse button.

3. Select **Add to Favorites** to add the bookmarklet to the favorites list.

Citation Examples

In this section, we will provide citation examples using established citation formats. The styles that we will be using are MLA and APA. The types of resources we will cite are Web pages, email messages, discussion group messages, Usenet newsgroup messages, and FTP resources. The common elements in citations for different types of resources will be listed, and a citation example for each type of Internet resource will be given in one of the styles. The information provided is general and is not meant to cover every situation. If you have a specific citation question that is not covered here, go to one of the citation guides listed in the FYI on page 272 or visit your library. Librarians are usually willing to assist you in locating and using citation style guides as long as you indicate which style you have been instructed to use.

Web Pages

The major citation styles agree that the following elements should be included in a citation for a Web page:

- ☑ Author's name
- ☑ Document title
- ☑ Title of larger or complete work, if relevant
- ☑ Date of publication or last revision
- ☑ Date page was accessed
- ☑ URL

Citation Examples

MLA Style:

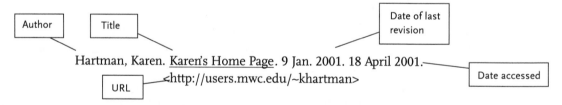

In the citation, note that the URL is placed in angle brackets. This is a feature of MLA style.

APA doesn't require brackets around the URL.

APA Style:

Hartman, K. (2001, January 9). *Karen's home page.* Retrieved April 18, 2001 from http://users.mwc.edu/~khartman.

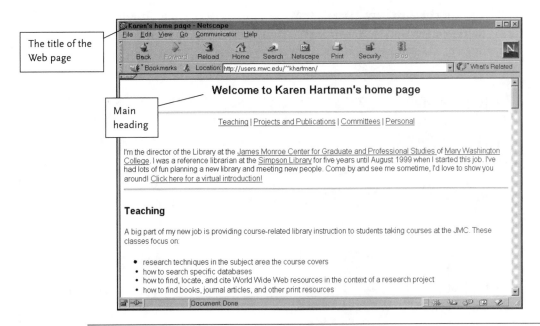

Figure B.1   Determining the Title of a Web Page

We determined the Web page title by using the title found at the top of the browser window.

Citing a Web Page That Is Part of a Larger or Complete Work

Many Web pages are parts of larger works or projects. In each of these cases, you need to not only provide the author and title of the individual document, but also the title of the larger work, its editor (especially when using MLA style), and the institution that sponsors the site (if applicable). In many instances, you'll want to include information about the complete work in order to put the document in its proper context and to credit the institution that has helped to make the work available. This additional information may help the reader find the Web page again if the URL changes. The following shows how you would cite a page that was part of a larger work.

Citation Examples

MLA Style:

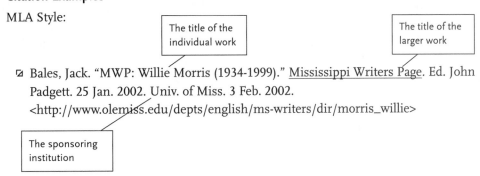

☑ Bales, Jack. "MWP: Willie Morris (1934-1999)." <u>Mississippi Writers Page</u>. Ed. John Padgett. 25 Jan. 2002. Univ. of Miss. 3 Feb. 2002.
 <http://www.olemiss.edu/depts/english/ms-writers/dir/morris_willie>

APA Style:

☑ Bales, J. (2002 January 25). MWP: Willie Morris (1934-1999). In *Mississippi Writers Page*. Retrieved February 3, 2002 from the University of Mississippi Web site: http://www.olemiss.edu/depts./English/ms-writers/dir/morris_willie.

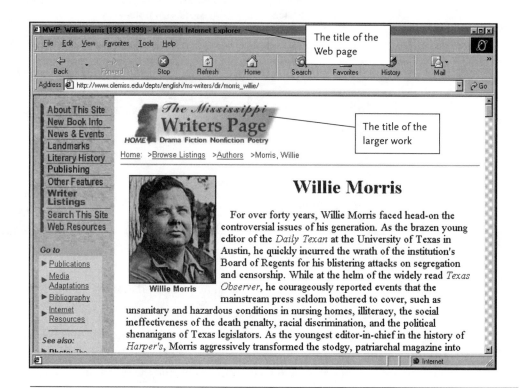

Figure B.2   A Web Page That Is Part of a Larger Work

In this citation, we determined:

☑ The title of the Web page was found at the top of the browser window. Because MWP is uninformative, we could, if we wished, change the title to simply Willie Morris. If we did so, we would be required to place square brackets around the title, indicating that we had changed it. But in this case, we have decided to leave the Web page title as MWP: Willie Morris (1934-1999). The date range indicates the years Mr. Morris lived.

☑ The author of this page was found by scrolling down to the end of the article, as shown in Figure B.3.

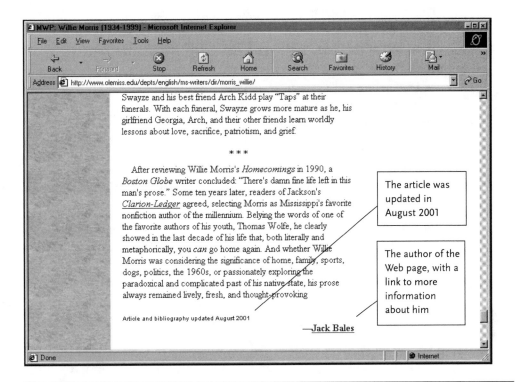

Figure B.3   Finding the Author of the Willie Morris Page

Determining the date of last revision proves to be a bit more difficult. Near the author's name there is a statement that the article was updated in August of 2001, but if we scroll down to the end of the page, the revision date is listed as January 25, 2002, as shown in Figure B.4. This is the date we will use.

The editor of the larger work, *Mississippi Writers Page*, is John Padgett. His name is also found at the end of the Web page, as shown in Figure B.4. Note that MLA requires the editor's name as part of the citation, but APA does not.

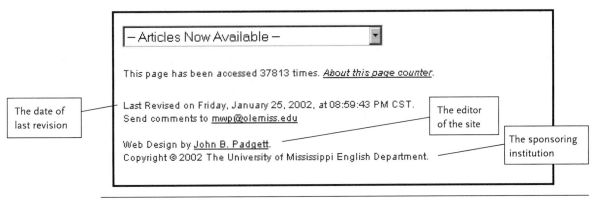

Figure B.4   Important Information Located at the End of the Web Page

Personal Email Messages

The elements required to cite a personal email message are:

- ☑ Author's name
- ☑ Subject of message
- ☑ Date message was sent
- ☑ Description and recipient of message

All of these are usually displayed by the software you use to read email and are available as standard headers in a message.

Citation Examples

MLA Style:

- ☑ Ackermann, Ernest. "Working on Post-Tenure Review." Email to the author. 31 Jan. 2001.

APA Style:

Personal email messages in APA style are cited within the text of a paper only and should not be included in the References section. Within the text of a document, a personal email message may be cited like this:

- ☑ Ernest Ackermann (personal communication, Jan. 31, 2001) stated that the post-tenure review process could be streamlined by using departmental guidelines.

Discussion Group or Listserv Messages

A citation for an email message that was generated in a discussion group or listserv needs to include the discussion group's address. If the message can be retrieved through an archive, the citation needs to include the URL of the Web page that allows access to the archive. The elements usually required to cite discussion group or listserv messages are:

- ☑ Author's name
- ☑ Subject of message or title of posting
- ☑ Date of posting
- ☑ Description of posting
- ☑ URL of discussion group or archive
- ☑ Date of access (MLA only)

Citation Examples

MLA Style:

> Description

Ackermann, Ernest. "Bookmark Files With Netscape 4.0." Online posting. 7 March 2000. Nettrain. 10 Nov. 2000. < http://listserv.buffalo.edu/cgi-bin/wa?S1=nettrain >.

> Access date

APA Style:

> Date of posting

> Subject of message

Ackermann, E. (1999, March 7). Re: Bookmark files with Netscape 4.0. Message posted to Nettrain discussion group, archived at http://listserv.buffalo.edu/cgi-bin/wa?S1=nettrain

Usenet Newsgroup Articles

Usenet news consists of a collection of articles, each part of a specific newsgroup. The articles, as email messages, have headers that give us the information we need for the citation. These are the items to include in the citation of a Usenet article:

- ☑ Author's name
- ☑ Subject of message
- ☑ Name of newsgroup
- ☑ Date message was posted
- ☑ Date of access (MLA only)

Citation Examples

MLA Style:

> Ackermann, Ernest. "Question About Keeping Bay Plant Indoors." Online posting.
> 3 Dec. 2000. 13 Feb. 2001 <news:rec.gardens>.

APA Style:

> Ackermann, E. (2000, December 3). Question about keeping bay plant indoors. Message
> posted to news:rec.gardens.

Electronic Journal Articles

An article in an electronic journal can be cited very much like any other Web resource. If you were citing an article in a journal, it would be reasonable to include the journal name, volume, issue, and date. If you were citing a resource from a printed journal, you would also include page numbers, but that doesn't apply in this case. Some citation styles require a paragraph count instead. The URL gives the location of the article. The citation should contain the following elements:

- ☑ Author's name
- ☑ Title of article
- ☑ Title of journal, volume and issue numbers, date of publication
- ☑ Number of paragraphs if possible (not always necessary)
- ☑ Date of last revision, if known and different from date of publication
- ☑ Date accessed
- ☑ URL

Citation Examples

MLA Style:

> Hartman, Karen, and Ernest Ackermann. "Finding Quality Information on the Internet."
> <u>Syllabus Magazine</u> 13,1 1999. 20 Jan. 2002 <http://www.syllabus.com/syllabusmagazine/
> qualityinfoontheinternet.html>.

APA Style:

> Hartman, K., & Ackermann, E. (1999). Finding Quality Information on the Internet.
> *Syllabus Magazine, 13,1.* Retrieved January 20, 2002 from
> http://www.syllabus.com/syllabusmagazine/qualityinfoontheinternet.html.

Full-text journals that are part of proprietary databases, for example, InfoTrac or Lexis-Nexis, will require more information as part of the citation. When in doubt about how to cite a particular online journal, ask a librarian for help.

FTP Resources

FTP stands for File Transfer Protocol. Before Web browsers came into popular use, FTP was the most popular way to retrieve and send files from one computer to another on the Internet. A citation for a file available by FTP usually contains the following elements:

- ☑ Name of author or institution
- ☑ Title of document
- ☑ Size of document, if relevant
- ☑ Date of last revision
- ☑ URL
- ☑ Date accessed

Citation Examples

MLA Style:

- ☑ American Civil Liberties Union, <u>Briefing Paper Number 5, Drug Testing in the Work Place</u>.
2 Nov. 1992. 3 Oct. 2001. <ftp://ftp.eff.org/pub/Privacy/Medical/ aclu_drug_testing_workplace.faq>

Example of an FTP image file:

> Size of the file

"Mars1.gif" [535K]. 16 Jan 1995. 13 May 1999. <ftp://ftp.jpl.nasa.gov/pub/images/ browse/mars1.gif>.

If there is no obvious title for a file, as in the case of a file that holds an image, you may use the file name as the title of the work or create a descriptive title and enclose it in square brackets.

[Photograph of Mars, 535 K]. 16 Jan. 1995. 13 May 1999. <ftp://ftp.jpl.nasa.gov/pub/ images/browse/mars1.gif>

Note that we have included the size of the file as well.

APA Style:

American Civil Liberties Union. (1992, November 2). *Briefing Paper Number 5, Drug Testing in the Work Place.* Retrieved October 3, 2001 from ftp://ftp.eff.org/pub/Privacy/ Medical/aclu_drug_testing_workplace.faq.
Mars1.gif (1995, January 16). 535K. Photograph of Mars. Retrieved May 13, 1999 from ftp://ftp.jpl.nasa.gov/pub/images/browse/mars1.gif.

Recording Citation Information

When doing research on the Internet, it's smart to record the document information by either printing the resource or making a browser bookmark so that you can return to the resource easily. Bookmarking resources is a good habit to get into. The bookmark saves the Web page title and URL accurately so you don't have to write it down and risk losing it. Even if you share a computer with others, you can save your bookmarks to a file on a disk and import them to your computer later. Netscape Navigator's Bookmark Properties option allows you to describe the bookmark, which is an efficient way to create a bibliography entry.

**How to Create Browser
Bookmarks or Favorites**

Web pages
In Netscape: Click Bookmarks and select Add Bookmark from the Bookmarks menu while the selected Web page is in the browser window.

In Internet Explorer: Click on Favorites and select Add to Favorites while the selected Web page is in the browser window.

Frames
In Netscape: Right-click inside the frame you want to bookmark. Select Add Bookmark from the resulting menu.

In Internet Explorer: Right-click in the frame and select Add to Favorites.

Security and Privacy on the Web

It's easy to get the impression that we're browsing the Web and using Internet services in an anonymous manner. But that's not the case. Every time you visit a Web site, some information about your computer system is transmitted to the server. When you fill out a form, the information you provide is passed to a server. You also need to be aware of the risks involved with giving out personal information through email, chat groups, and forms. Children especially need to be informed of the risks and dangers involved with using the Internet.

Let's look at some issues related to security or the secure transmission of information and privacy when using a Web browser.

Computer and Network Security

When you use a computer system connected to the Internet, you're able to reach a wide variety of sites and information. By the same token, any system connected to the Internet can be reached in some manner by any of the other computer systems connected to the Internet.

Partaking of the material on the Internet also means that you have to be concerned about the security of your computer system and other systems. The reason for the concern about your system is obvious—you probably don't want unauthorized persons accessing your information or information belonging to others who share your system. You can protect your system from malicious or unintentional actions that could destroy stored information or halt your system. You also don't want other people masquerading as you. At the same time, you need to be concerned about the security of other systems so that you can have faith in the information you retrieve from those systems and so that you can conduct business transactions on the Internet. A lack of security can result in damage, theft, and what can be worse in some cases: a lack of confidence or trust.

Maintaining security becomes more important as we use the Internet for commercial transactions or transmitting sensitive data. There is always the chance that new services introduced to the Internet won't be completely tested for security flaws or that security problems will be discovered. While it's exciting to be on the cutting edge, there's some virtue in not adopting the latest service or the latest version of software until it has been around for a while. This gives the Internet community a chance to discover problems. Several agencies are dedicated to finding, publicizing, and dealing with security problems. The U.S. Department of Energy maintains the "CIAC (Computer Incident Advisory Capability) Website," **http://www.ciac.org/ciac/.**

Passwords

When you access the Internet by using a login name, your primary defense against intrusion is your password. You need to choose a password that will be difficult to guess. This means choosing a password that's at least six characters long. You also should use a password that contains upper- and lowercase letters and some nonalphabetic characters. In addition, the password shouldn't represent a word, and it shouldn't be something that's easy to identify with you such as your phone number, room number, birth date, or license number. Some bad choices are Skippy, 3451234a, or gloria4me. Better choices might be All452on, jmr!pmQ7, or sHo=7otg. Naturally, you have to choose something that you'll remember. Never write down your password; doing that makes it easy for others to find.

Firewalls

Because connecting a network to the Internet allows access to that network, making the connection raises concerns with system administrators and others responsible for network security. One device or part of a network that can help enhance security is called a firewall. A firewall can be a separate computer or some other network device that allows only certain packets into a network. (Remember that all information is passed throughout the Internet as packets.) By using a firewall and configuring it correctly, only certain types of Internet services can be allowed through to the network. Organizations with firewalls often place their Web, FTP, and other servers on one part of their network and put a firewall system between those servers and the rest of the network. The firewall restricts access to the protected internal network by letting through only packets associated with certain protocols. If you are on the protected portion of the network, behind the firewall, then you can access Internet and Web sites on the Internet, but they may not be able to gain direct access to you. Firewalls also perform logging and auditing functions so that if security is breached, the source of the problem may be determined.

Viruses

One type of program that causes problems for Internet users is called a virus. A virus doesn't necessarily copy your data or attempt to use your system. However, it can make it difficult or impossible to use your system. A virus is a piece of code or a set of instructions that attaches itself to an exisiting program. Just like a biological virus, a computer virus can't run or exist on its own but must be part of an executing program. When these programs are run, the added instructions are also executed. Sometimes the virus does nothing more than announce its presence; in other cases, the virus erases files from your disk. A virus moves from system to system by being part of an executable program. Be careful where you get programs. You can obtain a program that scans your system for viruses and also checks programs you load onto your system for known viruses. Use these antivirus programs to check any new programs that you load onto your system. Also be sure to have a backup copy of your files so that everything can be restored if is inadvertently or maliciously erased.

Getting documents and images from other sites on the Internet won't bring a virus to your system. Viruses come only from running programs on your system. Viruses can exist in executable programs and also have been found in word-processing documents that contain portions of code called macros.

Security is your responsibility, and being paranoid about it isn't a solution. You need to take appropriate steps to protect the security of your computer, your information, and your network.

Secure Transmission of Information with a Web Browser

To keep the transmission of information secure, we need to guarantee that unauthorized persons cannot view the information and that the received information isn't forged. Both of these guarantees are crucial for reliable commercial transactions via a Web browser. Potential buyers might be reluctant to make a purchase using a Web page if they feel uncomfortable about transmitting their credit card numbers on the Internet. Sellers or buyers might be reluctant to conduct business on the Internet unless they can somehow be sure of the identity of the party that they are dealing with.

Encryption

As packets travel from network to network, there's really very little to prevent someone (with the proper expertise and equipment) from viewing the contents of the packets. Several encryption schemes or algorithms have been devised to convert messages or any other form of information (even a Web page) into a coded form. To read or decode the message, the recipient needs to supply a password. Another way to handle encryption is to set up a secure path through the Internet. Requiring a password to enter "secure-server mode" does this. The server and the browser encrypt and decrypt all the packets passed between the two sites.

Digital Certificates

A packet of information on the Internet contains the Internet address of the sender, but this can be forged. One method of protecting against this type of forgery is through the use of digital certificates. A digital certificate identifies the holder of the certificate. The certificates are used to encrypt and decrypt information as well as to provide digital signatures to guarantee the identity of the sender and the authenticity of a certificate. A digital signature is a code that's used to guarantee the identity of the sender and the authenticity of a certificate. An individual or organization obtains a certificate from a company, called a certificate authority, that guarantees the identity of the holder of the certificate. The certificate is attached to the message or Web page and can be used to guarantee the authenticity of information.

Privacy on the Web

When you retrieve Web pages while visiting sites on the Web, you leave a trail of your activity behind. Much of the trail is generated automatically. Web servers record information about every request, and your client also records information about the sites you visit. Sometimes we give out information about ourselves. That's fine as long as we're aware of who is collecting the information and how it will be used.

What Happens When You Go to a Web Site—What the Server Knows

When you go to a Web site, either by clicking on a hyperlink or by typing in a URL in the location field, your browser (the client program) sends a request to a Web server. This request includes the IP address of your computer system, the URL of the file or Web page you've requested, the time the request was made, and whether the request was successful. If you clicked on a hyperlink from a Web page, the URL of the Web page is also passed to the server. All of this information is kept in log files on the server. It's possible to have the log files analyzed and track all access to a Web server.

The Trail Left on Your Computer

We've seen that each server keeps log files to identify requests for Web pages. So, in that sense, you leave a trail of your activities on each of the Web servers that you contact. There's also a trail of your activities kept on the computer you use to access the Web. If you're using a computer to access the Web in a public place, such as a lab or a library, then it's possible for someone to check on your activities.

Cache

Most Web browsers keep copies of recently accessed Web pages, images, and other files. Netscape and other browsers call this the cache; Microsoft Internet Explorer calls these "Temporary Internet Files." When you return to a Web page you've visited recently, the browser first checks to see if it's available in the cache and retrieves it from your computer rather than retrieving it from a remote site. It's much faster to retrieve a Web page from the cache rather than from a remote site. This is convenient, but it also leaves a record of your activities. It is possible to clear the cache or remove the temporary files.

Netscape

If you're using Netscape: Bring up the **Preferences** panel by clicking on **Edit** in the menu bar and selecting **Preferences**; next bring up the **Cache** panel by clicking on **Advanced** and then clicking on **Cache**; and finally clear the disk cache by clicking on **Clear Disk Cache**.

Internet Explorer

If you're using Internet Explorer. Click on **Tools** in the menu bar, select **Internet Options**, then click on the tab **General** (if it's not already in the foreground). Now click on **Delete Files** in the section titled "Temporary Internet Files."

History List

The Web browser keeps a record of the path you've taken to get to the current location. To see the path and select a site from it,

Netscape

Click on **Go** in the menu bar.

Internet Explorer

Click on **View** in the menu bar and select **Go To**.

The browser also keeps a list of all the Web pages visited recently in the history list. This list is kept around for a time period specified in days. You can set the number of days an item may be kept on the list. You also can delete the files from the history list.

Netscape

Click on **Edit** in the menu bar, select **Preferences**, and then click on **Navigator**. Set the number of days items are to be kept in the history list or delete the entire list (click on **Clear History**) here.

Internet Explorer

Click on **Tools** in the menu bar, select **Internet Options**, then click on the tab **General** (if it's not already in the foreground). Set the number of days items are to be kept in the history list or delete the entire list (click on **Clear History**) here.

Cookies

A cookie is information that's passed to a Web server by the Web browser program. A Web server requests or writes a cookie to your computer only if you access a Web page that contains the commands to do that. Cookies are used to store information such as a login name and password or information about what portions of a Web site were visited on your computer. When you request a Web page, a server can retrieve the information that it stored on your computer. Netscape developed the terms and methods for working with cookies.

Cookies are sometimes viewed as an invasion of privacy, but they are useful to you in some cases. Suppose you frequently visit a site that requires you to give a password or a site that you can customize to match your preferences. The protocol HTTP is used when you visit a Web site. When a Web page is requested, a connection is made between the client and the server, and the server delivers a Web page. Once the page has been transmitted, the connection is terminated. If you visit a site again, the server, through HTTP, has no information about a previous visit. Cookies can be used to keep track of your password or keep track of some preferences you've set for every visit to that site. That way, you don't have to enter the information each time you visit.

☑ F Y I **Cookies**

- ☑ "cookie – Webopedia Definition and Links," http://webopedia.internet .com/TERM/c/cookie.html

- ☑ "The Truth About Cookies," http://www.kifka.com /Cookies.htm

- ☑ "An Introduction to Cookies," http://hotwired .com/webmonkey /geektalk/96/45/index3a .html?tw=backend

---

Web browsers allow you to control how you will deal with cookies:

Netscape

You have the option to not accept any cookies, to accept only cookies that get returned to the server that put them on your computer, or to be warned before accepting a cookie. To set this option, click on **Edit** in the menu bar, select **Preferences**, and then click on **Advanced**.

Internet Explorer

You can set security zones for different types of Web sites. To set security zones, click on **Tools** in the menu bar, select **Internet Options**, then click on the tab **Security** (if it's not already in the foreground). To customize how cookies are dealt with, click on **Customize**.

Giving Out Information About Yourself and Your Family

There are a number of situations in which you might be asked or tempted to give out personal information, such as when filling out a form, downloading software, signing up for a service on the Web, or being asked for your address or phone number through email or a chat group.

Any information you put into a form will be passed to a Web server and find its way into a database. Disclosing your street address to a business sometimes results in your receiving junk mail, and disclosing your email address may result in your getting unsolicited junk email, or "spam" as it's called. You can't be sure how the information will be used or marketed unless the organization gathering the data makes some explicit guarantees. We often hear about situations of fraudulent practices and schemes that swindle money from unsuspecting individuals, and we're just as likely to come across those types of situations ourselves when we're using the Internet. It's relatively easy to create an Internet or Web presence that makes an individual, a company, or an organization appear to be legitimate and trustworthy. Because of this, we need to be all the more skeptical and cautious when conducting personal or commercial dealings on the Internet.

☑ F Y I   **Privacy and Snooping**

☑ "Analyze Your Internet Privacy," http://privacy.net/analyze/

☑ "Privacy Initiatives," http://www.ftc.gov/privacy/index.html

☑ "someone to watch over you," http://salon.com/sept97/21st/article970918.html

More dangerous situations can arise when we develop a relationship with someone through email or a chat group. These situations can arise because when we're communicating with someone on the Internet, most of the communication is through text. We don't get to hear the person's voice or see them. They might send us a picture or tell us about themselves, but we may never really *know* the person with whom we are communicating. For example, I could be involved in a long series of email messages or have several conversations in a chat room with a person who claims to be my age and gender. The person might even send me a photograph. However, it could be that the person is not telling the truth. So we need to be very careful about giving out any personal information, and we certainly wouldn't make arrangements to meet the person without having the meeting take place in a public location. It's also not a bad idea to take other precautions, such as letting a friend or family member know where you are going.

The Web page "Staying Street Smart on the Web!" **http://www .yahooligans.com/docs/safety**, is a good place to find information about Internet safety issues for children and parents.

Children particularly need to discuss these issues with their parents, and they need to understand clearly stated rules about not giving out any personal information or telling someone where they go to school or play.

Common sense tells us not to give out personal information, home phone numbers, or home addresses to people we don't know. We're likely not to do that in our daily lives when we don't know the person who is asking for the information, and it is just as important to apply the same rules when we're using the Internet or the World Wide Web. The Internet and the World Wide Web give us lots of opportunities for learning, recreation, and communication. We don't need to be rude or unfriendly, but we do need to be careful, safe, and secure.

Glossary

404 error

A response code or error transmitted by a Web server to a client when a requested Web page or file is not present on the server.

administrative address

The address to use to join an email discussion group or interest group and to send requests for services.

alternate text

A description of a hyperlink or image, put in by the author of a Web page, that pops up when you move the mouse pointer over the hyperlink or image.

anonymous FTP

A means of using FTP to make files readily available to the public. When you start an FTP session with a remote host, you give the login or user name "anonymous" and enter your email address as the password. When you use a URL that starts with **ftp://** and a domain name with a Web browser, an anonymous FTP session begins, and you don't have to enter a user name or password.

article

A message or file that is part of a Usenet newsgroup.

ASCII (American Standard Code for Information Interchange)

A code for representing characters in a numeric form. An ASCII file is one that contains characters that can be displayed on a screen or printed without formatting or using another program.

asynchronous communication

Communication where the sender and receiver don't participate at the same time, for example, email or voicemail.

attachment

A file that is sent as part of an email message but that is not in the body of the message. Images, programs, and word-processing files are usually sent as attachments, because most email programs allow only plain text in the body of the message.

binary file

A file containing information such as a compressed archive, an image, a program, a spreadsheet, or a word-processing document. The items in the file usually cannot be displayed on a screen or printed without using some program.

BinHex

An encoding scheme that converts binary data into ASCII (American Standard Code for Information Interchange) characters.

bookmark list

A list of links to items on the World Wide Web. Bookmark lists are usually created by individuals as they use Netscape. A good way to keep track of favorite or important sites, since they are saved and can be used at any time. See also *favorites list*.

case sensitivity

The ability of a search tool to distinguish between uppercase and lowercase letters. Some search tools aren't case sensitive; no matter what you type, the tool picks up only lowercase matches. Search engines that are case sensitive strictly follow a search request; they'll return documents containing the words in the case in which they were entered in the search expression.

CGI (Common Gateway Interface)

A specification for transferring information between programs that execute on a Web server and the server software itself. A typical situation is for a so-called CGI program to take input from the server software, process it, and write the output in the form of a Web page that is then passed to a client by the server.

chat room

A conference or forum that allows two or more people to converse with each other at the same time by taking turns typing messages.

client/server

A program or Internet service that sends commands to and receives information from a corresponding program, often at a remote site, called a server. Most Internet services run as client/server programs. Telnet, for example, works this way. A user starts a client program on his computer that contacts a Telnet server.

commercial database

A database that requires you to pay a subscription cost before accessing it. It is also referred to as a proprietary database.

Communications Decency Act of 1996

Legislation approved by Congress that made it a criminal offense to include potentially indecent or offensive material on the Internet. The U.S. Supreme Court ruled in June of 1997 that this act abridged the freedom of speech that is protected by the First Amendment, and the act was ruled unconstitutional.

concept searching

A feature enabling a search engine to find synonyms in its database. When you type in a word or phrase, the engine automatically searches for the word or phrase you want, plus words or phrases that may mean the same thing. For example, if the word teenage is in your search expression, the search engine also looks for the word adolescent.

content area

The part of a Web browser window that contains the current Web page; it contains images, text, or hyperlinks.

cookie

A relatively small piece of information that is initially placed on a client's computer by a Web server. Once a cookie is present, the same Web server may read or rewrite the cookie. A Web server requests or writes a cookie to your computer only if you access a Web page that contains the commands to do that. Cookies are used to store information such as your login name and password or information about what portions of a Web site were visited on your computer. Sometimes viewed as an invasion of privacy, cookies are useful to you in some cases. Cookies can be used to keep track of your password or keep track of some preferences you've set for every visit to that site. You can set preferences in your browser to accept or reject cookies.

copyright

The right to copy or duplicate material such as images, music, and written works. Only the owners of the information can grant this right. Regardless of whether information on the Internet or a Web page is accompanied by a statement asserting copyright, it is still protected by the copyright laws of the United States, the Universal Copyright Convention, and the Berne Convention.

cross-posting

Posting an article to more than one Usenet newsgroup.

decoded

Describes a file recreated in binary format that has been encoded or translated from binary to ASCII or text format. Binary files that are sent as attachments to email have to be encoded (translated from binary to ASCII) before they are sent and decoded (translated from ASCII to binary) when they are received before they can be used.

default setting

The configuration a search engine uses unless you override the setting by specifying another configuration. For example, in some search engines, the Boolean operator OR is the assumed relationship between two words unless you type AND between the words.

directory

A topical list of Internet resources, arranged hierarchically. Directories are meant to be browsed, but they can also be searched. Directories differ from search engines in one major way—the human element involved in collecting and updating the information.

discussion group

A group that discusses a single topic via email messages. An individual subscribes to or joins a discussion group electronically, and all messages sent to the group are distributed to the members by email.

domain name

See *Internet domain name.*

domain name system

A system of computers and protocols on the Internet through which an Internet domain name is translated into an IP address.

download

To transfer or copy a file from another computer (the remote computer) to the computer you're using (the local computer). This term is often applied to the process of retrieving a file from a software library or FTP archive.

ECPA (Electronic Communications Privacy Act)

The U.S. law that prevents U.S. investigative agencies from intercepting or reading email messages without first obtaining a warrant.

electronic mail (email)

A basic Internet service that allows users to exchange messages electronically.

email client

The program you use to work with your email. Also called the mail user agent.

email discussion group

See *discussion group*.

emoticon

A symbol that can be typed using one or more characters to foster more expressive and efficient communication. For example, :-) and :) are used to represent a grin or smile. These are also used to denote that a sentence is to be interpreted as a joke.

encoded

Describes a file that's been translated from binary format to ASCII (American Standard Code for Information Interchange). This is done so the file can be sent using email.

encryption

A procedure to convert a file or message from its original form to one that can only be read by the intended recipient.

fair use

A provision in most copyright conventions or statutes that makes it possible for individuals to copy portions of a document or other piece of work for short-term use.

fan-in

The receiving by an individual in a group of all the messages to the group. One person asks a question, and replies can come from anywhere in the world.

fan-out

The sending of one message to a group and having it automatically distributed or made available to every member of the group.

FAQ (frequently asked questions)

A list, often associated with Usenet newsgroups, of commonly asked questions and answers on a specific topic. This is usually the first place users should look to find answers to questions or to get information on a topic.

favorites list

The name that Internet Explorer gives to an individual's collection of favorite URLs. The browser includes menu bar and toolbar links to the favorites list. This list is similar to the bookmark list kept by Netscape. See also *bookmark list*.

field

Part of a Web page or bibliographic record that is designated for a particular kind of data or text.

field searching

A strategy in which you limit a search to a particular field. In a search engine, you might search only the URL field. By narrowing the scope of searchable items, field searching helps to eliminate the chance of retrieving irrelevant information.

filter

Software that filters out certain Web sites from the results of a search.

flame

An email message or article in a Usenet newsgroup that's meant to insult someone or provoke controversy. This term is also applied to messages which contain strong criticism of or disagreement with a previous message or article.

follow-up

An article posted in response to another article. The follow-up has the same subject as the original article.

frame

Some Web pages are divided into rectangular regions called frames. Each frame has its own scroll bar, and in fact, each frame represents an individual Web page.

freeware

Computer programs that have been made available to the public free of charge.

frequently asked questions (FAQ)

See *FAQ*.

FTP (File Transfer Protocol)

A means of transferring or sharing files across the Internet from one computer system to another.

FTP archive

A collection of files available through anonymous FTP.

full-text indexing

A search engine feature in which every word, significant or insignificant, is indexed and retrievable through a search. See also *stop word*.

group address

The address to use to send email to each member of a discussion group, interest group, listserv list, or mailing list.

hierarchy

A list of subjects in a directory. The subjects are organized in successive ranks with the broadest listed first and with more specific aspects or subdivisions listed below.

high precision/high recall

A phenomenon that occurs during a search when you retrieve all the relevant documents in the database and retrieve no unwanted ones.

high precision/low recall

A phenomenon that occurs when a search yields a small set of hits. Although each one may be very relevant to the search topic, some relevant documents are missed.

home page

The first screen or page of a site accessible through a Web browser.

HTML (Hypertext Markup Language)

The format used for writing documents to be viewed with a Web browser. Items in the document can be text; images; sounds; or links to other HTML documents, sites, services, and resources on the Web.

HTTP (Hypertext Transfer Protocol)

The standard protocol that World Wide Web servers and clients use to communicate.

hyperlink

A word, phrase, image, or region of an image that is often highlighted or colored differently and that can be selected as part of a Web page. Each hyperlink represents another Web page; a location in the current Web page; an image, audio, video, or multimedia file; or some other resource on the World Wide Web. When the hyperlink is selected, it activates the resource that it represents.

hypermedia

An extension to hypertext that includes graphics and audio.

hypertext

A way of viewing or working with a document in text format that allows you to follow cross-references to other Web resources. By clicking on an embedded hyperlink, the user can choose her own path through the hypertext material.

IMAP (Internet Message Address Protocol)

A protocol used to retrieve email from a mail server. It is similar to POP3 but has additional features.

implied Boolean operator

The characters + and -, which can be used to require or prohibit a word or phrase as part of a search expression. The + acts somewhat like AND, and the - acts as NOT would in a Boolean expression. For example, the Boolean expression rivers AND lakes NOT swamps may be expressed as +rivers +lakes -swamps.

interest group

A group that discusses and shares information about a single topic via email.

Internet

The collection of networks throughout the world that agree to communicate using specific telecommunication protocols, the most basic being Internet Protocol (IP) and Transmission Control Protocol (TCP), and the services supplied by those networks.

Internet domain name

The Internet name for a network or computer system. The name consists of a sequence of characters separated by periods, such as www.mwc.edu. The domain name is often the first part of the URL that follows ://. For example, the domain name in the URL http://www.ckp.edu/technical/reference/swftp.html is www.ckp.edu.

IP (Internet Protocol)

The basic protocol used for the Internet. Information is put into a single packet, containing the addresses of the sender and the recipient, and then sent out. The receiving system removes the information from the packet.

IP address

An Internet address in numeric form. It consists of four numerals, each in the range of 0 through 255, separated by periods. An example is 192.65.245.76. Each computer connected to the Internet has an IP address assigned to it. The IP address is sometimes used for authentication.

IRC (Internet Relay Chat)

A synchronous communication system on the Internet. An individual uses an IRC client to contact one of the several IRC servers on the Internet. Once connected, the individual joins a channel or chat room and can communicate in realtime with others using the channel.

ISP (Internet service provider)

A usually commercial service that provides access to the Internet. Fees often depend on the amount of time and the maximum possible speed, in bits per second, of access to the Internet.

Java

A programming language that was originally designed to be used to develop applications in networked devices. It has been used very successfully to make small applications available through Web pages in a platform-independent format as bytecodes.

JavaScript

A programming language used exclusively within Web pages. The statements in the language are made part of a source file to enable some interactive features such as mouse clicks and input to forms. JavaScript is not based on or part of Java.

keyword

A descriptive or significant word in a Web document.

limiting by date

A search tool feature that allows you to limit search results to pages that were indexed after, before, or between certain dates.

list address

See *group address*.

listserv

The type of software used to manage a listserv list.

low precision/high recall

A phenomenon that occurs during a search when you retrieve a large set of results, including many irrelevant documents.

lurking

Reading the email or articles in a discussion group or newsgroup without contributing or posting messages.

mail user agent

See *email client.*

mailing list

See *discussion group.*

menu bar

The sequence of pulldown menus located across the top of the Web browser window. All commands are accessible from the menu bar.

meta-search tool

A tool that provides either the ability to search more than one search engine or directory simultaneously or a list of search tools that can be accessed from its site. These two major types of meta-search tools are called parallel search tools and all-in-one search tools.

meta-tag

A keyword inserted in the meta-tag portion of an HTML source document by the Web page author. If Web pages don't have much text, meta-tags help them come up in a keyword search.

MIME (multipurpose Internet mail extensions)

Extensions to standard email programs making it easy to send, receive, and include nontext files.

MOO

Similar to a MUD, but the enabling software is written in an object-oriented manner. This allows persons unfamiliar with the intricacies of the software to be able to set up and manage a MOO.

MUD

Multiuser dimension or multiuser dungeon. Software that enables synchronous communication in a virtual world. It was originally designed to represent dungeons-and-dragons-type role-playing games.

natural language searching

The capability of entering a search expression in the form of a question or statement.

nested Boolean logic

The use of parentheses in Boolean search expressions. For example, the nested expression **((rivers OR lakes) AND canoeing) NOT camping** will find resources that contain first either the words *rivers* or *lakes* and then the term *canoeing,* but not resources that contain the term *camping.*

news server

A computer that is used to hold the collections of articles that make up newsgroups, and to run the programs that pass any new articles posted to its newsgroups on to any other server that carries the same newsgroups.

newsgroup

A collection of Usenet articles arranged by topic. Some are specialized or technical groups (such as **comp.protocols.tcp-ip.domains**—topics related to Internet domain style names), some deal with recreational activities (such as **rec.outdoors.fishing .saltwater**—topics related to saltwater fishing), and one, news.newusers.questions, is dedicated to questions from new Usenet users.

newsreader

The software you use to read, reply to, and manage Usenet news.

packet-switched network

A message delivery system in which information is broken into small units (packets) and routed through a computer network using the most efficient route available for each. The packets may travel along different paths, but are reassembled into one message by the receiving computer.

PGP

Pretty Good Privacy, the name given to a public key encryption system for exchanging email in a secure, encrypted format. PGP was developed by Philip R. Zimmerman in 1991.

phrase searching

A search feature supported by most search engines that allows you to search for words that usually appear next to each other. It is possibly the most important search feature.

post

A message sent to an email discussion group or a Usenet newsgroup. Also, to send a message to an email discussion group or Usenet newsgroup.

POP (Post Office Protocol)

The way many email programs retrieve messages from a mail server. Email is delivered on the Internet to the mail server and an email program running on a personal computer retrieves that email through POP.

PPP (Point-to-Point Protocol)

A standard protocol that allows a computer with a modem to communicate using TCP/IP.

proprietary database

See *commercial database.*

protocol

A set of rules for exchanging information between networks or computer systems. The rules specify the format and the content of the information, and the procedures to follow during the exchange.

proximity searching

A search feature that makes it possible to search for words that are near each other in a document.

public key encryption

An encryption method that involves the use of two codes or keys. The two keys, one called the private key and the other called the public key, are assigned to an individual. Using the public key anyone can encrypt a message or file that can only be decrypted or decoded by the use of the corresponding private key.

reference work

A resource used to find quick answers to questions. Traditionally thought of as being in the form of books (such as dictionaries, encyclopedias, quotation directories, manuals, guides, atlases, bibliographies, and indexes), a reference source on the World Wide Web closely resembles its print counterpart. A reference book doesn't necessarily contain hyperlinks to other resources, although it will often have hyperlinks within the document itself.

relevancy ranking

A ranking of items retrieved from a database. The ranking is based on the relevancy score that a search engine has assigned.

results per page

A feature of some search engines that allows you to designate the number of results listed per page. Search engines usually list 10 results per page.

robot

See *spider*.

scroll bar

The rectangular area on the right side of a window that allows you to move up or down in an open document. You move by clicking and dragging it or clicking on the arrow at the bottom of the bar.

search engine

A collection of programs that gather information from the Web (see also *spider*), index it, and put it in a database so it can be searched. The search engine takes the keywords or phrases you enter, searches the database for words that match the search expression, and returns the results of the search to you. The results are hyperlinks to sources that have descriptions, titles, or contents matching the search expression.

search expression

The keywords and syntax that you enter into a search form. With this expression, you ask a search tool to seek relevant documents in a particular way.

search form

The rectangular pane or oblong box that appears on the home pages of most search tools. In this space, you enter a search expression.

shareware

Software that you are allowed to download and try for a specified period free of charge. If you continue to use the program after that time, you are expected to pay a usually modest fee to continue using the product legally.

signature

An optional portion of an email message consisting of information about the sender such as his full name, mailing address, phone number, etc. The signature is stored in a file and automatically included with each message.

smiley

The emoticon used to denote a smile, a grin, or a joke. Two common forms of this emoticon are :) and :-).

SMTP (Simple Mail Transfer Protocol)

The Internet standard protocol used to transfer electronic mail from one computer system to another.

source file

The text file that contains the HTML tags for a Web page. A browser reads the source for a Web page from this file and then, using the HTML tags, displays the Web page.

spam

Unwanted and unsolicited email. The electronic equivalent of paper junk mail.

specialized database

A self-contained index that is searchable and available on the Web. Items in specialized databases are often not accessible through a keyword search in a search engine.

spider

A computer program that travels the Internet to locate Web documents and FTP resources. It indexes the documents in a database, which is then searched using a search engine (such as AltaVista or Google). A spider can also be referred to as a robot or wanderer. Each search engine uses a spider to build its database.

status bar

The bar or rectangular region at the bottom of the browser window that shows several items of information regarding the transfer of a Web document to the browser. When the mouse is moved over a hyperlink it shows the hyperlink's URL. When a Web page is requested it gives information about contacting and receiving information from a server. During transmission it tells, in terms of a percentage, how much of the document has been transferred and indicates whether transmissions are being carried on in a secure manner.

stemming

See *truncation*.

stop word

A word that an indexing program doesn't index. Stop words usually include articles (*a*, *an*, and *the*) and other common words.

subject category

A division in a hierarchical subject classification system in a Web directory. You click on the subject category that is likely to contain either the Web pages you want or other subject categories that are more specific.

subject guide

A collection of URLs on a particular topic. Most easily found listed in virtual libraries, they are also referred to as meta-pages.

subscribe

To join a discussion group, interest group, listserv list, or mailing list. You use this term when writing commands to join such a group and to list a Usenet newsgroup on your newsreader.

synchronous communication

Communication where the participants participate at the same time. Chat is an example of synchronous communication.

tag

A code used in HTML that identifies an element so that a Web browser will know how to display it.

TCP (Transmission Control Protocol)

A protocol used as the basis of most Internet services. It is used in conjunction (actually on top of) the Internet Protocol. It allows for reliable communication oriented to process-to-process communication.

text file

A file containing characters in a plain human-readable format. There are no formatting commands such as underlining or displaying characters in boldface or different fonts. It is also called an ASCII file.

thread

A collection of articles that all deal with a single posting or email message.

thumbnail

A representation of an image in a size that's usually much smaller than its true size. For example, we may represent an image whose size is 100-by-200 pixels as a thumbnail of 25-by-50 pixels.

toolbar

A sequence of icons or items in the window above the content area of a Web browser. Clicking on an icon or item executes a command or causes an action.

top-level category

One of several main subjects in the top of a hierarchy in a directory's list of subjects.

truncation

In the formulation of a search expression, truncation is used when you want to find all endings of a word. It is done by cutting off the end of the word back to the root, and replacing it with a symbol, usually the asterisk (*). When given such a request, a search engine or database will look for all possible ends of the word, in addition to the root word itself.

unsubscribe

To leave, sign off from, or quit a discussion group, interest group, listserv list, or mailing list. You use the term when writing commands to end a relationship with a discussion group or to remove a Usenet newsgroup from the list of those you would regularly read.

upload

Transfer a file from the computer system being used to a remote system.

URL (Uniform Resource Locator)

A way of describing the location of an item (document, service, or resource) on the Internet and also specifying the means by which to access that item.

Usenet news

A system for exchanging messages, called articles, arranged according to specific categories called newsgroups. The articles are passed from one system to another, not as email between individuals.

virtual community

A collection of individuals who form a bond through electronic communication.

virtual library

A directory that contains collections of resources that librarians or other information specialists have carefully chosen and organized in a logical way.

Web browser

A program used to access the Internet services and resources available through the World Wide Web.

Web hosting service

A commercial service (in most cases) that provides a Web server to host a Web site. Fees often depend on the amount of disk space available, monthly traffic measured in bytes, and types of services that are provided.

Web page

The information available and displayed by a Web browser as the result of opening a local file or opening a location (URL). The contents and format of the Web page are specified using HTML.

Web server

A computer that runs the software and has the Internet connections so that it can satisfy HTTP requests from clients. In other words, it is a properly configured computer system that makes it possible to make Web pages available on the Internet.

white page service

A Web search service that helps locate email or street addresses for individuals. Similar services for businesses and government agencies are called yellow page services.

wildcard

A character that stands in for another character or group of characters. Most search tools use an asterisk for this function. Although a wildcard is most often used in truncation, it can also be used in the middle of words (for example, **wom*n**).

World Wide Web

The collection of different services and resources available on the Internet and accessible through a Web browser.

XHTML (Extensible Hypertext Markup Language)

A well-defined and well-formed definition or formulation of HTML with rules that are more strict than HTML. It also allows for the possibility of extending HTML to include other tags and meanings we can apply to those tags.

Index

404 error, 27–28

A

administrative address, 144–145
advertising, unsolicited, 118–119
All the Web, 62–66
AltaVista, 66–70
alternate text, 34, 209
American Library Association, 72
anchor tag, 206–208
anonymous FTP, 169, 171, 188–190, 208
antivirus software, 174
AOL Instant Messenger, 109
ASCII (American Standard Code for Information Interchange), 132, 193, 212, 220, 225–226
asynchronous communication, 100, 123, 165
attributes (Web page), 209
avatars, 104

B

background colors, 197, 210–211
Basic Search Strategy: The 10 Steps, 49, 61–70, 74
Berners-Lee, Tim, 9
binary files, 132
BinHex, 132
blocking devices, 72
bookmark list, 35–36, 274
Boole, George 56
Boolean operators 56–57, 68–71, 74

capitalizing, 56
implied, 57
nested 57
browsers, introduction to 9–18, 28–45
bulleted lists (Web page), 202–204
bulletin boards, 142

C

cache, 281
capturing and using text, 246–251, 255–258
capturing data, 252–255, 259
capturing images, 251–252, 258
case sensitivity, 59
CAUCE (Coalition Against Unsolicited Commercial Email), 119
Censorship, 49, 155
CERN, European Organization for Nuclear Research, 9
CGI (Common Gateway Interface), 225
Chat, 99, 101, 119
privacy and security, 104, 283
Children's safety 283–284
citing Web and Internet information, 260, 266–274
difficulties of, 268
discussion group messages, 274
electronic journal articles, 275
examples of, 270–276
FTP resources, 276
guidelines, 268–270